NEW
MATHS
IN ACTION

S3²

Members of the
Mathematics in Action Group
associated with this book:

D. Brown
R.D. Howat
G. Meikle
E.C.K. Mullan
R. Murray
K. Nisbet

Published in 2004 by:
Nelson Thornes Ltd
Delta Place
27 Bath Road
CHELTENHAM
GL53 7TH
United Kingdom

04 05 06 07 08 / 10 9 8 7 6 5 4 3 2 1

A catalogue record of this book is available from the British Library

ISBN 0 7487 8538 8

Illustrations by Oxford Designers and Illustrators
Page make-up by Tech-Set Ltd

Printed and bound in Croatia by Zrinski

Acknowledgements
Ben Curtis/Press Association: 102, 220; Corel 28 (NT): 237; Corel 62 (NT): 157;
Corel 168 (NT): 137, 200, 219; Corel 278 (NT): 142 bottom; Corel 407 (NT): 181;
Corel 628 (NT): 222; Corel 684 (NT): 198; Corel 745 (NT): 154; Corel 760 (NT): 32;
Digital Vision 9 (NT): 27; Digital Vision 12 (NT): 142 top; Gerry Ellis and Michael
Durham/Digital Vision LC (NT): 4; Greek postal service: 124 (TRIPOD); Kazuyoshi
Nomachi/Science Photo Library: 14; NASA: 138; NASA/Science Photo Library: 228;
Photodisc 75 (NT): 17; Science Photo Library: 20, 122; Stockpix 3 (NT): 84.

The publishers have made every effort to contact copyright holders but apologise if
any have been overlooked.

Contents

Introduction

This book has been specifically written to address the needs of the candidate attempting the Standard Grade Mathematics course at General Level. It is a two-year course and Book S4[2] will be required to complete the syllabus.

The content has been organised to ensure that the running order of the topics is consistent with companion volumes S3[1] and S3[3], aimed at Foundation and Credit Level candidates respectively. This will permit the flexibility of dual use, and facilitate changing sections during the course if required.

Throughout the book, chapters follow a similar structure.

- A review section at the start of each chapter ensures that knowledge required for the rest of the chapter has been revised.
- Necessary learning outcomes are demonstrated and exercises are provided to consolidate the new knowledge and skills. The ideas are developed and further exercises provide an opportunity to integrate knowledge and skills in various problem solving contexts.
- Challenges, brainstormers and investigations are peppered throughout the chapters to provide an opportunity for some investigative work for the more curious.
- Each chapter ends with a recap of the learning outcomes and a revision exercise which tests whether or not the required knowledge and skills addressed by the chapter have been picked up.

The final chapter of the book contains revision exercises, one for each of the twelve preceding chapters.

A teacher's resource pack provides additional material such as further practice and homework exercises and a preparation for assessment exercise for each chapter.

1 Calculations and the calculator

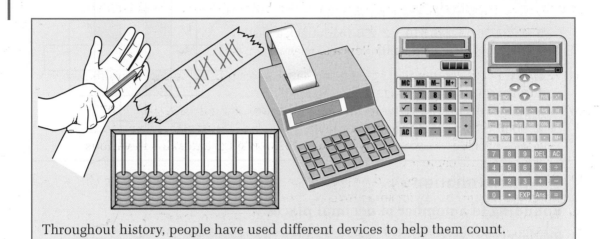

Throughout history, people have used different devices to help them count.

1 REVIEW

◀◀ **Exercise 1.1**

Do not use a calculator for questions **1** and **2**.

1 a 143 + 714 **b** 847 + 19 + 215 **c** 289 − 144
  d 3000 − 1762 **e** 405 × 6 **f** 263 × 9
  g 854 ÷ 7 **h** 4496 ÷ 8 **i** 50 + 40 + 20
  j 300 − 60 **k** 50 × 30 **l** 400 × 20
  m 60 ÷ 20 **n** 70 × 500 **o** 500 ÷ 50

2 a 7·6 + 2·3 **b** 16·5 + 7·9 **c** 8·25 + 17·6
  d 6·7 − 3·5 **e** 9·4 − 4·8 **f** 11·6 − 5·7
  g 20 − 6·8 **h** 1·5 × 3 **i** 30·8 × 9
  j 18·5 ÷ 5 **k** 6·18 ÷ 3 **l** 14·31 ÷ 9
  m $\frac{1}{8}$ of £10 **n** $\frac{5}{8}$ of 184 metres

3 Use your calculator to do these.
  a 94·7 + 38·6 **b** 155 − 76·8 **c** 57 × 17·5
  d 20 502 ÷ 9 **e** 0·4 × 460 **f** 19 548 ÷ 36

4 Round to the nearest
  a ten: **i** 77 **ii** 32 **iii** 65 **iv** 181 **v** 469
  b hundred: **i** 512 **ii** 763 **iii** 1280 **iv** 5625 **v** 10 868
  c whole number: **i** 4·7 **ii** 8·1 **iii** 13·5 **iv** 2·7143 **v** 0·896 734

5 When a calculator is turned
   upside-down some numbers look
   like words. 35009 becomes 'GOOSE'.

a Copy the crossword grid below.

b Calculate the answer to each clue, then turn your calculator upside-down to find
   the word to be entered into each space.

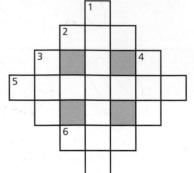

Across

2 $252 \div 9 \times 34 - 14$ (ask for money)

5 $1\,234\,567 + 246\,810 + 2\,450\,161$ (attack a castle)

6 $7 \times 11 \times 10 + 1$ (unwell)

Down

1 $26 \times 268 \times 543 - 1687$ (able to be read)

3 half of $64 \times 27 + 73$ (you can stand on one)

4 $1000 - 72 + 65$ (Humpty Dumpty!)

---

2 Approximation

Rounding to a number of decimal places

Reminder

To round to 1 decimal place:
- examine the digit in the second decimal place, p
- if p is 4 or less then round down
- if p is more than 4 then round up.

Example 1
Round 1·83 to 1 d.p.
1·83
The digit in the second decimal
place is '3'
1·83 = 1·8 to 1 d.p.

Example 2
Round 7·384 to 1 d.p.
7·384
The digit in the second decimal
place is '8'
7·384 = 7·4 to 1 d.p.

Similarly, we can make a rule for rounding to 2 decimal places.

To round to **2** decimal places:
- examine the digit in the **third** decimal place, p
- if p is 4 or less then round down
- if p is more than 4 then round up.

When working with **money** we usually work to 2 decimal places.
When working with **weight** and **volume** we often work to 3 decimal places.

Example 3   2·375 = 2·38 to 2 d.p.

Example 4   0·123 456 tonne = 0·12 tonne to 2 d.p.

Your calculator can be set to work to a fixed number of decimal places.
Find out how to **FIX** your calculator to work to 2 decimal places.

Exercise 2.1

1 Round each length to 1 decimal place.

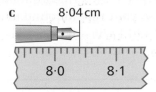

   a   8·33 cm   **b**   12·28 cm   **c**   8·04 cm

   8·3   8·4   12·2   12·3   8·0   8·1

2 Round each number to 1 decimal place.

   a 4·29   **b** 7·83   **c** 11·47   **d** 0·88
   e 9·04   **f** 3·99   **g** 6·82 seconds   **h** 24·47 cm
   i 52·69 litres   **j** 0·35 kg   **k** 43·125 metres

3 When rounded to 1 decimal place:
   a which **one** of these would **not** be 8·2?
      8·24   8·17   8·149   8·2066
   b which **one** of these would round to 14·6?
      14·666 666 667   14·65   14·5493   14·55   14·681 14

4 Round the number on each calculator display to
   i 1 decimal place
   ii 2 decimal places.

   a   **b**   **c**

   5.3687   3.141592654   28.083

FIX your calculator to 1 decimal place. Type in each of the above numbers and check your answers.

5 Round the following to 2 decimal places:
   a 1·571   **b** 6·046   **c** 21·285
   d 403·202   **e** 0·747 47   **f** 13·994

6 After some money calculations, the following are recorded on the calculator display.
   Round each amount of money to the nearest penny.
   a £4·723   **b** £16·554   **c** £29·968   **d** £344·51847
   e £100·06584   **f** £0·0475   **g** £33·333333

FIX your calculator to 2 decimal places to check your answers.

7 Kiera was working out £710 ÷ 14.
   The calculator display shows her answer.
   a Round her answer to the nearest penny.
   b FIX your calculator to 2 decimal places and then
      perform the calculation.

   50.71428571

8 Perform each calculation, giving your answer to 2 decimal places.
   a 1 ÷ 3   **b** 17·5 × 2·63   **c** 67 ÷ 9   **d** $\frac{1}{11}$ of 59   **e** $\frac{1}{13}$ of 100

9 At the beginning of this exercise you were given a rule for rounding numbers to 1 and to 2 decimal places.

   a Write down a rule for rounding to 3 decimal places.

   b Use your rule to round the following to 3 decimal places:

     i 3·714 56   **ii** 78·190 23   **iii** 0·049 65 (careful)

     iv 0·092 06   **v** 0·2496

Significant figures

The significant figures in a number are those that give us an idea of
i   the value of a number or   **ii**   the accuracy to which it was made.

A beekeeper counted of 874 bees in a swarm.
There are 3 significant figures here.
The 8 adds the most value (800). It is the **most significant digit**.

To the nearest 10 there are 870 bees.
There are now only 2 significant digits.

To the nearest hundred there are 900 bees.
There is now only 1 significant digit.

The trailing zeros don't seem to count … but be careful!
The 20 on a twenty pence coin has 2 significant figures.
There are exactly 20 pennies … not 19 … not 21.

When working with whole numbers we generally have to be told how many digits are significant.
When working with decimal fractions, **every digit after the most significant digit is significant**. (In this case **only** leading zeros are not significant.)

Examples
To 1 significant figure:
18 = 20 (1 s.f.)   234 = 200 (1 s.f.)   4567 = 5000 (1 s.f.)   0·57 = 0·6 (1 s.f.)

To 2 significant figures:
1351 = 1400 (2 s.f.)   0·0246 = 0·025 (2 s.f.)   0·504 = 0·50 (2 s.f.)   4·009 = 4·0 (2 s.f.)

Exercise 2.2

1 When rounding to 1 significant figure should:

   a 42 become 40 or 50   **b** 79 become 70 or 80

   c 120 become 100 or 200   **d** 389 become 300 or 400

   e 1760 become 1000 or 2000   **f** 5·3 become 5 or 6

   g 0·76 become 0·7 or 0·8   **h** 0·006 23 become 0·006 or 0·007?

2 Round to 2 significant figures:

   a 374   **b** 516   **c** 445   **d** 4380   **e** 9·843

   f 56·894   **g** 0·133 333 333   **h** 0·6035   **i** 0·0419   **j** 0·070 62

   k 0·008 42   **l** 0·060 41   **m** 50·09   **n** 0·000 456 **o** 0·999

   p 0·7049   **q** 0·009 95   **r** 146·79   **s** 9·708

3 Round each number to 1 significant figure:
  a 41 kg   **b** 8·6 cm   **c** 265 minutes   **d** 0·714 litre   **e** £1631
  f 0·078 g   **g** 0·008 52 mm   **h** 0·0102 s   **i** 0·6705 m^2 **j** 460 kg

4 Express 84 291 correct to:
  a 1 s.f   **b** 2 s.f   **c** 3 s.f   **d** 4 s.f

5 Calculate, correct to 2 significant figures:
  a 16 ÷ 15   **b** 0·025 × 3·14   **c** 300 ÷ 13   **d'** 0·40 × 0·50
  e 3·16 − 3·005   **f** £5·00 ÷ 12   **g** 2·001 + 0·617   **h** 1 ÷ 11

---

3 Estimate, calculate and check

Press the wrong key, press too often, or press too lightly ... and the displayed answer will be wrong!

It is good practice to have an idea of what the answer should look like before reaching for the calculator.

Example   Calculate 849 × 7·9

Estimate
- Working to 1 s.f. the calculation becomes 800 × 8 so I expect an answer round about 6400 = 6000 (1 s.f.).
- A last digit check: 849 × 7·9 ... 9 × 9 = 81 I expect an answer that ends in 1.

> 800 × 8 is about 6000

Calculate   On my calculator I get 6707·1.

Check   My answer is reasonably close to 6000 and ends in a 1. I'm probably correct.

It is often worthwhile doing the calculation twice as a check.

Key to Success   Estimate Calculate Check

Exercise 3.1

1 Pick a reasonable estimate for each calculation from the choice given.
  a 47 × 22   **i** 10   **ii** 100   **iii** 1000   **iv** 10 000
  b 97 + 51 + 38   **i** 100   **ii** 200   **iii** 300   **iv** 400
  c 7180 − 1856   **i** 500   **ii** 900   **iii** 5000   **iv** 9000
  d 3·8 + 5·2 + 6·6   **i** 16   **ii** 26   **iii** 36   **iv** 160

2 For each calculation:
  i estimate the answer to 1 significant figure
  ii say what the last digit of the answer should be
  iii use your calculator to get an answer. Check it against your estimate.
  a 68 + 13   **b** 92 + 57   **c** 263 + 157
  d 75 − 49   **e** 1047 − 521   **f** 37·4 + 44·2
  g 85·2 − 31·4   **h** 48·1 + 30·2 + 19·9   **i** 5·03 − 0·91 − 0·85

Remember always to **estimate, calculate and check.**

3 **a** Tom bought a shirt for £12·99, a jumper for £25·20 and underwear for £9·99.
How much did he spend altogether?

b In The Good Read Bookshop, 31 identical books
were piled up on top of each other.
Each book was 2·9 cm thick.
How high was the pile of books?

c Fiona had £532·60 in her bank account.
She spent £17·80 and £33·12 and paid by direct debit card.
(The money comes straight out of the account.)
How much is left in her account?

4 Edwin Good won £20 000 in a golf competition.
His expenses were: hotel £953·50, travel £415 and caddie's fee £1500.
How much of his prize money did he have left?

5 Aleta is writing a 3000 word essay. So far she has written 1650 words.
a How many words has she still to write?
b She writes 250 words per page. How many pages does her essay take?

6 Calculate the area of each rectangle, correct to 1 decimal place.

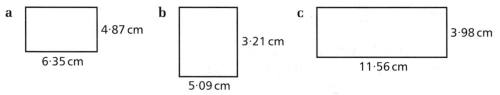

a 4·87 cm 6·35 cm   **b** 3·21 cm 5·09 cm   **c** 3·98 cm 11·56 cm

7 Calculate the total cost of: 25 tins of paint at £14·55 per tin
4 paint brushes at £5·50 each
3 packs of sanding paper at £2·99 each.

8 Steve looks at the exchange rates before his holiday in Florida.
£1 can be exchanged for $1·59.
a How much does he get for £240, to the nearest cent (hundredth of a dollar)?
b Later he changes $85 back to pounds at the same rate.
How much does he receive, to the nearest penny?

9 Ms Smith pays her council tax in ten monthly instalments.
Calculate each payment if her annual charge is:
a £1355 **b** £845·36 (to the nearest penny).

10 To calculate each competitor's final score in a diving competition, the three judges'
scores are added together and then multiplied by the 'degree of difficulty' for the dive.
a Elaine is awarded 5, 5·5 and 5·5 for a dive with a degree of difficulty of 1·4.
What was her final score?
b Alan has scores of 6, 6·5 and 5·5 for a dive with degree of difficulty 1·8.
Find his final score.
c The judges awarded Joyce 5·5, 5·5 and 6 for her dive.
If her final score was 28·9, what was the degree of difficulty of this dive?

Exercise 3.2

1 Without using a calculator, work out which of the following cost about £1000.

   a    **b**    **c**

   210 trophies £4·95 each   52 payments of £38   12 chairs at £90·50 each

2 The distance by rail between two towns is 37 km.
A day return ticket costs £11·24.
Calculate the cost in pence per kilometre.

3 Helen's phone call to her cousin in India lasted 17 minutes and cost £22·98.
Work out, to the nearest penny, the cost of the phone call per minute.

4 A unit of electricity costs 5·87 pence.
   a *Estimate* the cost of
      i   8 units
      ii 32 units
      iii 96 units.
   b Calculate the actual costs, to the nearest penny.
   c How many whole units can be bought for £50?

5 All-Bright toothpaste comes in two sizes.

   The small tube holds 125 ml and costs £1·54.
   The large tube holds 175 ml and costs £1·98.
   a Divide £1·54 by 125 to work out the cost per millilitre for the small tube.
   b Work out the cost per millilitre for the large tube.
   c Compare the costs to work out which is the better buy.

6 Best buys! In a similar fashion, work out which is the best buy in each of the
following situations.
   a Java coffee: small £1·56 for 100 g;
                       large £3·97 for 250 g
   b Face cream: small £1·49 for 75 ml;
                       large £2·15 for 110 ml
   c Corn flakes: small £1·84 for 550 g;
                       medium £2·45 for 750 g;
                       large £3·49 for 1 kg

4 Get your priorities right!

In a string of calculations, the order in which you do them is important.

Brackets:	Any calculation in brackets must be tackled first.
Of:	Next do any calculation that involves the word 'of', e.g. $\frac{1}{2}$ of 36.
Divide/Multiply:	These have equal priority, but usually doing division first will make the problem easier.
Add/Subtract:	Do any additions and subtractions last of all.

Many people remember the order using the 'word' **BODMAS**.

Example 1 $5 + 2 \times 3$ *Example 2* $6 \div 2 + 1$ *Example 3* $(10 - 4) \times 2$

          $5 + 2 \times 3$ $6 \div 2 + 1$ $(10 - 4) \times 2$

       $= 5 + 6$ $= 3 + 1$ $= 6 \times 2$

       $= 11$ $= 4$ $= 12$

Exercise 4.1

1 Evaluate:

   a $8 + 3 \times 4$ **b** $10 \times 1 + 4$ **c** $6 + 7 \times 5$ **d** $2 \times 11 - 4$

   e $3 + 9 - 4$ **f** $6 \times 2 + 5 \times 8$ **g** $11 \times 3 - 6 \times 2$ **h** $40 \div 4 + 1$

   i $17 + 12 \div 3$ **j** $19 - 6 \div 2$ **k** $30 + 14 \div 7$ **l** $15 \div 3 + 24 \div 8$

   m $4 + 6 \times 2$ **n** $(4 + 6) \times 2$ **o** $(5 + 4) \times 6$ **p** $7 \times (4 + 3)$

   q $(3 + 8) \times (4 + 1)$ **r** $\frac{1}{2}$ of $6 + 4$ **s** $18 - \frac{1}{2}$ of 10 **t** $\frac{1}{3}$ of $(6 + 9)$

   u $30 \div (8 - 6)$ **v** $40 \times (7 - 5)$ **w** $\frac{1}{4}$ of $80 \times (9 - 6)$ **x** $\frac{1}{3}$ of $(\frac{1}{2}$ of $60)$

2 Key in the following on your calculator:

If you got the answer 20 then you have a **scientific** calculator, programmed with the BODMAS rules.

If you got 44 then you have an **arithmetic** calculator which is only programmed to combine two numbers at a time.

For this type of calculator you must take the responsibility of applying the rules.

You will need to type

     ... followed by   

to get the correct answer.

For the rest of the chapter we will assume you have a scientific calculator.

5 Squares, square roots and powers

When a number is multiplied by itself, the **square** of the number is produced.

Example 1 $3 \times 3 = 9$ ... 9 is the square of 3. This is written as 3^2.

Example 2 $7 \times 7 = 49$ ... 49 is the square of 7. This is written as 7^2.

Example 3 $0{\cdot}5 \times 0{\cdot}5 = 0{\cdot}25$ ... $0{\cdot}5^2 = 0{\cdot}25$

Your calculator will have this function. Look for

We can work this idea backwards.
What number squared gives us 49?
From the example above we see the answer is 7.
We say that 7 is the **square root** of 49.
We write $\sqrt{49} = 7$

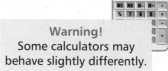

Warning!
Some calculators may behave slightly differently.

Again your calculator will have this function. Look for

Check the following: 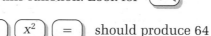   should produce 64

   should produce 9.

Exercise 5.1

1 Calculate:
  a 3^2 **b** 7^2 **c** 1^2
  d 8^2 **e** 10^2 **f** 13^2
  g 17^2 **h** 25^2 **i** $8{\cdot}4^2$
  j 107^2 **k** $0{\cdot}4^2$ **l** $3{\cdot}9^2$

2 Use the **square** function on your calculator to help you work these out.
  (Remember squaring is a form of multiplication.)
  a $3^2 + 4^2$ **b** $17^2 + 5^2$ **c** $1{\cdot}4^2 + 3{\cdot}7^2$ **d** $25^2 - 24^2$
  e $11^2 - 4^2$ **f** $6{\cdot}7^2 - 3{\cdot}8^2$ **g** 7×5^2 **h** $6 - 2^2$
  i $(5 + 1)^2$ **j** $4 \times 6^2 - 1$

3 Calculate:
  a $\sqrt{25}$ **b** $\sqrt{36}$ **c** $\sqrt{4}$ **d** $\sqrt{81}$ **e** $\sqrt{1}$
  f $\sqrt{144}$ **g** $\sqrt{1369}$ **h** $\sqrt{256}$ **i** $\sqrt{4356}$ **j** $\sqrt{11\,025}$
  k $\sqrt{11{\cdot}56}$ **l** $\sqrt{0{\cdot}16}$ **m** $\sqrt{31{\cdot}6969}$

4 Use the **square root** function on your calculator to work out the following, correct to 2 decimal places.
  a $\sqrt{38}$ **b** $\sqrt{59}$ **c** $\sqrt{79}$
  d $\sqrt{554}$ **e** $\sqrt{0{\cdot}85}$ **f** $\sqrt{0{\cdot}07}$

5 The area of a square can be calculated by squaring the side.
Calculate the area of each of the following square panes of glass.

$$A = l^2$$

47 cm

54·5 cm

104 cm

Window
Glass
30p per cm²

6 Use the square root function to find out the length of the side of a square whose area is:

a 36 cm²　　　　**b** 289 cm²　　　　**c** 1·96 m²　　　　**d** 0·64 m²

7 4 × 4 × 4 = 64. This can be written in a shorter form: $4^3 = 64$.
We say that **4 to the power of 3 is 64**.
Similarly $6 × 6 × 6 × 6 × 6 = 6^5 = 7776$ … **6 to the power of 5 makes 7776**.

This function is also on your calculator. Try

Use the **power** function to help you calculate:

a 3^3　　　　**b** 2^4　　　　**c** 1^5　　　　**d** 5^5
e 7^2　　　　**f** 3^4　　　　**g** 7^3　　　　**h** 2^7
i 11^4　　　**j** 10^6　　　**k** 123^3　　**l** $0·2^6$

8 Use your calculator to help you find out which is bigger in each pair.

a 3^5 or 6^3　　　　　　**b** 2^3 or 3^2　　　　　　**c** 3^4 or 4^3
d 2^4 or $\sqrt{144}$　　　　**e** $\sqrt{2·25}$ or $1·1^4$　　　**f** 21^2 or $\sqrt{190\,000}$

9 The volume of a cube can be calculated by finding **the length of a side to the power of 3**.
For example, a cube whose side is of length 5 cm has a volume of 5^3 cm³ = 125 cm³.
Calculate the volume of a cube whose side is of length:

a 12 cm　　　　**b** 23 cm　　　　**c** 27 mm　　　　**d** 1·2 m

Investigation

They say that the King of Persia was so pleased with the game of chess when it was invented that he offered the inventor anything he wished.

The inventor said 'Place one grain of rice on the first square of the board, place two on the second, place four on the third, place eight on the fourth and so on until you reach the sixty-fourth square.'

By using your calculator to look at the powers of 2, see if you can find the first square with more than 1 000 000 grains of rice upon it.

Should the king agree to the request?

6 Brackets and memory

Calculators will allow you to use brackets to 'force' the order in which the calculations are done.
Remember: brackets are tackled first.

Example 1 Calculate $\dfrac{3\cdot42 + 1\cdot56}{6\cdot14 - 2\cdot82}$

Think of it as $(3\cdot42 + 1\cdot56) \div (6\cdot14 - 2\cdot82) =$
Keying this into the calculator gives an answer of $1\cdot5$.

Sometimes it is useful to store a number in the calculator's memory, especially if it is going to be used more than once.

Example 2 When $x = 1\cdot6$ find the value of:
    a $3x$ **b** $2x + 4$ **c** $x^2 + 2x + 1$.

First store $1\cdot6$ in the calculator's memory, e.g. key in $1\cdot6$ and press $\boxed{\text{STO}}$
(The method will vary depending on the calculator.)

You can then use $\boxed{\text{RCL}}$:

a $3 \times \boxed{\text{RCL}} = 4\cdot8$ **b** $2 \times \boxed{\text{RCL}} + 4 = 7\cdot2$

c $\boxed{\text{RCL}}\ \boxed{x^2} + 2 \times \boxed{\text{RCL}} + 1 = 6\cdot76$

Many calculators have time-saving features such as 'constant facility' or 'last answer memory' which can save you a lot of work.
See if your calculator has any of these.

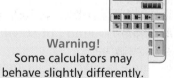

Warning!
Some calculators may behave slightly differently.

Exercise 6.1

1 Use brackets to help you evaluate the following:
  a $72 \div (39 - 21)$ **b** $4\cdot1 \times (2\cdot6 + 3\cdot5)$ **c** $17 \times (4\cdot5 - 1\cdot7)$ **d** $(9 + 14)^2$

  e $(83 - 26)^2$ **f** $(9\cdot2 + 3\cdot4)^3$ **g** $\dfrac{45}{3 \times 0\cdot6}$ **h** $\dfrac{1\cdot21}{25\cdot3 - 19\cdot8}$

  i $\dfrac{4\cdot7 + 3\cdot5}{5\cdot5 - 1\cdot4}$ **j** $\dfrac{7\cdot2^2}{2\cdot5^2 + 3\cdot75}$

2 Later in the course you will find a need for the following calculations.
  Work out the value of each one.
  a $\sqrt{(6^2 + 8^2)}$ **b** $\sqrt{(17^2 - 8^2)}$ **c** $\sqrt{5^2 + 12^2}$ **d** $\sqrt{6\cdot5^2 - 6^2}$

3 Use the memory in your calculator to help you here.
  a   When $x = 3\cdot14$ calculate (to 2 d.p.):
   i $5x$ **ii** $3x - 2\cdot1$ **iii** $x^2 + 4x$ **iv** $4x^3 \div 3$
  b   When $y = 4\cdot2$ evaluate:
   i $4y - 1$ **ii** $y + y^2$ **iii** $\dfrac{y + 5}{y - 5}$ **iv** $\sqrt{(y^2 + 1)}$

4 Which of the numbers from 1 to 10 divide 468 195 exactly?
(Hint: to save labour, put 468 195 into the memory.)

5 Terri went to Paris at a time when the rate was
1·623 euro (€) to the pound (£).
Her calculator has a memory that isn't scrubbed
when she switches it off.
See if yours can do that.
Terri stored 1·623 in the memory.

a Multiply by memory recall (RCL) to convert the following to euro:

   i £20   **ii** £65   **iii** £456   **iv** £724

b Divide by memory recall to convert the following amounts to pounds (£):

   i €30   **ii** €5000   **iii** €391   **iv** €885

c Pat went to America when $1·56 = £1. Use your calculator memory to convert the following to pounds:

   i $7   **ii** $20   **iii** $75   **iv** $150   **v** $6780

---

7 Fractions and ratios

Fractions

Modern calculators will let you enter common fractions using the $a^{b/c}$ button.

Example 1   Find $\frac{3}{4}$ of £6·40.   3 $a^{b/c}$ 4 × 6·40 = 4·80

Example 2   Write $5\frac{3}{4}$ as an improper (top heavy) fraction.

    5 $a^{b/c}$ 3 $a^{b/c}$ 4   enters the fraction

    then 2nd $a^{b/c}$ gives a display like 23 ⌋ 4 which means $\frac{23}{4}$.

    Note that pressing '=' will restore the fraction to a mixed number.

Example 3   Calculate $1\frac{1}{4} + \frac{2}{3}$.

    1 $a^{b/c}$ 1 $a^{b/c}$ 4 + 2 $a^{b/c}$ 3 = gives a display 1 ⌋ 11 ⌋ 12 which

    means $1\frac{11}{12}$.

Exercise 7.1

1 Calculate:

  a $\frac{1}{8}$ of £58·40   **b** $\frac{1}{9}$ of £307·80   **c** $\frac{1}{14}$ of 784 m   **d** $\frac{3}{8}$ of £132

  e $\frac{5}{6}$ of 34·8 tonnes   **f** $\frac{11}{25}$ of £168·75   **g** $\frac{19}{100}$ of £17   **h** $\frac{35}{41}$ of £779

2 Convert the following to improper fractions:

  a $4\frac{2}{3}$ **b** $1\frac{1}{4}$ **c** $2\frac{3}{5}$ **d** $3\frac{1}{2}$ **e** $7\frac{5}{8}$ **f** $4\frac{5}{6}$

3 By entering the fraction and then pressing '=', convert these improper fractions into mixed numbers:

a $\frac{17}{3}$ **b** $\frac{28}{9}$ **c** $\frac{31}{6}$ **d** $\frac{53}{5}$ **e** $\frac{11}{8}$ **f** $\frac{17}{12}$

4 Calculate the following with the aid of a calculator:

a $\frac{1}{2} + \frac{1}{4}$ **b** $\frac{1}{2} - \frac{1}{4}$ **c** $\frac{2}{3} + \frac{1}{6}$ **d** $\frac{5}{6} - \frac{1}{3}$

e $\frac{2}{3} - \frac{5}{9}$ **f** $\frac{3}{4} - \frac{3}{8}$ **g** $\frac{7}{8} + \frac{3}{4}$ **h** $1\frac{1}{2} + \frac{3}{8}$

i $2\frac{1}{5} - 1\frac{3}{4}$ **j** $3\frac{1}{6} + 4\frac{1}{8}$ **k** $5\frac{1}{7} + 1\frac{2}{5}$ **l** $4\frac{5}{6} - 2\frac{3}{5}$

m $\frac{3}{4} \times \frac{1}{5}$ **n** $\frac{2}{7} \times \frac{1}{4}$ **o** $\frac{6}{11} \times \frac{2}{9}$ **p** $1\frac{1}{2} \times 2\frac{1}{3}$

5

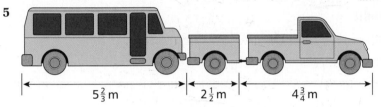

$5\frac{2}{3}$ m $2\frac{1}{2}$ m $4\frac{3}{4}$ m

The lengths of the minibus, trailer and truck are all given.

a What is the total length of the queue?

b What is the difference in length between the trailer and the truck?

Ratio

Ratios are often used when sharing or mixing amounts.

Example 1   Share £28 between Jordan and Asha in the ratio 3 : 1.

                 This means Jordan gets 3 parts and Asha gets 1 part … 4 parts in all.
                 If £28 is split into 4 parts then each part is worth 28 ÷ 4 = £7.
                 So Jordan gets £7 × 3 = £21 and Asha gets £7 ×1 = £7.

Example 2   Thyme and tea are mixed in the ratio 1 : 9 to produce a herbal tea.
                 How much of each is in a 1 kg (1000 g) bag of the mixture?

                 1 part is thyme and 9 parts are tea … 10 parts in all.
                 If 1000 g is split into 10 parts then each part is worth 1000 ÷ 10 = 100 g.
                 So there are 100 × 1 = 100 g of thyme and 100 × 9 = 900 g of tea.

Exercise 7.2

1 Tom and Sarah share £500 in the ratio 1 : 4. How much does each receive?

2 Split each quantity in the ratio shown.

     a 140 g in the ratio 6 : 1   **b** 56 m in the ratio 1 : 7
     c 450 tonnes in the ratio 4 : 1   **d** 8100 seconds in the ratio 1 : 8
     e 84 ml in the ratio 5 : 1   **f** 1 kg in the ratio 1 : 3
     g 1320 mm in the ratio 1 : 10   **h** 325 days in the ratio 12 : 1

3 Sand and cement are mixed in the ratio 3 : 1 to produce a concrete.
How much of each is needed to make 360 kg of the concrete?

4 Bashir spends his day sleeping or working. The ratio of sleep to work is 1 : 3. How many hours does he spend at each activity?

5 Diluting orange is made drinkable by mixing the concentrate and the water in the ratio 1 : 11.
   a How much water is in 600 ml of the mixture?
   b How much concentrate is used to make 1080 ml of the mixture?

6 Laura and Kirsty are to share £360.
   a Split £360 in the following ratios:
      i 1 : 2   **ii** 1 : 3   **iii** 1 : 4   **iv** 1 : 5   **v** 1 : 1
   b Which split would benefit
      i Laura most
      ii Kirsty most?

---

8 Standard form

Large numbers

In America some years ago, a swarm of locusts covered an area of 200 000 square miles.
There were over 125 000 000 000 000 locusts.
Together they weighed over 25 000 000 tonnes!

Some of these numbers are too big for the calculator to handle *normally*.
A shorter way of writing these large numbers has been developed.

Example 1
$200\,000 = 2 \times 10 \times 10 \times 10 \times 10 \times 10 = 2 \times 10^5$

Example 2
$25\,000\,000 = 2{\cdot}5 \times 10 \times 10 \times 10 \times 10 \times 10 \times 10 \times 10 = 2{\cdot}5 \times 10^7$

Example 3
$125\,000\,000\,000\,000 = 1{\cdot}25 \times 10^{14}$

Every number can be expressed in this way.

> $a \times 10^n$ ... A number between 1 and 10 (a) multiplied to a power of 10 (10^n).
> It is known as **standard form** or **scientific notation**.

First take a number   ...   3481·5

Put the point after the first significant digit   ...   3·4815   (giving a)

Count the number of digits that the point would need to jump over to get back to its position   ...   3·4815, in this case 3   (giving n)

$3481{\cdot}5 = 3{\cdot}4815 \times 10^3$

Exercise 8.1

1 Express each number in the form $a \times 10^n$, i.e. in standard form.

a 600	**b** 6000	**c** 60 000	**d** 600 000	**e** 600 000 000
f 200	**g** 90	**h** 4000	**i** 500 000	**j** 100 000 000
k 320	**l** 5800	**m** 9130	**n** 645 000	**o** 87 000
p 2430	**q** 46	**r** 455 000	**s** 301 000	**t** 176 400 000 000
u 79·2	**v** 81·4	**w** 6·15	**x** 9·04	**y** 104·45

2 Rewrite each sentence, expressing each number in scientific notation.
  a A car engine size is 2000 cc.
  b There are 365 days in a year.
  c The town population was 17 500.
  d The diameter of the Earth is 12 700 km.
  e You have lived for roughly 442 000 000 seconds.

Happy
442 000 000th
Birthsecond

3 Express the numbers mentioned here in standard form.
  a Dinosaurs roamed the Earth 169 000 000 years ago.
  b Light travels at 30 000 000 000 cm/s.
  c The mass of the Earth is 5980 000 000 000 000 000 000 000 kg.
  d The sun is 149 000 000 km away.
  e The most fertile creature is the cabbage aphid.
    One pest can give rise to 822 million descendents in one year!

4 Write these numbers in the *normal* decimal notation.

a 4×10^3	**b** 5×10^6	**c** 2×10^5	**d** 4×10^4
e $4{\cdot}2 \times 10^3$	**f** $6{\cdot}7 \times 10^4$	**g** $5{\cdot}8 \times 10^2$	**h** $8{\cdot}9 \times 10^6$
i $1{\cdot}25 \times 10^3$	**j** $9{\cdot}04 \times 10^5$	**k** $6{\cdot}55 \times 10^2$	**l** $2{\cdot}357 \times 10^8$
m $2{\cdot}18 \times 10^0$	**n** $6{\cdot}1 \times 10^1$	**o** $4{\cdot}11 \times 10^0$	**p** $7{\cdot}17 \times 10^1$

5 When the answer to a calculation is too large for the display, a calculator will give it in standard form.
  a Calculate 13 000 000 × 50 000 000.
  b Which of the following displays is most like yours?

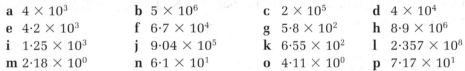

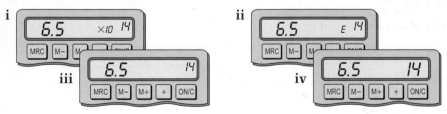

  Each of these displays represents the same number …
  $6{\cdot}5 \times 10^{14}$ or   650 000 000 000 000

6 Perform the following calculations, expressing your answer in both standard form and normal decimal form.
  a 45 000 000 × 74 000
  b 810 000 × 650 000
  c 81 400 × 516 200
  d 99 999 999 + 99 999 999

7 8 500 000 people on holiday spent an average of £1800 each.
   a Use your calculator to find the total amount spent.
   b Write out this amount in normal decimal form.

8 There are 365 days in a year, 24 hours in a day, 60 minutes in an hour and 60 seconds in a minute.
   Calculate, in standard form, the number of seconds:
   a in 1000 years (ignoring leap years)
   b that you had lived by your last birthday.

9 The circumference of the Earth is roughly 25 000 miles.
   There are 1760 yards in a mile and 3 feet in a yard.
   a Calculate the circumference of the Earth in feet.
   b If you travelled round the Earth 200 times, how many feet would you have travelled?
   c Write this number in normal decimal form.

Investigation 1

1 a Look for a pattern as you calculate these.
   i 999 999 × 2   **ii** 999 999 × 3   **iii** 999 999 × 4
b Can you write down an answer to
   i 999 999 × 5   **ii** 999 999 × 9?

2 a Look for a pattern as you calculate:
   i 11 × 11   **ii** 111 × 111   **iii** 1111 × 1111
b Can you write down an answer to
   i 11 111 × 11 111   **ii** 111 111 × 111 111?

3 a Calculate:
   i 9 × 9   **ii** 99 × 99   **iii** 999 × 999   **iv** 9999 × 9999
b Can you write down an answer to
   i 99 999 × 99 999   **ii** 999 999 × 999 999?
Check all your answers on the calculator.

Investigation 2

You should be able to enter numbers in standard form into your calculator.

For example, 3.14×10^5 is entered by keying in 3·14 (EXP) 5.

When you press '=' you get 314 000. What is this telling you?

1 Use your calculator to turn the following into normal decimal form.
   a 7×10^6 **b** 5×10^3 **c** 8×10^4 **d** 3×10^2
   e 8.1×10^0 **f** 6.3×10^1 **g** 7.01×10^6 **h** 1.31×10^7

2 0.561×10^5 is **not** in standard form. Why not?

Can you still use (EXP) to work it out?

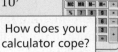

How does your calculator cope?

Small numbers

Example 1
Human hair grows at the rate of 0·000 000 5 cm per second.
Write this in standard form.

Again put the point after the first significant
digit ... 5·0   (giving *a*)

Count the number of digits that the point would
need to jump over to get back to its position
... 0·000 000 5, in this case 7 to the left   (giving *n*)

$0·000\ 000\ 5 = 5·0 \times 10^{-7}$
Note the negative sign suggesting 'to the left'.

Example 2
The eye of a needle has been measured as 0·085 cm wide.
In standard form $0·085 = 8·5 \times 10^{-2}$.

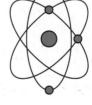

Exercise 8.2

1 Express each of the following in the form $a \times 10^n$ ... i.e. standard form.
  a 0·05   **b** 0·007   **c** 0·00002   **d** 0·01   **e** 0·9
  f 0·053   **g** 0·043   **h** 0·025   **i** 0·000 031   **j** 0·0069
  k 0·035 6   **l** 0·001 74 **m** 0·000 086 2 **n** 0·333 3   **o** 0·000 000 000 005 5

2 Rewrite each sentence, expressing the number in standard form.
  a The thickness of a sheet of paper is 0·113 mm.
  b A film of oil is 0·000 000 8 mm thick.
  c The mass of an electron is 0·000 000 000 000 000 000 000 000 000 911 kg.

3 Express the number in each sentence in standard form.
  a There is 0·000 28 of an hour in a second.
  b There is 0·000 001 9 of a year in a minute.
  c A millimetre is equal to 0·000 001 kilometre.
  d A proton weighs 0·000 000 000 000 000 000 000 001 64 g.

4 Write each of these numbers in normal decimal form:
  a 2×10^{-3} **b** 5×10^{-4} **c** 6×10^{-2} **d** 3×10^{-1}
  e $8·6 \times 10^{-4}$ **f** $2·32 \times 10^{-3}$ **g** $4·7 \times 10^{-5}$ **h** $6·67 \times 10^{-9}$

5 Work each of these out on your calculator and give your answer in both standard and
  normal decimal form:
  a 0·000 000 6 ÷ 80   **b** $(0·000\ 005)^2$ **c** 0·000 06 × 0·000 6 × 0·006 × 0·06
  d 0·002 316 ÷ 940 000   **e** $(0·00\ 234)^3$ **f** 0·001 ÷ 1000 000

6 We were on holiday for $3·85 \times 10^{-2}$ of a year.
  How long is that in days?

◀◀ RECAP

Rounding

To round to 1 decimal place:
- examine the second decimal place, p
- if p is 4 or less then round down
- if p is more than 4 then round up.

To round to 2 decimal places:
- examine the third decimal place, p
- if p is 4 or less then round down
- if p is more than 4 then round up.

For whole numbers you will generally be told how many figures are significant, unless the number is exact, e.g. there are 360° in a complete turn (3 s.f.).
For numbers containing a decimal point, all digits after the most significant digit are significant.

Good practice: estimate, calculate and check

Estimate   Work with numbers correct to 1 significant figure to get your estimate.
Calculate   Perform the calculation on the calculator.
Check   Does your answer broadly agree with your estimate?
             Is a last-digit check possible?
             Is it worth calculating again?

Get your priorities right: BODMAS

In a string of calculations, the order in which you do them is important.
Brackets: Any calculation in brackets must be tackled first.
Of: Then do any calculation which involves the word 'of', e.g. $\frac{1}{2}$ of 36.
Divide/Multiply: These have equal priority, but usually doing division first will make the problem easier.
Add/Subtract   Do any additions and subtractions last of all.

Some particular keys

Squares $[x^2]$ ... 5 $\boxed{x^2}$ = 25   Square roots $[\sqrt{}]$ ... $\boxed{\sqrt{}}$ 49 = 7

Powers $[y^x]$ ... 2 $\boxed{y^x}$ 3 = 8   Brackets $\boxed{(}$ $\boxed{)}$
                                                       Calculations in brackets get done first.

Fractions $\boxed{a^{b}/_{c}}$ allows fractions to be entered ... 3 $\boxed{a^{b}/_{c}}$ 4 $\boxed{a^{b}/_{c}}$ 5 enters $3\frac{4}{5}$.

Standard form/scientific notation

This form is more convenient when working with very large or very small numbers.
The calculator will use this form when the answer can't be displayed normally.

Example 1 $3.19 \times 10^4 = 31\ 900$

Example 2 $3.19 \times 10^{-4} = 0.000\ 319$

Check how your calculator displays such numbers.

Use a calculator only where you feel it is appropriate.

1 Calculate:
  a $5 + 6 \times 2$ **b** $20 - 3 \times 4$ **c** $22 - \frac{1}{2}$ of 36   **d** $(4 + 8) \div 6$

2 Evaluate:
  a 3^2 **b** $8 \cdot 2^2$ **c** 2^4 **d** $3 \cdot 1^3$ **e** $\sqrt{0 \cdot 49}$ **f** $\sqrt{1 \cdot 21}$

3 **a** Round each number to 1 decimal place:
   i $3 \cdot 87$ **ii** $8 \cdot 641$ **iii** $1 \cdot 25$
   iv $345 \cdot 57$ **v** $2 \cdot 479238$ **vi** $4 \cdot 2994$

  b Give each number correct to 2 decimal places:
   i $7 \cdot 3457$ **ii** $35 \cdot 0479$ **iii** $0 \cdot 878787$
   iv $0 \cdot 0496$ **v** $0 \cdot 0076$

  c Round each number to 1 significant figure:
   i 130 **ii** 4650 **iii** $4 \cdot 72$ **iv** $0 \cdot 0222$

  d Round each number to 2 significant figures:
   i 365 **ii** 4076 **iii** $4 \cdot 005$ **iv** $0 \cdot 007\,091$

  e Give an answer correct to 2 significant figures:
   i £7 ÷ 2   **ii** 25 g ÷ 5   **iii** $6 \div 3 \cdot 141\,592\,6$

4 For each calculation **i** write down an estimate **ii** suggest, where possible, what the last digit will be **iii** perform the calculation **iv** check that parts **i**, **ii** and **iii** agree.
  a $234 + 456$ **b** $620 - 149$ **c** 26×47 **d** $441 \div 9$

5 Calculate:
  a $3 \cdot 69 + 9 \cdot 87$ **b** $5 \cdot 8^2$ **c** $\sqrt{256}$
  d 12^4 **e** $5 \cdot 72 \times 0 \cdot 91$ **f** $1 \cdot 68^2$
  g $\sqrt{(9^2 + 40^2)}$ **h** $5 \cdot 8 \times (8 \cdot 7 - 4 \cdot 9)$ **i** $5 \cdot 5^2 + 3 \cdot 1^3$

6 **a** Philip spent three-elevenths of his salary on rent for his flat.
     Philip's monthly salary was £1309. What was his monthly rent?
  b Divide £467 by 19. Round your answer to the nearest penny.

7 Use your calculator's memory to help you convert the following amounts into dollars (£1 = \$1·53).
  a £10   **b** £54   **c** £1200   **d** £12·60

8 **a** Express the following as mixed numbers: **i** $\frac{19}{7}$ **ii** $\frac{25}{2}$ **iii** $\frac{39}{10}$
  b Express the following as improper fractions: **i** $3\frac{1}{5}$ **ii** $1\frac{2}{7}$ **iii** $4\frac{3}{11}$
  c Calculate:
   i $\frac{1}{5}$ of 60   **ii** $\frac{2}{9}$ of 45   **iii** $\frac{3}{10}$ of 70   **iv** $\frac{2}{5} + \frac{3}{8}$ **v** $4\frac{1}{2} - 2\frac{3}{8}$ **vi** $\frac{5}{6} \times \frac{3}{10}$

9 **a** Share £216 in the ratio 8 : 1.
  b James made a mint creme mixture using mint extract and mashed potato in the ratio 1 : 20. He made 147 ml of the mixture. How much of each ingredient is there?

10 **a** Write in standard form:
    i 1200 **ii** 40 **iii** $305\,000\,000$ **iv** $0 \cdot 0034$ **v** $0 \cdot 008$
  b Write out these numbers in full:
    i $1 \cdot 5 \times 10^6$ **ii** $5 \cdot 6 \times 10^{-3}$ **iii** 9×10^{-5} **iv** $3 \cdot 7 \times 10^0$

REVISE

2 Integers

Anders Celsius was a Swedish astronomer who lived between 1701 and 1744. He devised a way of measuring temperature which was adjusted and improved after his death. This Swedish postage stamp shows his image.

100 °C was chosen as the temperature at which water boils. 0 °C was chosen as the temperature at which ice forms … but what do we do if it gets colder than that?

1 REVIEW

a Temperature

On a really cold day the temperature can fall below zero.
Two degrees below zero is written as -2 °C.
We read -2 °C as 'negative 2 degrees Celsius' or
'2 degrees below zero'. On a weather report you may hear it read as 'minus 2 degrees Celsius'.
The negative sign ($-$) is taken to mean 'below zero'.

b Coordinates

The position of any point in two dimensions can be described using a coordinate diagram and positive and negative coordinates.
The position of A is (4, 3), B is (-2, 4), C is (-5, -2) and D is (4, -5).
The negative sign is taken to mean
- 'to the left of the origin' on the x axis
- 'below the origin' on the y axis.

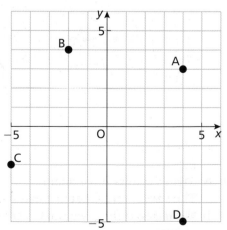

c Sea level

The height of an object on Earth is measured from sea level.
The top of Ben Nevis is 1344 m above sea level.
The maximum depth of Loch Ness is 230 m.
We can write this as −230 m.
The negative sign is taken to mean 'below sea level'.

d Profit and loss

A business can make a profit or a loss.
A loss of £3000 can be recorded as a negative profit, e.g. −£3000.
The negative sign is taken to mean 'a loss of'.

◀◀ **Exercise 1.1**

1 Here are the temperatures around Britain one night
  in winter:

Aberdeen	−5 °C	Edinburgh	−6 °C
Ayr	−1 °C	Glasgow	−4 °C
Belfast	0 °C	Lerwick	−2 °C
Cardiff	4 °C	Liverpool	3 °C
Dover	2 °C	London	1 °C
Dundee	−7 °C	Plymouth	5 °C

  a Re-write this list in order of temperature.
    Start with the coldest.
  b How many degrees colder was Aberdeen than London?
  c How many degrees warmer was Lerwick than Aberdeen?
  d How many degrees are there between the warmest and coldest places?

2 This map of Adam's Isle has its origin at Bruce, the island's capital city.

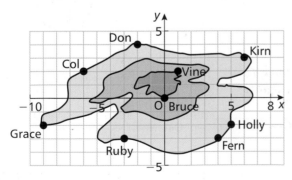

  a Make a list of the places marked on the map and write their coordinates beside
    them.
  b The islanders have decided to change the capital to Vine.
    The new map of Adam's Isle will have Vine as its origin.
    Write down the coordinates of the places on the new map when the origin is
    at Vine.

3

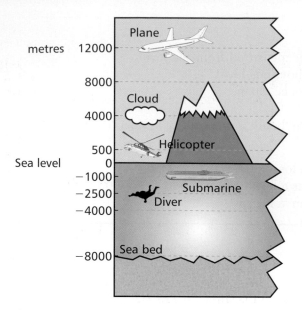

a What is the height of the mountain?
b How far above the helicopter is the cloud?
c How deep is the sea bed?
d How far from the bottom of the sea is the diver?
e How far above the diver is the submarine?
f How far is it from:
   i   the plane to the bottom of the sea
   ii the helicopter to the bottom of the sea
   iii the cloud to the diver
   iv the helicopter to the submarine?

4 Bert the Butcher sometimes makes a profit and sometimes makes a loss.
The bar graph shows the 'profit' made each month last year.

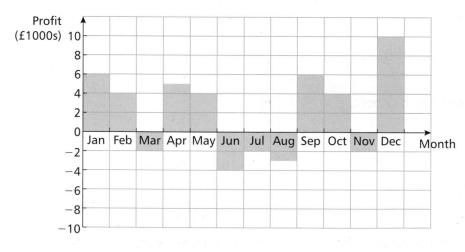

a For how many months did Bert make a profit?
b For how many months did he make a loss?
c Did Bert the Butcher make an overall profit or loss over the year?

2 Ordering integers

Positive and negative whole numbers are called **integers**.
Integers can be represented on a number line.
The further to the right a number is on the number line, the bigger it is.

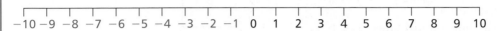

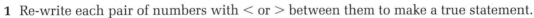

Example 1   4 is to the right of 3 on the number line, so 4 is bigger than 3.
We write '4 > 3'   '>' means 'is greater than' or 'is bigger than'.

Example 2   −1 is to the right of −2 on the number line, so −1 is bigger
than −2.
We write '−1 > −2'.

Example 3   −4 is to the left of −2, so −4 is smaller than −2.
We write '−4 < −2'   '<' means 'is less than' or 'is smaller than'.

The number line can also be drawn vertically, in which case bigger numbers
are above smaller numbers.

Exercise 2.1

1 Re-write each pair of numbers with < or > between them to make a true statement.
  a 5 ☐ 3   **b** 0 ☐ 4   **c** 3 ☐ −4   **d** 6 ☐ −2   **e** −3 ☐ −6
  f −2 ☐ −5   **g** −6 ☐ −5   **h** −4 ☐ 0   **i** 0 ☐ −1   **j** −1 ☐ −9

2 Write these numbers in order of size, smallest first.
  a 3, −2, 0, −1   **b** −1, 1, −2, −3   **c** 1, −2, 3, −6
  d 5, −4, −1, 2   **e** −3, −4, −1, 3   **f** 4, −2, 7, −6

3 Write down the number that is 1 bigger than:
  a 7   **b** −6   **c** −3   **d** −8   **e** −1

4 Write down the number that is 1 smaller than:
  a 5   **b** −1   **c** −7   **d** 0   **e** −3

5 Which number is:
  a 2 less than 7   **b** 5 greater than 3
  c 4 less than 3   **d** 3 less than 1
  e 2 less than 0   **f** 3 greater than −1
  g 5 less than −2   **h** 4 greater than −7?

6 These cold temperatures from around the world were recorded at 6 am:
  Moscow −8 °C; Anchorage −10 °C; Ontario −5 °C; Godthab −6 °C; Helsinki −2 °C.
  By 3 pm each of the above temperatures had risen by 7 °C.
  What was the temperature in each place by 3 pm?

7 The corners of square ABCD have the coordinates A(-7, -6), B(-3, -6), C(-3, -2) and D(-7, -2).
The x coordinate of each corner is increased by 2.
The y coordinate of each point is increased by 5.
Find the new coordinates of A, B, C and D.

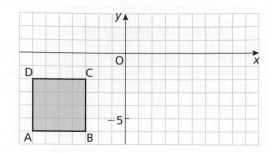

Challenge

When working with spreadsheets it is sometimes useful to turn a decimal number into the nearest integer that is smaller than it. For example 3·7 would turn into 3.

	A	B	C	D
1	3	INT(3.7)		
2	2	INT(2.1)		
3	5	INT(5.3)		
4	=INT(-4.3)	INT(-4.3)		

SUM ▼ ✗ ✓ = =INT(-4.3)

To get this to happen we type =INT(3.7) and 3 appears in the cell.
The illustration shows that =INT(2.1) gives 2 and =INT(5.3) gives 5.
What does =INT(-4.3) give?

If you have access to a computer, try different positive and negative decimals. Explore what is happening when you type in =INT(N+0.5) where N is some decimal number.

3 Adding integers

Treat an addition as a set of instructions.
Start at the first number and do what the second number tells you
(where 4 means four steps to the right, and -4 means four steps to the left).

Example 1 $3 + 4$ means '3 add 4'.
Start at 3 and go 4 to the right.
$3 + 4 = 7$

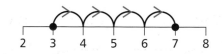

Example 2 $-2 + 3$ means '-2 add 3'.
Start at -2 and go 3 to the right.
$-2 + 3 = 1$

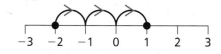

Example 3 $2 + (-5)$ means '2 add (-5)'.
Start at 2 and go 5 to the left.
$2 + (-5) = -3$

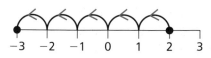

Example 4 $-1 + (-2)$ means '-1 add (-2)'.
Start at -1 and go 2 to the left.
$-1 + (-2) = -3$

Exercise 3.1

1 Find the values of the following. Use a number line if it helps you.

a $-3 + 5$ **b** $-1 + 4$ **c** $-2 + 6$

d $-4 + 1$ **e** $-6 + 6$ **f** $-5 + 4$

g $-8 + 5$ **h** $-3 + 7$ **i** $-9 + 6$

j $-7 + 8$ **k** $3 + (-4)$ **l** $1 + (-5)$

m $4 + (-7)$ **n** $2 + (-8)$ **o** $4 + (-4)$

2 Evaluate the following:

a $5 + (-3)$ **b** $3 + (-1)$ **c** $7 + (-2)$

d $0 + (-3)$ **e** $6 + (-5)$ **f** $-3 + (-2)$

g $-2 + (-4)$ **h** $-1 + (-5)$ **i** $-7 + (-2)$

j $-4 + (-3)$ **k** $-5 + (-4)$ **l** $-1 + (-1)$

m $-6 + (-3)$ **n** $-3 + (-3)$ **o** $-1 + (-8)$

3 Here are some number patterns formed by adding the same amount each time.

   i   Continue each pattern for three more terms.

   ii   What number is being added each time?

a 2, 6, 10, 14, ☐, ☐, ☐

b 21, 18, 15, 12, ☐, ☐, ☐   (-3 is being added)

c 50, 45, 40, 35, ☐, ☐, ☐

d $-5, -4, -3, -2,$ ☐, ☐, ☐   (1 is being added)

e 7, 5, 3, 1, ☐, ☐, ☐

f 9, 6, 3, 0, ☐, ☐, ☐

g $-20, -15, -10, -5,$ ☐, ☐, ☐

h $-10, -7, -4, -1,$ ☐, ☐, ☐

i $-8, -6, -4, -2,$ ☐, ☐, ☐

j 17, 12, 7, 2, ☐, ☐, ☐

4 What is the OUT number for each of these number machines?

5 Calculate each of these pairs:

a **i** $3 + (-1)$ **ii** $3 - 1$

b **i** $5 + (-1)$ **ii** $5 - 1$

c **i** $4 + (-2)$ **ii** $4 - 2$

d **i** $7 + (-3)$ **ii** $7 - 3$

e **i** $5 + (-5)$ **ii** $5 - 5$

f **i** $6 + (-4)$ **ii** $6 - 4$

What do you notice about each pair of answers?

4 Subtracting integers

This subtraction table is partially complete.

We know that a number subtracted from itself gives zero, for example $4 - 4 = 0$, $-2 - (-2) = 0$, so we have a diagonal of zeros in the table.

We know that zero subtracted from a number doesn't alter the number, for example $4 - 0 = 4$, so we can fill in the column headed '0'.

Some of the subtractions do not involve negative numbers, so we can fill these in.

						Second number					
−	−5	−4	−3	−2	−1	0	1	2	3	4	5
5						5	4	3	2	1	0
4						4	3	2	1	0	
3						3	2	1	0		
2						2	1	0			
1						1	0				
0						0					
−1					0	−1					
−2				0		−2					
−3			0			−3					
−4		0				−4					
−5	0					−5					

First number (labels the rows)

Exercise 4.1

1 Copy the table above.
  a Notice that as we move to the left, each number is 1 bigger than the one before it. Use the pattern to help you complete the top six rows.
  b Notice that as we move down, each number is one less than the number above it. Use this pattern to help you complete the table.

2 Use your completed table to help you write down the answers to these:
  a $5 - (-1)$ b $5 - (-2)$ c $4 - (-3)$ d $3 - (-2)$ e $1 - (-3)$
  f $3 - 5$ g $1 - 3$ h $0 - (-4)$ i $-1 - 2$ j $-4 - 1$
  k $-2 - 5$ l $-3 - (-5)$ m $-1 - (-2)$ n $-4 - (-3)$ o $-1 - (-1)$

3 Perform each pair of calculations:
  a i $4 - 1$ ii $4 + (-1)$ b i $1 - 2$ ii $1 + (-2)$
  c i $3 - 5$ ii $3 + (-5)$ d i $0 - 4$ ii $0 + (-4)$
  e i $-3 - 1$ ii $-3 + (-1)$ f i $-2 - 5$ ii $-2 + (-5)$
  g i $-3 - (-4)$ ii $-3 + 4$ h i $-5 - (-2)$ ii $-5 + 2$

The negative of 5 is -5. The negative of -3 is 3.
In Exercise 4.1 we saw that:

subtracting a number is the same as adding its negative.

Example 1 $4 - 5 = 4 + (-5) = -1$ *Example 2* $3 - (-1) = 3 + 1 = 4$

Express the subtraction as an addition.
Then use the number line.

Exercise 4.2

1 Use a number line to help you with these calculations:

a $2-3$	**b** $4-6$	**c** $1-5$	**d** $0-2$	**e** $3-7$
f $1-9$	**g** $-3-2$	**h** $-1-3$	**i** $-4-6$	**j** $-2-1$
k $3-(-1)$	**l** $5-(-2)$	**m** $1-(-4)$	**n** $2-(-2)$	**o** $0-(-3)$
p $-1-(-2)$	**q** $-3-(-5)$	**r** $-4-(-7)$	**s** $-2-(-1)$	**t** $-6-(-2)$

2 Find the value of:

a $3-5$	**b** $-4+9$	**c** $-5-1$	**d** $-6+1$	**e** $-7+7$
f $4-(-4)$	**g** $3+(-8)$	**h** $-9-(-2)$	**i** $8-2$	**j** $-6-(-6)$
k $-3-4$	**l** $5+(-4)$	**m** $-4+(-1)$	**n** $7-(-8)$	**o** $-3+(-7)$

3 For each of the following points, increase the x coordinate by 4 and decrease the y coordinate by 3:

a $(2, 5)$ **b** $(-7, 3)$ **c** $(-5, 1)$ **d** $(-3, 0)$ **e** $(-1, -3)$

4 The table shows the temperatures at noon at various places around the world. How many degrees each temperature had changed by 6 pm is also recorded.

	Moscow	Oslo	Calgary	Bergen	Anchorage	Stanley	Hobart	Dunedin
Temp. at noon	$6\,°C$	$-3\,°C$	$-1\,°C$	$1\,°C$	$-9\,°C$	$-5\,°C$	$3\,°C$	$-4\,°C$
Temp. change by 6 pm	$+4$	-2	$+3$	-3	$+1$	$+2$	-4	$+3$

Write down the temperature of each place at 6 pm.

5 Calculate the total profit or loss made by Daisy's Dairy over the year. ($+1$ stands for a profit of £1000; -1 stands for a loss of £1000.)

	Jan	Feb	Mar	Apr	May	Jun	Jul	Aug	Sep	Oct	Nov	Dec
Profit/Loss	3	1	-2	-1	2	-1	2	-6	-3	-1	2	5

6 What is the OUT number for each of these number machines?

a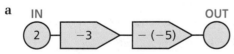

b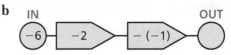

7 The table gives some information about the average surface temperatures on the planets of the solar system.

	Mercury	Venus	Earth	Mars	Jupiter	Saturn	Uranus	Neptune	Pluto
Temp. (°C)	179	453	8	4	-153	-185	-214	-225	-236

a How much hotter is Venus than
  i Mercury   **ii** Jupiter?
b What is the difference in temperature between
  i Jupiter and Saturn   **ii** Mars and Pluto?
c Which has the hotter temperature, Neptune or Pluto?

d i The maximum temperature recorded on Mercury is 427 °C. The minimum temperature is −92 °C. What is the range in temperature on Mercury?

ii The maximum temperature recorded on Earth one day was 37 °C. The range in temperature was 50 degrees. What was the minimum temperature on Earth that day?

8 The diagram shows the highest point and the lowest point on Earth.
It also gives the average height of land and the average depth of the sea bed.
a What is the difference in height between the Mariana trench and the top of Everest?
b What is the difference between the average height of the land and the average depth of the sea bed?

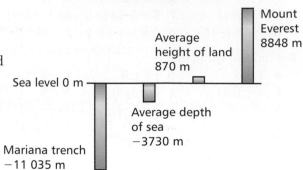

Challenge

These are magic squares. The total of any row, column or diagonal is the same.
i Find the magic total for each square. **ii** Copy and complete each square.

a

4		0
−3		
2		

b

	−3	2
	−1	
−4		

c

7		−7	4
−4	1		
0		−2	
	6		−8

5 Multiplying integers

Here is a partially completed multiplication table.
The following clues have been used to make the entries.

- We know how to multiply positive integers by positive integers.
- Any number times zero equals 0, e.g. $3 \times 0 = 0$.
- Zero times any number equals 0, e.g. $0 \times 2 = 0$.
- Any number multiplied by 1 remains the same, e.g. $4 \times 1 = 4$.
- 1 times any number equals the number, e.g. $1 \times 5 = 5$.

Second number

First number

×	−5	−4	−3	−2	−1	0	1	2	3	4	5
5						0	5	10	15	20	25
4						0	4	8	12	16	20
3						0	3	6	9	12	15
2						0	2	4	6	8	10
1	−5	−4	−3	−2	−1	0	1	2	3	4	5
0	0	0	0	0	0	0	0	0	0	0	0
−1						0					
−2						0					
−3						0					
−4						0					
−5						0					

Exercise 5.1

1 a Copy the table.
  b 5×5 means *five fives*
      $\Rightarrow 5 \times 5 = 5 + 5 + 5 + 5 + 5 = 25.$
      In the same way, $5 \times (-5)$ means *five negative fives*
      $\Rightarrow 5 \times (-5) = (-5) + (-5) + (-5) + (-5) + (-5) = -25.$
      Use this idea to fill in the top section of the table.
  c $1 \times 2 = 2 \times 1 = 2.$
      Similarly, $(-1) \times 2 = 2 \times (-1) = -2.$
      Use this idea to fill in the lower right section of the table.

2 From your completed table, find the value of:
  a $4 \times (-1)$ **b** $3 \times (-5)$ **c** -2×3 **d** -3×5 **e** -4×4
  f $2 \times (-4)$ **g** -5×2 **h** $5 \times (-3)$ **i** -4×0 **j** 3×4

Multiplying a negative integer by a whole number produces a negative integer.

Example 1 $4 \times 5 = 20$

Example 2 $-3 \times 4 = -12$

Example 3 $2 \times (-3) = -6$

---

3 Use this set of rules to calculate these:
  a 6×7 **b** -3×6 **c** $4 \times (-9)$ **d** $8 \times (-5)$ **e** -3×8
  f $5 \times (-9)$ **g** $7 \times (-4)$ **h** -6×5 **i** -1×8 **j** $6 \times (-7)$
  k $7 \times (-8)$ **l** -9×6 **m** -8×8 **n** $6 \times (-8)$ **o** -7×7

4 What is the OUT number for each of these number machines?
  a
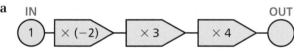
  b
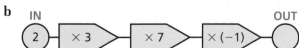

If you have a string of numbers to multiply, take them two at a time.

Example 1 $3 \times (-1) \times 2$

$3 \times (-1) \times 2$
$= -3 \times 2$
$= -6$

Example 2 $2 \times 4 \times (-7)$

$2 \times 4 \times (-7)$
$= 8 \times (-7)$
$= -56$

---

5 Evaluate:
  a $3 \times (-2) \times 5$ **b** $-2 \times 4 \times 1$ **c** $1 \times (-8) \times 6$
  d $-4 \times 1 \times 7$ **e** $3 \times (-3) \times 8$ **f** $4 \times 2 \times (-1)$
  g $-3 \times 2 \times 9$ **h** $2 \times (-3) \times 5$ **i** $7 \times 1 \times (-4)$

6 Integers on the calculator

You can add, subtract and multiply integers on your calculator using the (+/−) button. Calculators may vary.

It is always good practice to include brackets when they are given in the text.

Example 1 $-4 + (-5)$ (+/−) (4) (+) ((+/−) (5)) (=) -9

Example 2 $-3 - (-6)$ (+/−) (3) (−) ((+/−) (6)) (=) 3

Example 3 $2 - (-5)$ (2) (−) ((+/−) (5)) (=) 7

Example 4 -3×4 (+/−) (3) (×) (4) (=) -12

Exercise 6.1

1 Try these without a calculator, then use your calculator to check your answers.

  a $-6 + (-7)$ **b** $-5 + (-8)$
  c $-1 - (-9)$ **d** $-8 - (-3)$
  e $7 - (-4)$ **f** $2 - (-7)$
  g -8×4 **h** $3 \times (-9)$
  i -5×6 **j** -9×4
  k $7 \times (-5)$ **l** $9 \times (-4)$
  m $-1 - (-8)$ **n** $5 + (-8)$
  o $8 - (-9)$ **p** $7 + (-3) + (-6)$
  q $-5 - (-1) + (-4)$ **r** $-6 - (-3) - (-5)$
  s $3 \times 2 \times (-1)$ **t** $4 \times (-1) \times 7$
  u $-2 \times 2 \times 8$

2 Remember that integers obey the rules of priority: BODMAS.
Evaluate the following:

  a $-2 + 5 \times 3$ **b** $6 - 3 \times (-4)$
  c $(5 - (-2)) \times 4$ **d** $-3 \times 5 + (-2) \times 4$
  e $-3 + (-2) \times 2$ **f** $1 - (-1) \times 4$
  g $(4 + (-1)) \times 3$ **h** $1 \times (-2) + (-1) \times 5$

3 The Vulcan Cave system starts at a height of 345 m and goes down in four stages of 100 m.

  a Evaluate $345 - 4 \times 100$.
  b Describe how high the end of the cave system is.

4 Express the following numbers in the form $a \times 10^n$ where a is a number between 1 and 10 $(1 \leq a < 10)$ and n is an integer.

  a 34 000   **b** 255 000 000
  c 275 000 000 000   **d** 0·000 185
  e 0·004 56   **f** 0·000 000 000 12

Challenge

You start with 0. What do you end with?
Use your calculator to help you.

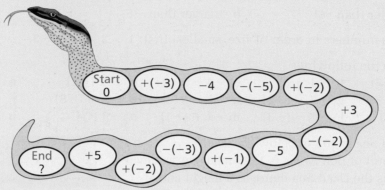

◀◀ RECAP

Integers are positive or negative whole numbers.
You should be able to order, add, subtract and multiply integers.

Integers can be represented on a number line:

$$-10\ -9\ -8\ -7\ -6\ -5\ -4\ -3\ -2\ -1\ \ 0\ \ 1\ \ 2\ \ 3\ \ 4\ \ 5\ \ 6\ \ 7\ \ 8\ \ 9\ \ 10$$

The further to the right a number is on the number line, the larger it is.

Examples $4 > 3$; $-3 > -4$; $5 < 7$; $-4 < -1$
                    ('$>$' means 'is greater than'; '$<$' means 'is less than'.)

A number line can help to:

● add integers   Start at the first number and do what the second number tells you.

   Examples   **a** $2 + (-3) = -1$
                      b $-1 + (-4) = -5$

● subtract integers   Instead of subtracting an integer, add its negative.

   Examples   **a** $1 - 3 = 1 + (-3) = -2$
                      b $-2 - (-6) = -2 + 6 = 4$

● multiply integers by a whole number   Treat it as repeated addition.

   Example $-3 \times 4 = -3 + (-3) + (-3) + (-3) = -12$

You can multiply without the number line.

Multiplying a negative integer by a whole number produces a negative integer.

Examples   **a** $-2 \times 5 = -10$ **b** $6 \times (-2) = -12$

1 Which of these are true and which are false?
  a $6 > 4$
  b $0 < 3$
  c $-1 > -2$
  d $-3 < -5$
  e $2 < -4$
  f $-5 > -7$

2 Write down the number that is:
  a 1 smaller than -3
  b 1 larger than -5.

3 List these numbers in order of size, smallest first: $1, -2, 4, -5, -3$.

4 Calculate the following:
  a $6 + (-7)$ b $-1 + 3$ c $-4 - 2$ d $7 + (-2)$ e -3×1
  f $5 - (-3)$ g $-6 - (-2)$ h -5×9 i $-2 + (-8)$ j $7 \times (-7)$
  k -2×0 l $-3 - (-3)$ m $-1 + (-1)$ n -9×4 o $2 - 7$

5 The Dead Sea is 403 m below sea level.
  The summit of Ben Nevis is 1343 m above sea level.
  a Express the Dead Sea figure as a height above
     sea level.
  b Calculate the difference in height between the top
     of Ben Nevis and the Dead Sea.

6 Find the value of:
  a $4 \times (-2) \times 6$
  b $5 + (-7) - 4$
  c $-1 - (-5) + (-8)$

7 Triangle PQR has vertices P(-4, 3), Q(-1, -2) and R(-7, 1).
  The x coordinates of P, Q and R have 5 added to them.
  The y coordinates of P, Q and R have 4 subtracted from them.
  Write down the new coordinates of P, Q and R.

8 Evaluate:
  a $-5 + 2 \times 1$
  b $5 - 7 \times (-2)$
  c $(2 - (-8)) \times 2$
  d $-5 \times 2 + 1 \times (-3)$

REVISE

3 Brackets and equations

Katy spends £3 travelling to and from school every day. She also spends £2 on lunch.

Can you work out what she spends in a week ... in two different ways?

1 REVIEW

Reminder

Look at how these expressions can be written in shorter forms:

$a + a + a = 3a$ 3 lots of a

$5 \times y = 5y$ 5 lots of y

$6x - 2x = 4x$ 4 lots of x

$h \times h = h^2$

$4 \times a \times b = 4ab$

$y + 3x + 2y - x = 3y + 2x$

◀◀ **Exercise 1.1**

1 Write these in shorter form:

  a $b + b + b$ **b** $x + x$ **c** $4y + 3y$ **d** $5e - 2e$

  e $a \times a$ **f** $4 \times x \times y$ **g** $a + b + a + b + a$ **h** $x + 3y - x + 2y$

2 Write an expression for the total cost of each set of items:

  a

  b

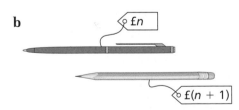

  c

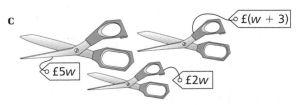

3 Find the OUT expressions:

a
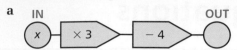

b
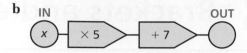

4 Find an expression for the perimeter of each shape. (All measurements are in centimetres.)

a
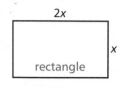

b

c

d
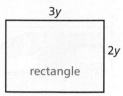

5 Find an expression for the area of each shape. (All measurements are in centimetres.)

a

b
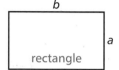

c
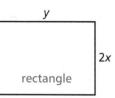

---

2 Brackets first

Reminder   If $a = 3$ then $2a + 4 = 2 \times 3 + 4 = 6 + 4 = 10$
and $2(a + 2) = 2(3 + 2) = 2 \times 5 = 10$

Exercise 2.1

1 If $x = 5$ find the value of:
  a i $3x - 3$ **ii** $3(x - 1)$ **b i** $5(x + 2)$ **ii** $5x + 10$
  c i $2(x - 4)$ **ii** $2x - 8$ **d i** $7x + 14$ **ii** $7(x + 2)$
  Comment on the answers to **i** and **ii** in each case.

2 If $y = 7$ evaluate:
  a i $2(y - 4)$ **ii** $2y - 8$ **b i** $3y + 18$ **ii** $3(y + 6)$
  c i $7(y + 3)$ **ii** $7y + 21$ **d i** $4y - 4$ **ii** $4(y - 1)$
  Comment on the answers to **i** and **ii** in each case.

3 $a = 9$ and $b = 5$. Calculate the value of:
  a i $6a - 30$ **ii** $6(a - 5)$ **b i** $4a + 16$ **ii** $4(a + 4)$
  c i $2(b + 1)$ **ii** $2b + 2$ **d i** $8b - 24$ **ii** $8(b - 3)$
  e i $3(a - 2)$ **ii** $3a - 6$ **f i** $7(b - 2)$ **ii** $7b - 14$
  g i $5(a + 3)$ **ii** $5a + 15$ **h i** $10(b + 6)$ **ii** $10b + 60$
  Comment on the answers to **i** and **ii** in each case.

4 If $k = 3$ find the value of:
  a i $k(k + 1)$ **ii** $k^2 + k$ **b i** $k(k - 2)$ **ii** $k^2 - 2k$
  c i $k(5 - k)$ **ii** $5k - k^2$ **d i** $6k + k^2$ **ii** $k(6 + k)$
  Comment on the answers to **i** and **ii** in each case.

3 With brackets and without brackets

$4x$ means 'four lots of x': $x + x + x + x$

$4(x + 3)$ means 'four lots of $x + 3$': $x + 3 + x + 3 + x + 3 + x + 3 = 4x + 12$

$3(y - 2)$ means 'three lots of $y - 2$': $y - 2 + y - 2 + y - 2 = 3y - 6$

When removing brackets, we multiply each term within the brackets by the term outside.

Example 1 $3(a + 2) = 3a + 6$

Example 2 $2(b - 5) = 2b - 10$

Example 3 $6(a - b) = 6a - 6b$

Example 4

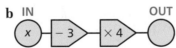

The OUT expression is $(x - 3) \times 2$, written $2(x - 3) = 2x - 6$.

Exercise 3.1

1 Remove the brackets (as in the examples above):

a $3(x + 2)$	**b** $2(y - 3)$	**c** $4(a + 2)$	**d** $3(t - 1)$	**e** $2(m + 6)$
f $4(c - 5)$	**g** $5(x + 3)$	**h** $2(h - 6)$	**i** $5(y + 7)$	**j** $4(n - 2)$
k $5(y + 1)$	**l** $7(w - 1)$	**m** $4(a + 7)$	**n** $3(e - 9)$	**o** $8(x + 4)$
p $3(k + 5)$	**q** $5(a - 6)$	**r** $4(x + 8)$	**s** $9(h - 8)$	**t** $3(u + 8)$
u $11(x - 3)$	**v** $8(y + 1)$	**w** $5(r - 6)$	**x** $7(n + 2)$	**y** $9(x + 9)$

2 Write the OUT expressions   **i** with and   **ii** without brackets:

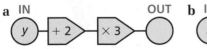

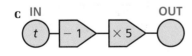

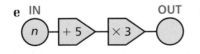

3 Multiply out these brackets:

a $8(5 - x)$	**b** $4(11 - m)$	**c** $11(3 + n)$	**d** $2(k + 3)$
e $5(m - 1)$	**f** $3(7 + y)$	**g** $5(2 + b)$	**h** $6(h + 10)$
i $7(y - 8)$	**j** $6(2 + k)$	**k** $3(5 - n)$	**l** $12(4 - c)$
m $8(9 - a)$	**n** $2(z + 5)$	**o** $7(6 - x)$	**p** $4(6 + e)$
q $9(8 - f)$	**r** $10(r - 9)$	**s** $9(4 - u)$	**t** $10(w + 7)$

Example 5 Expand: **a** $3(2a - 5)$ **b** $x(x - 3)$

$$\begin{array}{ll} \textbf{a} \ \ 3(2a - 5) & \textbf{b} \ \ x(x - 3) \\ \ \ \ = 6a - 15 & \ \ \ \ = x^2 - 3x \end{array}$$

Example 6 Expand the brackets and simplify the expression $2(x + 4) - x$.

$$\begin{aligned} 2(x + 4) - x \\ = 2x + 8 - x \\ = x + 8 \end{aligned}$$

Exercise 3.2

1 Remove the brackets:

a $2(3x - 3)$	**b** $4(5y + 2)$	**c** $6(2c - 1)$	**d** $5(4a - 5)$	**e** $7(6z + 1)$
f $5(8 - x)$	**g** $4(3e + 2)$	**h** $2(2y - 3)$	**i** $8(3w + 4)$	**j** $9(6x - 2)$
k $8(4y + 3)$	**l** $3(2a + 1)$	**m** $3(5k - 1)$	**n** $6(4c - 3)$	**o** $3(3y + 2)$
p $11(a + b)$	**q** $2(u - v)$	**r** $9(w - y)$	**s** $7(2a + 3)$	**t** $10(3b - 4)$
u $4(2a + 3b)$	**v** $5(4b - 3c)$	**w** $12(5x - y)$		

2 For each rectangle write two expressions for the perimeter, one with brackets and one without. (All measurements are in centimetres.)

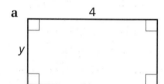

3 Multiply out the brackets, then simplify the expression:

a $3(y + 2) - 5$	**b** $2(m - 3) + m$	**c** $2x + 2(x + 3)$
d $7 + 3(a - 2)$	**e** $6(k - 2) - 5k$	**f** $2(5 + y) - 7$
g $7(n - 1) + 2n$	**h** $4 + 3(h - 1)$	**i** $10c + 5(2 - c)$
j $3(r + 1) - 2r$	**k** $2(y + 3) + 3(y - 2)$	**l** $4(x + 2) + 2(x - 1)$
m $3(n - 1) + 2(n + 2)$	**n** $4(a - b) + 5(a + b)$	**o** $5(x + y) + 3(x - y)$
p $7(m + n) + 2(m - n)$		

4 In each case find two different ways of writing the expression for the area:

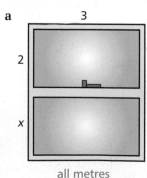

all metres

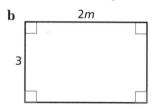

all millimetres

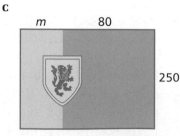

all centimetres

Challenge

In how many different forms can you write an expression for the perimeter of this window?

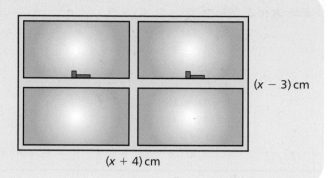

$(x - 3)$ cm

$(x + 4)$ cm

---

4 Old equations

Example 1   If $y - 5 = 8$, find the value of y.

$y - 5 = 8$

$\Rightarrow y - 5 + 5 = 8 + 5$

$\Rightarrow y = 13$

(check: $13 - 5 = 8$)

Example 2   Find x if $x + 6 = 11$.

$x + 6 = 11$

$\Rightarrow x + 6 - 6 = 11 - 6$

$\Rightarrow x = 5$

(check: $5 + 6 = 11$)

Example 3   Solve $3x = 24$.

$3x = 24$

$\Rightarrow 3x \div 3 = 24 \div 3$

$\Rightarrow x = 8$

(check: $3 \times 8 = 24$)

Example 4   Solve $3x + 5 = 17$.

$3x + 5 = 17$

$\Rightarrow 3x + 5 - 5 = 17 - 5$

$\Rightarrow 3x = 12$

$\Rightarrow 3x \div 3 = 12 \div 3$

$\Rightarrow x = 4$

(check: $3 \times 4 + 5 = 17$)

Exercise 4.1

1 Solve these equations. (Remember to check your solutions.)

  a $y + 2 = 7$ **b** $t - 3 = 9$ **c** $m + 2 = 6$ **d** $n + 11 = 11$ **e** $x - 5 = 1$

  f $y - 7 = 2$ **g** $5 + y = 8$ **h** $2 + k = 7$ **i** $z - 3 = 10$ **j** $x + 6 = 6$

2 Solve the following. Some of your answers may be fractions.

  a $6x = 12$ **b** $5m = 15$ **c** $8k = 56$ **d** $4n = 40$ **e** $2y = 3$

  f $3y = 4$ **g** $4a = 3$ **h** $2n = 7$ **i** $8 = 4t$ **j** $12 = 6x$

  k $11 = 2e$ **l** $5 = 2k$ **m** $26 = 26x$ **n** $2y = 1$

3 Find the value of the variable in each equation.

  a $3y - 1 = 8$ **b** $2x + 1 = 11$ **c** $4a + 7 = 15$

  d $5e - 3 = 12$ **e** $8k + 2 = 26$ **f** $11r - 6 = 27$

  g $7h - 5 = 23$ **h** $3c + 13 = 37$ **i** $31 = 7x - 4$

  j $20 = 2y + 2$ **k** $9m - 13 = 23$ **l** $36 = 12 + 4k$

Example 5 Solve $5x - 3 = x + 9$.

$$5x - 3 = x + 9$$
$$\Rightarrow 5x - 3 + 3 = x + 9 + 3$$
$$\Rightarrow 5x = x + 12$$
$$\Rightarrow 5x - x = x + 12 - x$$
$$\Rightarrow 4x = 12$$
$$\Rightarrow 4x \div 4 = 12 \div 4$$
$$\Rightarrow x = 3$$

(check: $5x - 3 = 5 \times 3 - 3 = 12$ and $x + 9 = 3 + 9 = 12$)

Exercise 4.2

1 Solve these equations and check your solutions:

    a $2y = y + 7$ **b** $3x = x + 4$ **c** $5m = 2m + 6$ **d** $2x - 5 = x$
    e $7k - 18 = k$ **f** $9h - 8 = h$ **g** $8y = 6y + 2$ **h** $9w = 7w + 5$
    i $5x = 3 + 3x$ **j** $4x = 1 + 2x$ **k** $5k + 3 = 8k$ **l** $2y + 15 = 7y$
    m $a = 5a - 8$ **n** $2c = 4c - 6$ **o** $12n = n + 33$ **p** $4r + 28 = 8r$
    q $7e - 1 = 6e$ **r** $3x - 17 = x$

2 The pairs of lengths in each picture are equal.
   Make an equation and solve it to find the length.
   (All measurements are in centimetres.)

a

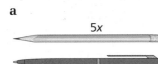

$5x$

$3x + 6$

b

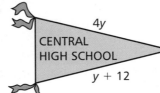

$4y$

CENTRAL
HIGH SCHOOL

$y + 12$

c

$2x - 7$

x

3 Solve these equations. Remember to check your solutions.

    a $4x - 1 = x + 5$ **b** $6y - 3 = 2y + 1$ **c** $7m + 2 = 5m + 8$
    d $3k + 2 = 10k - 12$ **e** $7x - 5 = 12x - 20$ **f** $24 + y = 8y + 3$
    g $5e - 3 = 2e + 18$ **h** $10 + 4k = 8k - 2$ **i** $9w - 3 = 5w + 25$
    j $23 + 3n = 10n - 5$ **k** $12 - x = 2x + 3$ **l** $y + 9 = 10 - y$

5 New equations

Example Find the value of y for which $3(y + 5) = 27$.

$$3(y + 5) = 27$$
$$\Rightarrow 3y + 15 = 27 \qquad \text{... removing the brackets}$$
$$\Rightarrow 3y + 15 - 15 = 27 - 15 \quad \text{... subtracting 15 from each side}$$
$$\Rightarrow 3y = 12$$
$$\Rightarrow 3y \div 3 = 12 \div 3 \qquad \text{... dividing each side by 3}$$
$$\Rightarrow y = 4$$

check: $3(y + 5) = 3(4 + 5) = 3 \times 9 = 27$

Exercise 5.1

1 Solve these equations by first removing the brackets.
  a $3(n - 2) = 6$ **b** $5(m + 1) = 40$ **c** $2(e - 5) = 4$
  d $9(d + 4) = 45$ **e** $3(h + 6) = 18$ **f** $6(a + 1) = 24$
  g $7(c + 3) = 63$ **h** $5(z - 10) = 15$ **i** $4(x - 7) = 28$
  j $10(m + 2) = 20$ **k** $8(w + 5) = 64$ **l** $5(b - 2) = 50$
  m $11(n - 5) = 66$ **n** $4(y + 3) = 16$

2 For each picture:
  i   write down an equation with brackets
  ii solve the equation by first removing the brackets
  iii use the solution to answer the question.
  a The total length of the queue of cars is 35 m. What is the length of one car?

  b The total amount of money saved is £27.
  How much is in each piggy bank?

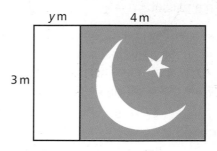

  c The total area of the wall and door is 40 m². What is the length of the wall?

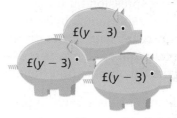

  d The total area of the giant flag is 15 m². What is the width of the white strip?

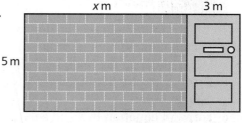

3 Solve these equations:
  a $18 = 2(y - 3)$ **b** $7(5 - x) = 21$ **c** $33 = 11(4 - m)$
  d $10(7 + n) = 80$ **e** $16 = 8(x + 2)$ **f** $0 = 3(k - 3)$
  g $14 = 2(y - 1)$ **h** $6(m - 1) = 48$ **i** $9(t + 4) = 63$
  j $4(n - 3) = 32$ **k** $45 = 5(x - 7)$ **l** $28 = 7(y + 4)$

4 a Pete bought seven CDs in a sale. They each cost the same amount.
There was £2 off the price of each. They cost him £56 in total.

    i Check that $7(x - 2) = 56$ represents the situation where £x is the original cost of one CD.

    ii Solve $7(x - 2) = 56$ to find the original cost of each CD.

  b A telephone company increased their phone charges by 3 pence a minute.
A 6 minute call now costs 72 pence.

    i Check that $6(y + 3) = 72$ represents the situation where y pence is the original charge per minute.

    ii Solve $6(y + 3) = 72$ to find the original charge per minute.

  c A crop of nine cabbage plants each increased their weight by 2 kg during the week.
Each cabbage originally weighed x kg. Together they now weigh 63 kg.

    i Check that $9(x + 2) = 63$ represents the situation.

    ii Solve $9(x + 2) = 63$ to find the weight of each plant at the start of the week.

5 A shopkeeper makes up bags of sweets, each holding the same amount.
The shopkeeper then adds four sweets to each bag.

  a Write an expression for the number of sweets in a bag given that the original number is represented by x sweets.

  b There were ten bags. Write down an expression for the total number of sweets.

  c The total number of sweets is 190. Form an equation in x.

  d Solve the equation to find the number of sweets originally in each bag.

6 A manufacturer sells screws in packets all holding the same amount.
Rather than put the price up, he removes two screws from each packet.
To fill a hundred packets he now needs 1000 screws.

  a Let x be the number of screws originally in a packet.
Write down an expression for the number of screws in a packet now.

  b Form an expression in terms of x for the number of screws needed for 100 packets.

  c Form an equation in x and solve it to find the number of screws originally in a packet.

7 The cost of a light bulb is reduced in the sales by 15p.
A packet of six bulbs now costs 384 pence.
Let x be the original cost of a light bulb.
Form an equation in x and solve it to find this amount.

Exercise 5.2

1 Solve these equations:

  a $3(2x - 1) = 15$ **b** $5(4 + 3y) = 50$ **c** $49 = 7(3n + 1)$

  d $12 = 2(1 + 5m)$ **e** $4(5y - 1) = 36$ **f** $66 = 6(2x + 3)$

  g $8(3x - 7) = 64$ **h** $9(5y - 10) = 45$ **i** $190 = 10(2n + 3)$

  j $2(7m - 20) = 2$ **k** $7(11x + 12) = 84$ **l** $0 = 9(3k - 15)$

2 Each diagram suggests an equation.

  i   Form the equation.

  ii Solve it to find the value represented by the letter.

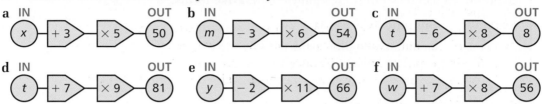

a IN x $+3$ $\times 5$ OUT 50

b IN m -3 $\times 6$ OUT 54

c IN t -6 $\times 8$ OUT 8

d IN t $+7$ $\times 9$ OUT 81

e IN y -2 $\times 11$ OUT 66

f IN w $+7$ $\times 8$ OUT 56

3 **a** I think of a number.   ... x

      I add 6.   ... $x + 6$

      I multiply this by 7. ... $7(x + 6)$

      My answer is 70.   ... $7(x + 6) = 70$

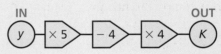

      Solve the equation to find the number.

  b In each case, write an equation and solve it to find the number thought of.

     i   'I think of a number. I subtract 6. I then multiply by 2 . My answer is 6.'

     ii 'I think of a number. I add 7. I multiply this by 3. I get 45.'

     iii 'I add 12 to a number and then double the result to get 38.'

Challenges

1 Each number machine in a pair has the same IN number and produces the same OUT number. What is the IN number?

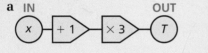

a IN x $+1$ $\times 3$ OUT T IN x -1 $\times 4$ OUT T

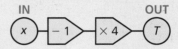

b IN y $\times 3$ $+6$ $\times 2$ OUT K IN y $\times 5$ -4 $\times 4$ OUT K

2

I thought of a number, added 7, multiplied by 3, then subtracted 10.

I thought of a number, subtracted 3, then multiplied by 7.

They both thought of the same number *and got the same answer*!

Find: **a** the number they both thought of **b** their final answer.

3 Brackets and equations

◀◀ **RECAP**

Expressions can be **simplified** if they contain **like terms**.

Example   Simplify $5x + y - 3x + 2y$

$5x$ and $3x$ are like terms with $5x - 3x = 2x$
y and $2y$ are like terms with $y + 2y = 3y$
$\Rightarrow 5x + y - 3x + 2y = 2x + 3y$

Expressions multiplied together can be simplified.

Examples $4 \times x = 4x$; $2a \times 3b = 6ab$; $y \times y = y^2$

An expression with brackets can be expanded to give an expression without brackets.
Each term within the brackets is multiplied by the term outside.

Example 1 $5(x + 2)$ ...   5 lots of $x + 2$
            $= 5x + 10$ ...   5 lots of x and 5 lots of 2

Example 2 $6(y - 5)$ ...   6 lots of $y - 5$
            $= 6y - 30$ ...   6 lots of y minus 6 lots of 5

Equations contain an equal sign, '=', and a letter representing an unknown amount.
Equations can be solved to find the value of the letter that makes the equation true.
This value is called the **solution** of the equation.
When solving an equation, always do the same thing to both sides of the equation.

Example   Solve $3x - 2 = x + 8$

$3x - 2 = x + 8$
$\Rightarrow 3x - 2 + 2 = x + 8 + 2$ ... add 2 to both sides
$\Rightarrow 3x = x + 10$
$\Rightarrow 3x - x = x + 10 - x$ ... subtract x from both sides
$\Rightarrow 2x = 10$
$\Rightarrow 2x \div 2 = 10 \div 2$ ... divide both sides by 2
$\Rightarrow x = 5$ ... this is the solution of the equation

Always check your solution by swopping it for the letter in the equation:

$3x - 2 = 3 \times 5 - 2 = 15 - 2 = 13$ and $x + 8 = 5 + 8 = 13$

Both sides are equal.

1 If $x = 2$ and $y = 7$ find the value of:
   a $2(x + 3)$ **b** $3(y - 5)$ **c** $x(x + 6)$

2 Remove the brackets:
   a $5(m + 1)$ **b** $6(n - 3)$ **c** $3(2 - x)$ **d** $4(3a + 2b)$

3 Write an expression
   i   with brackets   **ii**   without brackets for:
   a the OUT number

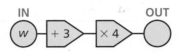

   b the perimeter of the rectangle.

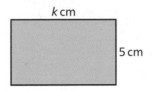

4 Multiply out the brackets and simplify:
   a $5(x - 3) + 15$ **b** $2(n + 4) - n$ **c** $12 + 3(h - 2)$

5 Solve each equation, remembering to check your solutions:
   a $x + 9 = 12$ **b** $y - 7 = 8$ **c** $5y = 35$
   d $3 = 2x$ **e** $3x + 2 = 17$ **f** $8m - 7 = 9$
   g $8n = 7n + 4$ **h** $5k = 2k + 24$ **i** $6x - 2 = x + 33$

6 Solve these equations by first removing the brackets:
   a $8(x - 5) = 56$ **b** $24 = 3(y + 4)$ **c** $8(2a + 1) - 6 = 50$

7 For each situation form an equation and solve it to answer the question.
   a 'I think of a number. I subtract 12 then multiply by 7 to get 21.
      What's my number?'

   b Total area is 28 m².
      What is the width of the left-hand pane of
      glass in this window?

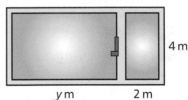

   c These two straws are the same length.
      What is this length?

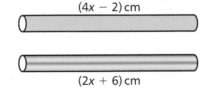

8 Gerry notices that the cost of a tyre for his car is £15 cheaper than usual.
   He buys five for his car. The total cost is £165.
   a Let £x be the usual cost of a tyre. Form an equation in x.
   b Solve the equation to find the usual cost of a tyre.

REVISE

4 Money

The euro became an official currency for non-cash transactions at the beginning of 1999.

In 2002 the euro notes and coins replaced the old currencies of Germany, France, Holland, Eire, Belgium, Luxembourg, Italy, Greece, Finland, Spain, Portugal and Austria.

1 REVIEW

◀◀ Exercise 1.1

1 Calculate:
- **a** £3·25 + £1·47
- **b** £5·68 + 75p
- **c** £8·85 − £2·26
- **d** £4·30 − 84p
- **e** £15 + £4·68 + 96p
- **f** £31 − £6·53 + 84p
- **g** £0·455 + £0·627

2 Ian buys an electric kettle for £17·95. How much change does he get from a £20 note?

3 Alice pays £34·99 for a pair of walking boots and £21·45 for a camping stove.
- **a** How much does she spend altogether?
- **b** How much change does she get from £60?

4 Calculate:
- **a** £2·75 × 4
- **b** £8·48 × 100
- **c** £7·65 ÷ 5
- **d** £199 ÷ 100
- **e** £6·47 × 1000
- **f** £840 ÷ 1000

5 **a** Golf balls cost £1·45 each. Calculate the cost of a box of 6 balls.
  b The cost of printing 100 score cards is £14.
     How much does it cost to print each card?

6 **a** Round each amount to the nearest £1:   **i** £26·49   **ii** £51·95
  b Round each amount to the nearest 10p: **i** £7·83   **ii** £13·06

7 The amounts shown on these calculators are in pounds and pence.
Write each of these amounts in words.

a

b

8 Calculate:
   a 10% of £46   b 1% of £7   c 20% of £3   d 5% of £800

9

Badminton racket	Shoes	Box of shuttles
£26·75	**£32·29**	**£7·99**

a Estimate the total cost of the badminton racket, shoes and shuttlecocks.

b Calculate the exact cost.

10 A party of 17 adults and 12 children visited the castle. What was the total cost?

Craggy Castle
Adults £6·35
Children £3·80

11 Calculate:
   a 12% of £83   b 8% of £5·50   c 85% of £74·80

---

2 Shopping bills

Some shortcuts!

Example 1   Calculate £2·45 + £3·78 + £1·55
      £2·45 + £1·55 = £4
      Answer = £4 + £3·78 = £7·78

Example 2   Calculate £63·65 − £49·99
      £63·65 − £50 = £13·65
      Answer = £13·65 + 1p = £13·66

Example 3   Calculate £6·95 × 8
      £7 × 8 = £56; 5p × 8 = 40p
      Answer = £56 − 40p = £55·60

Example 4   Calculate £6·43 × 40
      Answer = £6·43 × 4 × 10 = £25·72 × 10 = £257·20

Exercise 2.1

1 Calculate:
   a £2·50 + 99p   b £2·50 − 99p   c £4·37 + £1·95   d £5·72 − £3·99

2 Jamie buys a suit for £63, a jacket for £48 and shoes for £37. How much does he spend altogether?

3 Johanna usually pays £32·15 for a replacement ink cartridge for her computer printer.
She finds one on the internet on special offer at £18·99.
How much cheaper is the internet offer?

4 Kylie's car goes in for a service.
  a Estimate the total cost.
  b Calculate the actual total cost.

Oil & filter	£24·75
Plugs	£9·79
Labour	£45·25

5 Calculate the cost of:
  a 20 rolls of wallpaper
  b 6 litres of paint
  c 4 brushes.

DREAMS DIY CENTRE
Wallpaper ...... £8·50 per roll
Paint .... £12·99 per litre
Brushes .... £3·49 each

6 Sam works part-time at a supermarket. He is paid £5·78 per hour.
On Saturday he works 6 hours. On Sunday he works for 4 hours.
How much does he earn altogether?

7 Simon is doing a night-school course on computers.
The 20 lessons cost him £95.
What is the cost of each lesson?

8 Gemma's weekly paper bill is shown.

Mon–Sat	Daily Newsprint	6 × 50p
Sun	The Weekly Reporter	£1·35
	The Green Gardener	£2·65

Calculate the total bill for: **a** 1 week   **b** 4 weeks.

9 Tony pulls his grocery bill from his pocket to check it.
He paid with a £10 note and got £2·84 change.
He can't remember how much the cheese cost.
Work out the cost of the cheese.

Eggs	£1·27
Butter	84p
Milk	76p
Bread	£1·78
Cheese	

10 It takes 40 litres to fill the petrol tank of Corrina's car.
The price shown on the pump is £33·16.
What is the cost of 1 litre of petrol?

11 Copy and complete Gordon's bill at the meat counter.

1·5 kg rump steak at £7·40 per kg   = ...
2 kg sausages at £2·85 per kg   = ...
1·75 kg chicken at £3·40 per kg   = ...
400 g of cooked ham at 74p per 100 g = ...

Total = ...

3 Profit and loss

The **cost price** is the price goods are bought for.
The **selling price** is the price the goods are sold for.

Example 1   Sarah buys 1000 shares in Magnet Media Plc.
Each share costs £3·42.
A year later she sells them for £2·87 each.
Calculate: **a** the loss on each share   **b** the total loss.

   a Loss on one share = £3·42 − £2·87 = £0·55
   b Loss on 1000 shares = £0·55 × 1000 = £550

Example 2   Galaxy Garages buy a 4-wheel drive vehicle for £8600.
The selling price is calculated to make a 15% profit.
Calculate the selling price.

10% of £8600 = £860
5% of £8600 = £430 (half of 10%)
So 15% of £8600 = £1290
Selling price = £8600 + £1290 = £9890

Exercise 3.1

1 A newsagent sells writing pads for £1·19p.
He buys them for 75p.
How much profit does he make on each pad?

2 A stationer buys scientific calculators for £7·80 each.
She sells them for £9·49.
Calculate the profit on each calculator.

3 Ken buys a car for £1200. A year later he sells it for £995.
Calculate the loss Ken makes on the car.

4 Calculate the profit or loss made on each of these items.

a
Fridge
Cost Price
£164·50
Selling Price
£205·49

b
Washing Machine
Cost Price
£263·80
Selling Price
£339·95

c
Cooker
Cost Price
£368·60
Selling Price
£425·75

5 A bookshop buys 12 copies of *The Complete Works Of Shakespeare*
for £12·80 each. It sells 9 of them for £15·30 each and the
remaining 3 for £9·95.
   a Calculate the total profit made on the 9 books.
   b Calculate the total loss made on the remaining 3 books.
   c Does the shop make an overall profit or loss? How much?

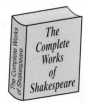

6 Jane and her friends run a tuck shop to raise money for charity.
They buy in bulk from a supermarket at these prices:

- one box of 10 ice creams costs £4·50
- one box of 50 toffee bars costs £8
- one box of 20 packets of crisps costs £3·60.

They sell all the goods at the prices shown.
How much profit do they make on a box of:
a ice creams **b** toffee bars **c** crisps?

7 Rocket Electronics pay these cost prices for the following items.

a  **b**  **c**

They aim to make a profit of 10% on each item they sell.
Calculate:
i the profit
ii the selling price for each item.

8 Toptread Plc pay a cost price of £18 for a pair of trainers.
They set the selling price to make 20% profit.
Calculate:
a the profit
b the selling price.

9 Smashing Shirts buy T-shirts for £6 each.
As a loss leader they sell them at a loss of 25%.
Calculate their selling price.

10 An art dealer buys three prints for £160 each.
He sells one for a profit of 30% and another for 5% profit.
He makes a loss of 15% on the third print.
Calculate the amount he gets for each print.

Calculating the profit as a percentage of the cost price

Example 3 A store buys a washing machine for £240.
It sells it for £283·20.
Calculate the profit as a percentage of the cost price.

Profit = £283·20 − £240 = £43·20

$$\text{Percentage profit} = \frac{43 \cdot 20}{240 \cdot 00} \times 100\% = 18\%$$

$$\text{Profit as a percentage of the cost price} = \frac{\text{profit}}{\text{cost price}} \times 100\%$$

Exercise 3.2

1 A newsagent pays 50p each for pens. He sells them for 55p.
   a How much profit is made on each pen?
   b Copy and complete: percentage profit = … ÷ 50 × 100% = …%

2 A music store buys CDs for £8. It sells them for £10.
   a How much profit is made on each CD?
   b Calculate the profit as a percentage of the cost price.

3 **i** Calculate the profit or loss on each of these transactions.
   ii Express the profit or loss as a percentage of the cost price.
   a Cost price   = £20   **b** Cost price   = 80p   **c** Cost price   = £125
   Selling price = £30   Selling price = 92p   Selling price = £100

4 A car dealer buys a second-hand car for £2000. He sells it for £2340.
   Calculate his profit as a percentage of the cost price.

5 Sara buys a ticket for a concert for £25.
   Unfortunately she can't go so she sells it for £19.
   Calculate the loss as a percentage of the cost price.

6 Calculate the profit or loss on each item as a percentage of the cost price.

   a
   | SNOWBOARD |
   | Cost Price £120 |
   | Selling Price £168 |

   b
   | SKIS |
   | Cost Price £180 |
   | Selling Price £226·80 |

   c
   | SKI BOOTS |
   | Cost Price £92 |
   | Selling Price £80·50 |

7 A wholesaler buys 20 mobile phones for £900.
   She sells them for £59·99 each.
   Calculate:
   a her profit on each phone
   b the profit as a percentage of the cost price, correct to 1 decimal place.

8 A grocer buys 144 eggs for £18.
   He sells them in boxes of 6 for 96p a box.
   Calculate his profit on each box as a percentage of the cost price.

9 Bernie bought a vase for £2·50 at a car boot sale.
   She sells it to an antique dealer for £15.
   a Calculate Bernie's profit as a percentage of the cost price.
   b The dealer sells it to a customer for £27·60.
         Calculate the dealer's profit as a percentage of his cost price.

10 A market stall trader buys a box of 40 towels for £120.
    He sells 25 of them for £4·99 each. The remainder he sells for £1·99 each.
    Calculate the profit or loss on the box of towels as a percentage of the cost price
    (correct to 1 decimal place).

4 Value Added Tax (VAT)

Teachers, civil servants, police, nurses, … schools, hospitals, … all these have to be paid for.

The government raises money by different taxes. One of these is called **Value Added Tax** or **VAT,** which is charged as a percentage on goods or services we purchase.

There are different rates of VAT:

- some items such as school books, children's clothes and medicines are **zero-rated**, meaning 0% or no VAT is charged
- on electricity and gas bills, VAT is charged at 5%
- on most other goods and services, for example cars, TVs, CDs, furniture, repair bills, or restaurant meals, VAT is charged at 17·5%.

Example 1   Calculate the VAT at 17·5% on a chair priced at £84.

Without a calculator: Note that 17·5% = 10% + 5% + 2·5%

10% of £84   = £8·40
5% of £84   = £4·20   (half of 10%)
2·5% of £84 = £2·10   (half of 5%)
17·5% of £84 = £14·70   (10% + 5% + 2·5%)

With a calculator: 17·5 ÷ 100 × £84 = £14·70

Example 2   The cost of the gas on Dave's gas bill came to £68·40.
Calculate: **a** the VAT at 5%   **b** the total bill including VAT.

a   10% of £68·40 = £6·84
So VAT = 5% of £68·40 = £3·42 (half of 10%)
b   Total bill = £68·40 + £3·42 = £71·82

Exercise 4.1

1 Find 10% of:
  a £50   **b** £9   **c** £583   **d** 60p   **e** £6400   **f** £7·50

2 Calculate 5% of:
  a £40   **b** £30   **c** £700   **d** £5
  e 80p   **f** £3700   **g** £9·20

3 Copy and complete:

10% of £36   = £….
5% of £36   = £….
2·5% of £36 = £….
17·5% of £36 = £….

4 Use the same method as question **3** to find 17·5% of:
  a £60   **b** £4   **c** £5000   **d** £48   **e** £2·60

5 Kay's electricity bill comes to £72 + VAT.
Calculate: **a** the VAT at 5%   **b** the total bill including VAT.

6 Calculate the VAT (17·5%) due on each item:
   a £200 mountain bike   **b** £18 soccer shirt
   c £1·20 tennis ball   **d** £1400 dinghy

7 Val's three course meal costs £26 + VAT.
Calculate: **a** the VAT due   **b** the total cost of the meal.

8 Gupta receives his electricity bill. The charge is £105·16 + VAT (5%).
Calculate, correct to the nearest penny:
   a the VAT due   **b** the total bill.

9 Calculate:
   i   the VAT due (17·5%)
   ii the total cost of each item (to the nearest penny).

   a   **b**   **c**   **d**

   £24·49   £2599   £167·75   £7999·99

A quick method

Where VAT is charged at 17·5% there is a quick method of finding the total cost.
Price + VAT = 100% of price + 17·5% of price = 117·5% of price,
i.e.   **1·175 × price**.

Example 3   Find the total price of a holiday that costs £650 + VAT.

   1·175 × £650 = £763·75

Exercise 4.2

1 Sue's plumbing bill comes to £86·50 + VAT.
Calculate the total bill.

2 Calculate the total cost of the picture and frame
including VAT.

Picture
£14·60

Frame
£28·40

3 George's gas bill is £62·60 + VAT (at 5%).
His electricity bill is £75·48 *including* VAT.
   a Which bill is the greater?   **b** By how much?

51

4 Calculate the total cost of each item, including VAT.

a    **b**    **c**    **d**

Mobile phone	Sun cream	Canoe	Caravan
£84·25 + VAT	£8·99 + VAT	£235·49 + VAT	£12 595 + VAT

5 Calculate this repair bill.

Roofing materials	£58·40
Labour: 5 hours at £35·80 per hour	£.......
Sub total	£.......
+ VAT at 17·5%	£.......
Total	£.......

6 The Taylors compare prices for a two week family holiday in Spain.
  a Which company is cheaper?
  b By how much?

SPANISH VILLAS
FLIGHTS:
£919·95
ACCOMODATION:
£859·99
All VAT included

EUROTRIP
FLIGHTS: £826·80 + VAT
ACCOMMODATION: £793·50 + VAT

Brainstormer

A new bathroom suite costs £799 including VAT.
Use a trial and improvement method to find the cost before VAT was added.

---

5 Telephone bills

With most telephone companies the cost of calls depends on:

the time of the day	weekday or weekend	the length of the call	how far you are phoning

There is also usually a basic charge called the **line rental**.
This is paid even if you make no calls.

Peak time is Monday to Friday between 8 am and 6 pm.
Off-peak is between 6 pm and 8 am.
The weekend is Saturday and Sunday.

The charges in the table show the rate in pence per minute for calls in the UK.

Note 1: The minimum charge for any call is 5p.

Note 2: Some telephone numbers are charged at a higher special rate.

	Local	Non-local
Peak time	4p	8p
Off-peak	1·5p	4p
Weekend	1p	2p

This table gives the international rates for calls to the USA and Europe.

	Charge per min
Peak time	24p
Off-peak	22p
Weekend	21p

Example 1   What is the cost of a 5 minute local call on Tuesday at 10.00 am?
Peak-time local rate is 4p per min.
Cost = 4p × 5 = 20p

Example 2   What is the cost of a non-local call on Saturday at 8 pm which lasts for 12 minutes?
Weekend non-local rate is 2p per minute.
Cost = 2p × 12 = 24p

Example 3   What is the cost of a 10 minute call to New York at 6 am on a Wednesday?
Off-peak international rate is 22p per minute.
Cost = 22p × 10 = £2·20

Exercise 5.1

1 Are calls at these times charged at peak, off-peak or weekend rate?
   a Sunday 3 pm   b Thursday 11 am
   c Friday 2 am   d Monday 6.30 pm

2 What is the rate per minute for each of these?
   a a local call on Wednesday at 11 am
   b non-local call on Saturday at 1 pm
   c an international call on Thursday at 9.30 am
   d non-local call on Friday at 5·30 pm

3 Wendy rings her friend on Monday at 7 pm. It is a local call and lasts for 8 minutes. What is the cost of the call?

4 Eric rings his uncle in the USA at 3 pm on a Saturday. They talk for 15 minutes. How much does the call cost?

5 Ms Smith makes a non-local call at 8.15 am on a Tuesday morning. The call lasts for 23 minutes. Calculate the cost of the call.

6 Mandy rings her friend, Gill, on Thursday at 8.30 pm. It is a local call. They chat for 20 minutes. On Sunday Gill calls her back and they talk for 25 minutes.
   a Which call costs the most?   **b** By how much?

7 Mike's mobile phone rate is 30p per minute for the first 3 minutes each day and then 5p for each extra minute. How much does it cost him on days when he uses it for a total of:

   a 4 minutes   **b** 10 minutes   **c** 20 minutes?

8 Tim is charged 12p for each of the first three text messages he sends on one day. Any further messages on that day cost 9p each. How much is he charged on days when he sends:
   a 3
   b 6
   c 12 text messages?

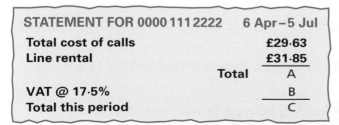

9 Jamila's telephone bill lists calls that cost over 40p.

Date	Time	Dialled number	Duration	Cost (£)
1 Apr	10:21	0870 1234567	00:14:03	0·898
5 Apr	14:43	0870 9876543	00:47:24	3·029
23 Apr	16:06	0870 1357913	01:16:08	4·864

Calculate the total cost of these calls, correct to the nearest penny.

Example 4   Here is a summary of a telephone bill.

STATEMENT FOR 0987 654 3210	6 Jan–5 Apr
Total cost of calls	£42·75
Line rental	£31·85
Total	£74·60
VAT @ 17·5%	£13·06
Total this period	£87·66

Exercise 5.2

1 Look at Jo's phone bill below. Calculate entries A, B and C.

STATEMENT FOR 0000 111 2222	6 Apr–5 Jul
Total cost of calls	£29·63
Line rental	£31·85
Total	A
VAT @ 17·5%	B
Total this period	C

2 This is Ken's phone bill.
Calculate entries A, B and C.

STATEMENT FOR 0444 555 6666   6 Jul–5 Oct

Total cost of calls	**£57·84**
Line rental	**£37·25**
Total	A
VAT @ 17·5%	B
Total this period	C

3 Draw up a phone bill like the one above.
Enter call charges of £124·63 and line rental of £37·25.
Complete the bill to calculate the total amount due.

4 This is Alana's phone bill.
Some of the bill is unreadable.
Calculate:
a the missing total
b the cost of the calls.

STATEMENT FOR 0444 777 8888   6 Oct–5 Jan

Total cost of calls	
Line rental	**£31·85**
Total	
VAT @ 17·5%	**£15·42**
Total this period	**£103·53**

6 Gas and electricity bills

A gas or electricity bill shows you:

- how many units have been used
- the VAT at 5%
- the charge for those units
- the total charge.

The amount of gas or electricity used can be calculated from meter readings.

Example 1   Calculate the number of units used in this period.

	Meter readings	
Period	Present	Previous
9 Apr–8 Jul	32 518	31 849

Units used = present − previous = 32 518 − 31 849 = 669 units

Power companies often charge two rates.
The first thousand or so units are charged at one rate.
Any units used above this number are charged at a lower rate.

Example 2   Find the cost of 6385 units when the first 1150 are charged at 1·792p
per unit and the rest at the rate of 1·428p per unit.

The first 1150 units at 1·792p = 2060·8p
= 2061p
= £20·61 (to nearest penny)
The rest, 6385 − 1150   = 5235 units at 1·428p
= 7475·58p
= £74·76 (to nearest penny)
Total = £95·37

Exercise 6.1

1 Calculate the number of units used over each of these periods.

Meter readings

Period	Present	Previous
a 9 Jan–8 Apr	4782	3916
b 9 Apr–8 Jul	73528	72384

2 Mr Watt's electricity bill shows that he used 450 units. The cost for each unit is 5·640p. How much is he charged? Write your answer in pounds and pence.

3 Calculate the cost in pounds and pence, correct to the nearest penny, of these amounts of electricity:

a 693 units at 6·420p each   **b** 1279 units at 7·837p each

4 These are the unit charges for Mrs Mantle's gas bill:
first 1200 units at 1·760p; next 4620 units at 1·325p.
Calculate in pounds and pence, to the nearest penny:

a the cost of   **i** the first 1200 units   **ii** the 4620 units
b the total cost.

5 VAT, at 5%, is added to gas and electricity bills.
This is part of Lisa's gas bill.

a Calculate A by finding 5% of £62·80.
b Calculate B by adding the VAT to £62·80.

Total gas and charges	....	**£62·80**
VAT at 5%	....	A
Amount due	....	B

6 Look at Frank's electricity bill below.
Calculate the entries A and B.

Reading dates	Present	Previous	Units	Cost/unit	Charges (£)
9 Jan–8 Apr	9847	9197	650	5·240p	£34·06
VAT at 5%					A
Amount due					B

Standing charges

Some power companies have a standing charge. This is paid even if no units are used.

Example 3   Look at this electricity bill.

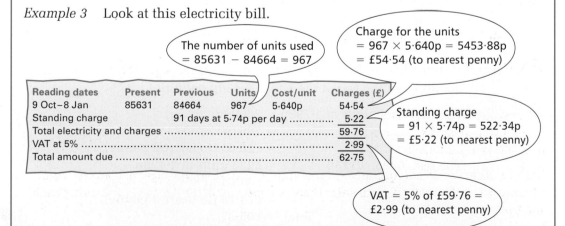

The number of units used
= 85631 − 84664 = 967

Charge for the units
= 967 × 5·640p = 5453·88p
= £54·54 (to nearest penny)

Reading dates	Present	Previous	Units	Cost/unit	Charges (£)
9 Oct–8 Jan	85631	84664	967	5·640p	54·54
Standing charge		91 days at 5·74p per day			5·22
Total electricity and charges					59·76
VAT at 5%					2·99
Total amount due					62·75

Standing charge
= 91 × 5·74p = 522·34p
= £5·22 (to nearest penny)

VAT = 5% of £59·76 =
£2·99 (to nearest penny)

Exercise 6.2

1 Calculate the entries A, B, C and D in this electricity bill.

Reading dates	Present	Previous	Units	Cost/unit	Charges (£)
9 Jan–8 Apr	8528	7648	A	5·640p	B
Standing charge		89 days at 5·74p per day			C
Total electricity and charges					D

2 Mr West uses 6483 units of gas.
The first 1185 units cost 1·794p per unit.
  a Calculate the cost of these units, in pounds and pence, correct to the nearest penny.
  b The remaining units cost 1·209p per unit.
    i How many units are remaining?
    ii Calculate the cost of these units, in pounds and pence, to the nearest penny.
  c What is the total charge for all the units used?

3 Over the same period of time, Mrs Yates uses 8241 units of gas.
Use the same prices as in question **2** to calculate the total charge for the units used.

4 Copy this electricity bill and fill in the missing entries.

Reading dates	Present	Previous	Units	Cost/unit	Charges (£)
9 Apr–8 Jul	6438	5718	...	5·640p	
Standing charge		90 days at 6·15p per day			
Total electricity and charges					
VAT at 5%					
Total amount due					

Investigation

One unit of electricity on a bill is 1 kilowatt hour (kWh).
A typical one-bar electric fire uses 1 kW to run and will use 1 unit per hour.
At 7p per kWh it would cost 7p to run the fire for 1 hour.

The cost of running a 100 W light bulb for one hour $= 7 \times \dfrac{100}{1000} = 0 \cdot 7p$

(1 kW = 1000 watts)

What would it cost to run:
a a 7 kW shower for 1 hour
b a 200 W light bulb for 1 hour?

$$\text{Hourly rate} = 7 \times \frac{\text{watts}}{1000}$$

Look at other electrical appliances. You should find their wattage written on them.
Make a list of the watts or kilowatts they use and calculate the cost of running each
for 1 hour.

7 Changing money abroad

This list gives the value of £1 when this book was written.

Country	Currency	£1 buys
Euro zone	Euro (€)	1·42
USA	Dollar ($)	1·62
Switzerland	Swiss franc	2·04
Japan	Yen	183·33
India	Rupee	76·51
Denmark	Kroner	10·04

Example 1   Change £45 into rupees.
£45 = 45 × 76·51 rupees = 3442·95 rupees

Example 2   Change 20 000 rupees into pounds.
20 000 rupees = 20 000 ÷ 76·51 = £261·40 (to nearest penny)

 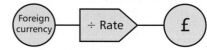

Exercise 7.1

Use the exchange rates given in the table to answer questions **1–4**.

1 Change £10 into:
  a euro   **b** dollars   **c** yen   **d** kroner.

2 Mrs Ryan and her daughter Meg are visiting the USA.
  Mrs Ryan changes £1000 into dollars ($). Meg changes £50.
  How much does: **a**   Mrs Ryan   **b**   Meg receive?

3 Terry is going on holiday to France and Switzerland.
  He changes £200 into euro and £80 into Swiss francs.
  How many:
  a euro   **b** Swiss francs does he get?

4 On a business trip to Japan, Mr Wheeler exchanges
  £600 into the local currency.
  How much does the exchange bureau give him?

5 This graph helps change between pounds (£) and
  euros (€) when the rate is €1·40 = £1.
  a Use the graph to change these amounts into euro:
    i   £20   **ii**   £50   **iii**   £75
  b Use the graph to change these amounts into
    pounds:
    i   €85   **ii**   €60   **iii**   €110

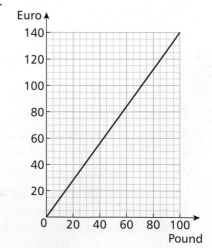

6 Use the exchange rates in the table at the start of this exercise to change these amounts into pounds, correct to the nearest penny:

    a €10   **b** $10   **c** 100 Swiss francs   **d** 1000 kroner

7 Diana bought these presents while on holiday in Europe.
Using the same table, change each price into pounds, correct to the nearest 10p.

    a   **b**   **c**   **d**

    Handbag €30   Shoes €65   Earrings €18   Watch €128

When foreign currency isn't spent and is changed back into pounds, the exchange rate can be different.

Example 3   Roger flies to Japan and changes £750 into yen at £1 = 183·33 yen.

        a How many yen does he get?

        b He spends 125 000 yen. On returning to Britain he changes his remaining yen back into pounds at a rate of £1 = 185·80 yen. How much does he get in pounds?

        a Amount received = 750 × 183·33 = 137 497·5 yen

        b Amount left = 137 497·5 − 125 000 = 12 497·5 yen

                = 12 497·5 ÷ 185·8 = £67·26 to nearest penny

Exercise 7.2

Use the exchange rates given in the table before Exercise 7.1 unless another rate is given.

1 On holiday in the USA, Ken buys a CD for $9.
His school friend Karl buys the same CD in Spain for €8.
Who got the better deal?
Show your working.

2 Giving your answers correct to 2 decimal places, change:

    a £5·70 into euro   **b** £62·75 into dollars

    c £128·50 into Swiss francs   **d** £284·30 into yen

    e £99·99 into rupees   **f** £450·80 into kroner

3 Change these amounts into pounds, correct to the nearest 10p.

    a €75·50   **b** $625·74   **c** 13·52 Swiss francs

    d 127 643 yen   **e** 739·50 rupees   **f** 3842·73 kroner

4 On holiday in Germany, Kay buys a watch for €174·99.
In Switzerland the same make and model of watch costs 284·49 Swiss francs.
In which country is the watch cheaper? By how much (in pounds)?

5 On holiday in Britain, Wilbur changes $840 into pounds at a rate of £1 = $1·62.
   a How much does he receive?
   b He spends £485·50. Back in the USA he changes his remaining pounds back into dollars at a rate of £1 = $1·70. How much does he get?

6 On business in Italy, Marie changes £725 into euro at a rate of £1 = €1·42.
   In Italy she spends €950·50. She changes the euro she has left into pounds at a rate of £1 = €1·49. How much does she receive, correct to the nearest £1?

---

8 Loans and hire purchase

Nicola doesn't have £1200 to buy the new 3-piece suite.
She has two choices. She could either
i   take out a loan or
ii buy it on Hire Purchase (HP).

3-piece suite
Cash Price
£1200

In each case the money is paid back in monthly instalments.
Nicola should shop around and find the best deal.

Example 1   Nicola arranges a loan of £1200 from her bank.
                She repays the loan by making six payments of £215.
                a Calculate her total repayments.
                b How much more than £1200 does she pay?

                a Total repayments = 6 × £215 = £1290
                b She pays £1290 − £1200 = £90 more.

Exercise 8.1

1 Jack borrows £2800 to pay for repairs to his roof.
   His total repayments over one year add up to £3108.
   How much does the loan cost him?

2 Paula takes out a bank loan for a new kitchen.
   She borrows £1800 and makes six repayments of £320.
   a Calculate her total repayments.
   b Paula borrowed £1800. How much more is paid back?

3 Austin borrows £5000 to replace his old car.
   His repayments are £268 a month for 20 months.
   a How much does he pay altogether?
   b How much more than £5000 does he pay?

In questions **4** to **8** calculate:

a the hire purchase price
b the difference between the HP and the cash price.

4 PERSONAL STEREO
Cash price £89·99
or
6 payments of
£16·49

5 MOUNTAIN BIKE
Cash price £195·49
or
10 monthly payments
of £22·99

6 DIGITAL CAMERA
Cash price £312·95
or
12 monthly
payments of £27·49

7 LAPTOP COMPUTER
Cash price £899·99
or
24 monthly payments
of £39·99

8 4 × 4 TRAILBLAZER
Cash price £16 999
or
36 monthly
payments of £519·99

With hire purchase sometimes a **deposit** has to be paid.
This payment must be paid before the goods can be taken home.
Often this deposit is a percentage of the cash price.

Example 2   Calculate:
    a the total cost of buying the suite on HP
    b the difference between the HP
       price and the cash price.

    a Deposit = 10% of £1200 = £120
       Instalments = 12 × £99·99 = £1199·88
       Total HP = £120 + £1199·88 = £1319·88
    b Difference = £1319·88 − £1200 = £119·88

3-PIECE SUITE
Cash price £1200 or
10% deposit + 12 monthly
instalments of £99·99

Exercise 8.2

1 There are two ways of buying a guitar: for a cash price of £89
or for a £20 deposit and 6 monthly instalments of £12·99.
Calculate:
  a the total monthly payments
  b the total HP price including deposit
  c the difference between the HP and the cash price.

2 Two ways of buying a DVD player are shown.
Calculate:
  a the total monthly payments
  b the total HP price including deposit
  c the difference between the HP and the
     cash price.

DVD PLAYER
CASH PRICE *£249·95*
or
£39·99 deposit &
12 monthly instalments
of
£19·99

For questions **3** and **4** calculate:

a the deposit
b the total monthly payments
c the total HP price including deposit
d the difference between the HP and the cash price.

3

> **COMPUTER & ACCESSORIES**
> **CASH PRICE £795**
> or 10% deposit &
> 12 monthly payments of £64·95

4

> **COMPACT CAR**
> **CASH PRICE £8990**
> or 12·5% deposit &
> 24 monthly payments of £349·95

5 a Calculate the cost of each of the instalment plans.
b How much would you save in each case if you paid cash?

> **KEYBOARD**
> **CASH PRICE £229**
> or 24 weeks at £10·99
> or 36 weeks at £7·99

6 a Calculate the cost of each of the instalment plans.
b How much would you save in each case if you paid the cash price?
c Which do you think is the best value? Give your reasons.

> **GOLF CLUBS**
> **CASH PRICE £599·99**
> or 10% deposit & 12 instalments of £49·99
> or 5% deposit & 24 instalments of £26·99

9 Car insurance premiums

By law, drivers must be insured in case they injure other road users or cause damage. This is called 'Third Party Insurance'.

Usually insurance against fire and theft is added to a Third Party policy.

If a car owner wants to insure against damage to himself and his own car he takes out a 'Comprehensive' policy.

Insurance rates vary according to the area where the driver lives and the type of car. If a driver makes no claims on his insurance he may get a discount, called a **no-claims bonus**.

The table gives comprehensive premiums for 12 months of cover with Crazy Car Insurance Plc.

		Area		
		low risk	medium risk	high risk
Car type	small	£380	£487	£625
	saloon	£490	£584	£986
	sports	£683	£839	£1264

Note: Drivers under 25 years of age pay an extra 50%

No-claims bonus:

No. of years	Discount
1	10%
2	20%
3	30%
4	40%
5	50%
6 or more	60%

Example Bee Green lives in a medium risk area and drives a saloon car. She is 28. She has 3 years no-claims bonus. Calculate the cost of a comprehensive policy.

Cost without no-claims bonus = £584
No-claims bonus of 30% = 30 ÷ 100 × £584 = £175·20
Actual cost = £584 − £175·20 = £408·80

Exercise 9.1

1 What is the annual cost of a comprehensive policy, before any no-claims discount, for each of these drivers?
   a Ahmed who lives in a low risk area and drives a small car
   b Yvonne who lives in a high risk area and drives a sports car
   c Eric who lives in a medium risk area and drives a small car

2 Mrs Ford drives a small car and lives in a high risk area.
   a How much is her insurance for 12 months?
   b She gets a no-claims bonus of £125. Calculate her premium.

3 **a** Linda's cover costs £584 less 50% no-claims bonus.
      How much does the no-claims bonus save her?
   b Dylan's insurance costs £986 less 30% no-claims bonus.
      How much does the no-claims bonus save him?

4 John is 21 years old. He is buying a small car and lives in a high risk area.
   Calculate the cost of his insurance.
   (Remember the extra 50% for drivers aged under 25.)

5 Tania lives in a high risk area and drives a saloon car.
   a How much is her insurance?
   b She has a one year no-claims bonus. Calculate her discount.
   c How much does she pay for her insurance?

6 Mr Grey drives a saloon car and lives in a low risk area.
   He has 4 years no-claims bonus.
   How much does he pay for a year's insurance?

7 Ms Davies lives in a medium risk area and drives a sports car.
   She has 6 years no-claims bonus.
   Calculate her annual insurance.

10 More insurance

Many things can go wrong on holiday and at home – theft, fire, medical bills, holiday cancellation, loss of money or valuables, injury or even death.

It is possible to take out insurance policies against any of these things happening.

Travel and valuables insurance

It is sensible to take out travel insurance when going on holiday in case:
- the trip has to be cancelled
- you are ill or injured and have to pay medical bills
- you lose your money or baggage, or they are stolen.

The table shows how much Tragic Travel Insurance Plc charge one person for insurance. The cost depends on destination and length of stay.

No. of days	UK (£)	Europe (£)	Worldwide (£)
1–3	8·25	14·50	30·50
4–6	9·75	16·80	36·70
7–9	11·52	22·60	39·45
10–17	14·83	24·85	42·50
18–25	18·56	26·90	45·37
26–35	22·85	30·25	48·52
each extra week	5·30	8·25	15·78

Note: these prices do not include skiing holidays. To include skiing all prices must be doubled.

Example   Wanda is going to spend a week sightseeing in Italy. How much will her travel insurance cost?

From the table, 7 days in Europe will cost £22·60.

Exercise 10.1

1 Sheila takes out a policy for a 3-day trip to Paris. What is the cost of her premium?

2 Phil is flying to the USA for three weeks. How much is his policy?

3 Karen is going for a short 5-day break in London. What would her insurance cost?

4 Vanessa has booked a fortnight skiing holiday in France. How much is her insurance premium?

5 Mr and Mrs Hill are going on a 6-week trekking holiday in Australia. How much will it cost to insure both of them?

6 It is possible to insure valuable items separately against theft or loss.
These might include cameras, computers, jewellery or sports equipment.
Home and Away Insurance have 12-month policies. Their charges depend on the
value of the item. For each £100 of the value the cost is £4·75.

Calculate the cost of insuring the following for 12 months:
a a camera, value £800   **b** a mountain bike, value £300
c a computer, value £1600 **d** jewellery, value £9500.

Building and contents insurance

Contents insurance
It is possible to insure furniture and other household items against fire, theft and
accidental damage. A separate policy is usually taken out for valuables.

Example 1   For one year's cover, The Happy Homes Insurance Company will
charge £3·57 for each £1000 of the value insured. Mr and Mrs Baker
calculate that the total value of their house contents is £45 000.
How much is the insurance premium for 1 year?

£45 000 ÷ 1000 = 45
Their policy will cost 45 × £3·57 = £160·65.

Building insurance
This usually covers damage by fire, storm, floods, lightning, subsidence, theft and
vandalism. For one year's cover, The Happy Homes Insurance Company will charge
53p for each £1000 of the value insured.

Example 2   Mr Jackson insures his bungalow for £85 000.
Calculate the cost of one year's insurance.

£85 000 ÷ 1000 = 85
Insurance cost = 85 × 53p = £45·05

Exercise 10.2

1 Jules rents a flat. He insures its contents for a total value of £5000.
Calculate the cost of one year's insurance with Happy Homes.

2 Donna lives in an apartment. She reckons that her contents would cost £12 000 to
replace. How much would a policy with Happy Homes cost?

3 Mr Castle lives in a house valued at £60 000.
How much would Happy Homes charge for a one year policy?

4 Mr and Mrs Temple own a detached house worth £230 000.
Calculate the cost of insuring the building with Happy Homes.

5 Josie takes out both building and contents policies with Happy Homes.
She puts values of £45 000 on her flat and £15 000 on the contents.
a Calculate the cost of insuring   **i** the building   **ii** the contents.
b What is the total cost of the policies?

6 Mike and Kay live in a house, value £115 000. They estimate the contents would cost £23 000 to replace.
  a Calculate the cost of insuring   **i** the building   **ii** the contents.
  b What is the total cost of the policies?

7 The Fitzwilliams own a large villa. The building is insured for £780 000. The contents are insured for £120 000.
  a Calculate the cost of insuring   **i** the building   **ii** the contents.
  b What is the total cost of the policies?

◄◄ **RECAP**

Profit and Loss
Cost price is the amount paid for goods.
Selling price is the amount the goods are sold for.
You should be able to calculate the profit or loss made when goods are bought and sold, and to work with percentages.
- profit = selling price − cost price (a loss if negative)
- percentage profit = $\frac{\text{profit}}{\text{cost price}} \times 100\%$

Value Added Tax (VAT)
You should be able to calculate the VAT on goods and services.
VAT is a tax added to the cost of goods.
- 0%   …   school books, children's clothes, medicines
- 5%   …   electricity and gas bills
- 17·5% …   most other items

Household bills
You should be able to calculate phone, gas and electricity bills.
- Units used = present reading − previous reading
- The bill may include the cost of the units, a standing charge and VAT (at 5% for gas and electricity).
- The first thousand or so units may be cheaper than the rest.

Hire Purchase (HP)
You should be able to calculate the cost of buying goods on HP.
A **deposit** may be asked for. This is often a percentage of the cost price.
The rest of the bill is made up of equal, regular payments called **instalments**.

Insurance premiums
An insurance **premium** is a yearly payment made to a company who will then cover you against financial loss.
You should be able to work with insurance premiums involving building and contents, cars, travel and valuables.
- The premiums for house and contents depend on the value of the goods insured.
- The premium for car insurance depends on the value of the vehicle and the length of time since the last claim was made, and is calculated using **no-claims bonus** tables.

Foreign currency exchange
You should be able to change from one currency to another.
The rate of exchange varies all the time and can be found in newspapers, on teletext and on the net.

1 Harry buys a CD, a DVD and a video.

CDs	£9·95
DVDs	£12·80
Videos	£7·20

  a Estimate the total cost.
  b Calculate:
    i the actual cost   **ii** the change from £40.

2 A shopkeeper buys 50 scientific calculators for £5·99 each.
  a What is the total cost of the calculators?
  b He sells them at £10·49 each.
    How much money, in total, does he get for them?
  c How much profit does he make?

3 Jani is charged 12p for each of the first three text messages she sends each day.
  Any further messages that day cost 9p each.
  How much is she charged for each of these days when she sends:

  a 2   **b** 4   **c** 10 text messages?

4 Twelve months' car insurance costs Christine £780, less her no-claims discount.
  For three years without a claim she gets a discount of 30%.
  Calculate:
  a the discount   **b** the amount she pays for her insurance.

5 **a** A store buys skateboards for £36 each.
    They want to make a profit of 12%.
    What should the selling price be?
  b The cost price of their roller blades is £58.
    The selling price is £69·99.
    Calculate the profit as a percentage of the cost price, correct to 1 decimal place.

6 **a** Mr Patel's gas bill comes to £84·60 before VAT is added.
    Calculate:
    i the VAT, at 5%   **ii** the total bill including VAT.
  b His phone bill is £91·58 before VAT.
    Calculate the total amount due including VAT, charged at 17·5%.

7 **a** Calculate the cost, in pounds and pence correct to the nearest penny, of 947 units
    of electricity at 6·473p per unit.
  b Calculate the entries A, B, C, D, E and F in this electricity bill.

Reading dates	Present	Previous	Units	Cost/unit	Charges (£)
9 Jul–8 Oct	3174	2393	A	5·820p	B
Standing charge		91 days at 6·15p per day			C
Total electricity and standing charge					D
VAT at 5%					E
Total amount due					F

8 Julie changes £280 into dollars at a rate of £1 = $1·63.
  a How many dollars is she given?
  b On holiday she spends $395. She changes the remaining dollars back into pounds
    at the same rate. How much does she get, correct to the nearest 10p?

9 Calculate:
  a the hire purchase price
  b the difference between the HP
   and the cash price.

CAR STEREO
CASH PRICE **£158**
or 10% deposit &
12 payments of £13·49

10 Illustrious Insurance charge these rates:

Building insurance   62p for each £1000 value of the property.
Contents insurance   £3·48 for each £1000 value of the goods.

Mr and Mrs Wright insure their house for £90 000 and the contents for £25 000.
Calculate the amount they pay to insure:
  a the building   **b** the contents.

5 Factors

It is often important to be able to reverse a process, although not all processes can be reversed.

 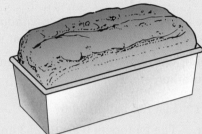

You can usually reverse a car ...   ... but try unbaking a loaf of bread!

1 REVIEW

Reminders

1 The **multiples** of 6 are 6, 12, 18, 24, ... They form the '6 times table'.

2 Some expressions are 'shorter forms' for multiplication, for example:

$a \times a = a^2; 4 \times a = 4a; 2a \times 3 = 6a; 2a \times 3a = 6a^2$

3 To expand brackets, each term inside the bracket is multiplied by the term outside, for example:

$3(2x + 4) = 3 \times 2x + 3 \times 4 = 6x + 12$

◄◄ Exercise 1.1

1 List the first five multiples of:

  a 2   **b** 9   **c** 7   **d** 11   **e** 100

2 **a** The multiples of 3 are 3, 6, 9, 12, 15, ...
     The multiples of 5 are 5, 10, 15, 20, 25 ...
     The multiples common to 3 and 5 are 15, 30, 45, ...
     What are these numbers multiples of?
  b List the first three common multiples of
     i   3 and 7   **ii**   2 and 5   **iii**   2 and 3.
  c 15 is the **lowest common multiple** (l.c.m.) of 3 and 5.
     State the lowest common multiple of
     i   3 and 7   **ii**   2 and 5   **iii**   2 and 3.

3 Write in shorter form:

  a $x \times 5$ **b** $w \times w$ **c** $5 \times 3c$ **d** $2y \times 3y$ **e** $5a \times 2b$

  f 5×5 **g** $t \times t \times t$ **h** $7k \times 2k$ **i** $y \times 4y$ **j** $4a \times 6a$

4 Remove the brackets:

  a $7(x - 3)$ **b** $5(2 - y)$ **c** $3(a + b)$ **d** $5(6x - 5)$

  e $x(x - 2)$ **f** $y(6 + y)$ **g** $a(a + b)$ **h** $5(6x - 5)$

  i $g(g - 1)$ **j** $m(8 + m)$ **k** $a(3a + 1)$ **l** $9(1 - 2x)$

2 Factors and primes

When one number divides another *without a remainder*, it is said to be a **factor** of that number.

Any number with only two factors is called a **prime number**.

$6 \div 1 = 6$ remainder 0 ✓
$6 \div 2 = 3$ remainder 0 ✓
$6 \div 3 = 2$ remainder 0 ✓
$6 \div 4 = 1$ remainder 2 ✗
$6 \div 5 = 1$ remainder 1 ✗
$6 \div 6 = 1$ remainder 0 ✓

Example 1   List the factors of 6.

    The factors of 6 are 1, 2, 3 and 6.

Example 2   **a** List the factors common to 42 and 30.

    b State the **highest common factor** (h.c.f.) of 42 and 30.

    a The factors of 42 are 1, 2, 3, 6, 7, 14, 21, 42.

      The factors of 30 are 1, 2, 3, 5, 6, 10, 15, 30.

      The numbers 1, 2, 3 and 6 are common to both lists. These are the common factors.

    b The number 6 is the highest number in this list so 6 is the h.c.f.

Example 3   Why is 1 not a prime number?

    1 has only one factor. Prime numbers have two.

Exercise 2.1

1 List all the factors of:

  a 10   **b** 13   **c** 8   **d** 12   **e** 25   **f** 50

2 For each pair of numbers below:

  i   list their factors

  ii list their common factor(s)

  iii state the highest common factor.

  a 16 and 30   **b** 24 and 84   **c** 63 and 8   **d** 100 and 40

3 Find the highest common factor of:

  a 132 and 99   **b** 200 and 75   **c** 81 and 50

4 **a** List the factors of each of the numbers from 1 to 10.

  b Which of these numbers have only two factors?

  c Any number with only two factors is called a prime number. List all the prime numbers less than 30.

5 **a** What is the only even prime number?

   b What is the smallest prime number after 49?

   c Two prime numbers are neighbouring if there are no prime numbers between them. 7 and 11 are neighbouring primes. There are three numbers between them. What is the biggest gap between neighbouring prime numbers less than 50?

6 Eratosthenes, a Greek mathematician who lived from 276 to 194 BC, suggested the following method for finding primes.

Step 1 Make a grid of numbers in columns as shown:

1	2	3	4	5	6	7	8	9	10
11	12	13	14	15	16	17	18	19	20
21	22	23	24	25	26	27	28	29	30
31	32	33	34	35	36	37	38	39	40
41	42	43	44	45	46	47	48	49	50
51	52	53	54	55	56	57	58	59	60
61	62	63	64	65	66	67	68	69	70
71	72	73	74	75	76	77	78	79	80
81	82	83	84	85	86	87	88	89	90
91	92	93	94	95	96	97	98	99	100

Step 2 Score out 1. It is not prime.

Step 3 Circle the first number not scored out (2) and then score out every number after that which can be divided by 2.

Step 4 Circle the first number not scored out (3) and then score out every number after that which can be divided by 3.

Step 5 Circle the first number not scored out (5) and then score out every number after that which can be divided by 5.

Step 6 Keep going until you run out of numbers.
You will have circled all the **primes** between 1 and 100.

This method is known as the **sieve of Eratosthenes**.

7 If a factor is also a prime number it is called a **prime factor**.
The prime factors of 6 are 2 and 3.
List the prime factors of:

   a 10 **b** 13 **c** 8 **d** 12 **e** 25 **f** 50 **g** 99

For big numbers a system should be used.

Example 1 Find the prime factors of 504.

Keep trying to divide
by the smallest
possible prime
until a result of 1
is achieved.

2	504
2	252
2	126
3	63
3	21
7	7
	1

So $504 = 2 \times 2 \times 2 \times 3 \times 3 \times 7$
The prime factors of 504 are 2, 3 and 7.

Example 2   Find *all* the factors of 60.

2	60
2	30
3	15
5	5
	1

Find the prime factors first.
Note that 60 = 1 × 2 × 2 × 3 × 5
So consider 1, 2, 2, 3, 5.

Using no prime factors: 1   1
Using one prime factor: 2, 3, 5   2, 3, 5
Using a product of two prime factors: 2 × 2, 2 × 3, 2 × 5, 3 × 5   4, 6, 10, 15
Using a product of three prime factors: 2 × 2 × 3, 2 × 2 × 5, 2 × 3 × 5   12, 20, 30
Using a product of four prime factors: 2 × 2 × 3 × 5   60

The factors of 60 are 1, 2, 3, 4, 5, 6, 10, 12, 15, 20, 30, 60.

Exercise 2.2

1 Find the prime factors of:

a 42	**b** 36	**c** 140
d 56	**e** 45	**f** 105
g 126	**h** 198	**i** 110
j 114	**k** 759	**l** 665

2 Find all the factors of:

a 12	**b** 35	**c** 48
d 71	**e** 78	**f** 240
g 300	**h** 405	**i** 325
j 165	**k** 221	**l** 1000

3 **a** Find the common factors of 60 and 45.
   b Write down the highest common factor (h.c.f.).
   c Work out the h.c.f. of:
      i   12 and 100   **ii**   32 and 88   **iii**   36 and 390

4 A town park had two paths. One was 2730 cm long and the other 2970 cm.
   The planners wanted to find a slab size that would pave both paths without cutting.
   Each slab size is a complete number of centimetres.
   a What slab sizes are possible (although not necessarily practical)?
      Hint: find the common factors of 2730 and 2970.
   b What is the largest practical size?

5 Bill has 1620 pennies and Jill has 4900.
   They each wish to split them into equal size bundles and have
   no coins left over.
   They want the same size of bundle as each other.
   a What is the biggest such a bundle can be?
   b How many such bundles will be made by
      i   Bill
      ii   Jill?

Challenges

a All the factors of a number, except the number itself, are called its **proper factors**.
For example, the proper factors of 6 are 1, 2 and 3.
Note that in this case the sum of the proper factors equals the number itself:
$1 + 2 + 3 = 6$.
When this happens, the number is called **perfect**.
There is another perfect number less than 30. Can you find it?

b The sixteenth century mathematician, Mersenne, suggested that many numbers of the form $2 \times 2 \times 2 \times \ldots \times 2 - 1$ were primes.
Investigate his claim when there are 1, 2, 3, 4, 5 twos.
To date the largest known prime is $2^{13\,466\,917} - 1$,
that is a Mersenne prime with 13 466 917 twos multiplied together then minus 1!

3 Factors and expressions

The factors of a number come in pairs which when multiplied together produce the number.

Example 1 **a** Find all the ways that 16 can be written as a product of two numbers.
b Hence state all the factors of 16.

a $1 \times 16 = 16$
$2 \times 8 \;= 16$
$4 \times 4 \;= 16$

> Being systematic, starting at 1, every time we found one factor we found a larger partner.

b The factors of 16 are 1, 2, 4, 8 and 16.

Example 2 Write down all the factors of 24 by considering factor pairs.
$1 \times 24 = 24$
$2 \times 12 = 24$
$3 \times 8 \;= 24$
$4 \times 6 \;= 24$
The factors of 24 are 1, 2, 3, 4, 6, 8, 12 and 24.

Expressions can also be **factorised** in this manner.

Example 3 Write down all the factors of $9a$ by considering factor pairs.
$1 \times 9a = 9a$
$3 \times 3a = 9a$
$9 \times a \;= 9a$
The factors of $9a$ are 1, 3, 9, a, $3a$ and $9a$.

Example 4 Write down all the factors of $2xy$.
$1 \times 2xy = 2xy$
$2 \times xy \;= 2xy$
$x \times 2y \;= 2xy$
$y \times 2x \;= 2xy$
The factors of $2xy$ are 1, 2, x, y, $2x$, $2y$, xy and $2xy$.

Exercise 3.1

1 List the different factor pairs whose product gives the number:

   a 6   **b** 9   **c** 10   **d** 15   **e** 18
   f 19   **g** 20   **h** 25   **i** 32   **j** 36

2 For each expression, find all the different ways it can be written as a product of two factors:

   a $3y$ **b** $7a$ **c** $5x$ **d** $4w$ **e** $9k$ **f** $6m$ **g** $10b$
   h mn **i** x^2 **j** pq **k** c^2 **l** $2ab$ **m** $3y^2$

3 Find the missing factor in these products:

   a $4 = 2 \times \ldots$ **b** $mn = m \times \ldots$ **c** $8r = 2 \times \ldots$
   d $9k = 3 \times \ldots$ **e** $12x = \ldots \times 4x$ **f** $10y = \ldots \times 5$
   g $7m = \ldots \times 1$ **h** $xy = y \times \ldots$ **i** $4s = 2s \times \ldots$
   j $a^2 = a \times \ldots$ **k** $2k^2 = 2 \times \ldots$ **l** $2n^2 = 2n \times \ldots$
   m $e^2 = 1 \times \ldots$ **n** $3ab = 3b \times \ldots$ **o** $6xy = 2y \times \ldots$

4 By considering factor pairs, list all the factors of the following:

   a $6k$ **b** $14b$ **c** $7ab$ **d** $12q$
   e $4kt$ **f** pqr **g** $13g$ **h** fg
   i $3x^2$ **j** $4x^2$ **k** $x^2 y$ **l** $2 x^2 y$

Challenges

1 Factors can be found by thinking of a **decision tree**.

  Example   Breaking $2ab$ into its basic parts gives us $2 \times a \times b$ ... 3 parts.
                 We can choose to have or not have each part in the factor.
                 See if you can follow the decision tree.

We can choose to have or not have 2.
Whatever we decide, we can choose to have or not have a.
Whatever we decide, we can choose to have or not have b.

We will end up with eight possible factors.

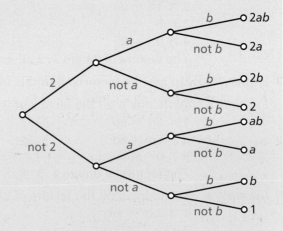

  a Make a decision tree to help you factorise:

     i $2a$ **ii** $7xy$ **iii** 70

    (Hint: think of it as prime factors $2 \times 5 \times 7$.)

  b Explore what happens when one part is duplicated, for example:

     i $2a^2$ **ii** $4a$ **iii** 12

    (Hint: think of it as $2 \times 2 \times 3$.)

2 The hunt for partners! Pairs of factors multiply to give $24a^2b$.
Can you match all the partners of the pairs?
Each one in the green set matches with one in the black set.

A. 1   B. $3a$ C. $3a^2$ D. ab
E. $2b$ F. $3a^2b$ G. a^2 H. $3ab$
I. 2   J. 4   K. a^2b L. $4b$
M. a N. $4a^2$ O. 3   P. $2a^2b$
Q. b R. $4a$ S. $4a^2b$ T. $2a^2$
U. $2ab$ V. $2a$ W. $4ab$ X. $3b$

1. $6a^2b$ 2. $12b$ 3. $6a^2$ 4. $24a^2$
5. $12ab$ 6. $24b$ 7. 6   8. $8a$
9. $8a^2b$ 10. $12a^2$ 11. $24a^2b$ 12. $24a$
13. $8b$ 14. $8a^2$ 15. $24ab$ 16. 12
17. $12a$ 18. 24   19. $12a^2b$ 20. $6a$
21. $6b$ 22. 8   23. $8ab$ 24. $6ab$

When working with expressions, we take the highest common factor to be the one with most parts and the biggest numerical part.

Example   a List the factors of   i $6a$ ii $9ab$.
b List the factors common to both lists.
c State the highest common factor of $6a$ and $9ab$.

a i   The factors of $6a$ are: 1, 2, 3, 6, a, $2a$, $3a$, $6a$.
ii   The factors of $9ab$ are: 1, 3, 9, a, b, $3a$, $3b$, $9a$, $9b$, ab, $3ab$, $9ab$.
b The common factors are 1, 3, a, $3a$.
c The highest common factor of $6a$ and $9ab$ is $3a$.

Exercise 3.2

1 a List the factors of   i $4a$ ii 8.
b List the factors common to both lists.
c State the highest common factor of $4a$ and 8.

2 a List the factors of   i $3xy$ ii $12y$.
b List the factors common to both lists.
c State the highest common factor of $3xy$ and $12y$.

3 Find the highest common factor of each of the following pairs.
a 6 and $3x$ b 12 and $8g$ c 7 and $21a$ d 18 and $24x$
e $24t$ and $36t$ f $6x$ and $36x$ g $21d$ and d h $25g$ and $40g$
i x and x^2 j y and y^2 k $4x^2$ and $8x$ l $21x^2$ and $7x$
m ab and a n $6ab$ and $42b$ o ab^2 and b p ab^2 and ab
q a^2b and ab r ab^2 and a^2b s $15ab$ and 10   t $18ab^2$ and $2ab$

4 For each expression:
  i expand the brackets to make it the sum of two terms
  ii state the highest common factor of the two terms.

  a $3(x + 4)$ **b** $7(2a + 5)$ **c** $5(t - 8)$ **d** $4(2x + 1)$
  e $x(2x + 5)$ **f** $g(4 - g)$ **g** $x(1 + x)$ **h** $2x(3x + 1)$
  i $3a(a + b)$ **j** $pq(3 + p)$ **k** $4f(3 - f)$ **l** $5d(d + 1)$

  Comment on your findings.

5 a Find the highest common factor of $2x$ and 4.
  b Expand $3(2x + 4)$ to make it the sum of two terms.
  c Find the highest common factor of the two terms.
  d Why is the h.c.f. not 3?

---

4 Using the highest common factor

We already know how to expand brackets, e.g. $4(3a + 2b) = 12a + 8b$.
Can we reverse the process? Can we put the brackets back?

If we start with $12a + 8b$,
we can see that the highest common factor is 4. $12a = 4 \times 3a$ and
                                                 $8b = 4 \times 2b$.

So 4 is outside the brackets and $3a$ and $2b$ are inside. $12a + 8b = 4(3a + 2b)$

When we put the brackets back, it is referred to as **factorising**.

Example 1   Factorise $15x + 20$.
                 The highest common factor of $15x$ and 20 is 5 $\begin{cases} 15x = 5 \times 3x \\ 20 = 5 \times 4 \end{cases}$
                 $\Rightarrow 15x + 20 = 5(3x + 4)$

Example 2   Factorise $4 - 12ab$.
                 The highest common factor of 4 and $12ab$ is 4
                 $\Rightarrow 4 - 12ab = 4(1 - 3ab)$ $\begin{cases} 4 = 4 \times 1 \\ 12ab = 4 \times 3ab \end{cases}$

Example 3   Factorise $14x + 21y$.
                 The highest common factor of $14x$ and $21y$ is 7
                 $\Rightarrow 14x + 21y = 7(2x + 3y)$ Check by mentally removing the brackets.

Exercise 4.1

1 Copy and complete to factorise these expressions:
  a $4x + 6 = 2($ $)$ **b** $3y + 9 = 3($ $)$ **c** $7m - 14 = 7($ $)$
  d $4k + 8 = 4($ $)$ **e** $6 - 3n = 3($ $)$ **f** $6a - 8b = 2($ $)$
  g $4k + 6m = 2($ $)$ **h** $7a + 7 = 7($ $)$ **i** $4a - 4 = 4($ $)$
  j $6e - 3 = 3($ $)$ **k** $14k - 7m = 7($ $)$ **l** $8x + 12y = 4($ $)$
  m $18y - 3 = 3($ $)$

2 Factorise each expression:

- **a** $3a + 6$
- **b** $5y - 10$
- **c** $6 - 2k$
- **d** $2m + 4$
- **e** $7k + 21$
- **f** $3a - 3b$
- **g** $5p - 10q$
- **h** $4x - 6$
- **i** $8 - 6y$
- **j** $6 - 4k$
- **k** $2a + 4b$
- **l** $7x - 14y$
- **m** $2a + 2$
- **n** $3y - 3$
- **o** $7r - 7$
- **p** $5 - 5x$
- **q** $2x + 10$
- **r** $16 - 2y$
- **s** $3a + 3$
- **t** $12a - 14b$

3 Factorise fully. Be sure to use the highest common factor each time.

- **a** $10x + 20$
- **b** $8y - 12$
- **c** $16 - 4a$
- **d** $18 - 9b$
- **e** $4a - 8b$
- **f** $6m + 18n$
- **g** $12 - 4w$
- **h** $6 - 12ab$
- **i** $20xy - 4$
- **j** $10x^2 + 40$
- **k** $8 - 4y^2$
- **l** $28 - 8mn$
- **m** $36k + 30$
- **n** $18x - 12y$
- **o** $50ab - 20$
- **p** $48y^2 + 36$

4 Factorise (where it is possible):

- **a** $6a + 24$
- **b** $5t - 81$
- **c** $8 - 4m$
- **d** $27m + 14$
- **e** $9k + 35$
- **f** $14 - 26g$
- **g** $34q - 13r$
- **h** $7x - 6y$
- **i** $9d - 4$
- **j** $71 - 3k$
- **k** $2a + 4b$
- **l** $7x - 14y$
- **m** $2a + 2$
- **n** $3y - 3$
- **o** $7r - 7$
- **p** $15 - t$
- **q** $44x + 39$
- **r** $81 - 45y$
- **s** $69m + 121$
- **t** $17a - a$

Example 4   Factorise $x^2 - 3x$.
$$x^2 - 3x = x(x - 3)$$ Check by mentally removing the brackets.

Example 5   Factorise $12ab - 16b$.
$$12ab - 16b = 4b(3a - 4)$$ Check by mentally removing the brackets.

Exercise 4.2

1 Factorise each expression fully:

- **a** $y^2 + 3y$
- **b** $x^2 - 5x$
- **c** $a^2 + 7a$
- **d** $t^2 - 2t$
- **e** $m^2 + 6m$
- **f** $k^2 - k$
- **g** $2a^2 + 4a$
- **h** $6a^2 - 3a$
- **i** $5n^2 + 15n$
- **j** $9w - 3w^2$
- **k** $4a + 12a^2$
- **l** $6p - 18p^2$

2 Complete these factorisations:

- **a** $ax + ay = a(\ldots)$
- **b** $ca - cb = c(\ldots)$
- **c** $ka + k = k(\ldots)$
- **d** $a^2 + ab = a(\ldots)$
- **e** $pq - q^2 = q(\ldots)$
- **f** $2x^2 + 6xy = 2x(\ldots)$

3 Factorise fully:

- **a** $ax - bx$
- **b** $mn - mp$
- **c** $2a + ab$
- **d** $mn - 5n$
- **e** $2x^2 - x$
- **f** $2x^2 - xy$
- **g** $a^2 - ab$
- **h** $xy + y^2$
- **i** $2x - 2xy$
- **j** $3a + 3ab$
- **k** $5mn - m^2$
- **l** $8x - 12x^2$
- **m** $6m^2 - 2m$
- **n** $2ax + ay$
- **o** $15k^2 - 6km$
- **p** $10p^2q + 12pq^2$

4 In each expression

- **i**   expand the brackets
- **ii**   simplify
- **iii** factorise.

- **a** $3(a + 4) + 4(a + 11)$
- **b** $5(x + 2) + 2(x + 9)$
- **c** $2(x + 6) + 7(x + 15)$
- **d** $8(y + 1) + 3(y + 12)$
- **e** $2(x - 4) + 3(x + 6)$
- **f** $5(y - 5) + 2(y + 2)$

Challenges

1 Common factors can be used in this way to make some problems easier, for example:
$$3 \times 98 + 3 \times 2 = 3(98 + 2) = 3 \times 100 = 300$$

a Using a similar trick, calculate these without the help of a calculator:
   i $7 \times 80 + 7 \times 20$
   ii $26 \times 4 \cdot 3 + 26 \times 5 \cdot 7$
   iii $13 \times 0 \cdot 9 + 13 \times 0 \cdot 1$

b Now try these:
   i $8 \times 102 - 8 \times 2$
   ii $14 \times 10 \cdot 3 - 14 \times 0 \cdot 3$
   iii $5 \cdot 1 \times 1 \cdot 9 - 5 \cdot 1 \times 0 \cdot 9$

c ... and these:
   i $5 \times \frac{3}{4} + 5 \times \frac{1}{4}$
   ii $7 \cdot 2 \times \frac{2}{5} + 7 \cdot 2 \times \frac{3}{5}$
   iii $8 \cdot 4 \times 9\frac{3}{4} + 8 \cdot 4 \times \frac{1}{4}$

d Write down the cost of:
   i 12 stamps at 28p each and 12 at 22p each
   ii 15 cans of fruit at 64p each and 15 at 36p each.

e Jackie did 20 press-ups, taking $3 \cdot 2$ seconds for each one, and 20 toe-touches at $1 \cdot 8$ seconds for each. How much time is that in total?

2 Ian says '$a + b$ is always a factor of $a^2 - b^2$.'
a Test his statement when:
   i $a = 3$ and $b = 1$
   ii $a = 4$ and $b = 3$
   iii $a = 7$ and $b = 3$

b Test his statement using your own pairs of values for a and b.
   (Make sure your a value is greater than your b value in each case.)
   Write a sentence about your results.

c Helen says '$a - b$ is always a factor of $a^2 - b^2$.'
   Test this statement and write a comment.

d Mark says '$2a - b$ is always a factor of $a^2 - b^2$.'
   Test this statement for $a = 6$ and $b = 3$.
   Comment.
   Now test it for other values and write another comment.

◀◀ **RECAP**

When one number divides another *without remainder*, it is said to be a **factor** of that number.

Any number with only two factors is called a **prime number**.

If a factor is a prime number it is called a **prime factor**.

Numbers can be expressed as a **product** of prime numbers, for example:

$12 = 2 \times 2 \times 3$

All the factors of a number can be found by considering this product and 1.
For example, the factors of 12 are: 1, 2, 3, 2×2, 2×3, $2 \times 2 \times 3$;
that is: 1, 2, 3, 4, 6, 12.
The factors can also be found by considering factor pairs, for example:

1×12; 2×6; 3×4.

Expressions have **factors**.
For example, $2a$ and $3b$ are factors of $6ab$ since $2a \times 3b = 6ab$.
All its factors are 1, 2, 3, 6, a, b, $2a$, $2b$, $3a$, $3b$, $6a$, $6b$, $6ab$.

Numbers may share factors. These are called **common factors**.
For example, 12 and 18 both have 1, 2, 3 and 6 as factors.
The largest of these, 6, is called the **highest common factor** (h.c.f.) of 12 and 18.

Expressions can also share factors.
For example, $6xy$ and $9x$ have 1, 3, x and $3x$ in common.
$3x$ is the highest common factor of $6xy$ and $9x$.

When two terms of a sum or difference have a common factor, the common factor can be taken outside the brackets. The process is called **factorising**.
The highest common factor should be used, for example:

$6xy + 9y = 3x(2y + 3)$ … always check by mentally removing the brackets.

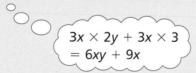

$3x \times 2y + 3x \times 3$
$= 6xy + 9x$

To *fully* factorise an expression, the highest common factor *must* be used.

1 List the factors of:　　　**a** 8　　　　　**b** 15　　　　**c** 36

2 List the common factors of 75 and 100.

3 Find the highest common factor of:
   a 24 and 108　　　　　　**b** 34 and 153

4 List all the prime numbers between 6 and 20.

5 Express 150 as a product of prime numbers.

6 **a** Write $6x$ as a product of two factors in as many different ways as you can.
   b List all of the factors of $6x$.

7 List all the factors of the expression $8pq$.

8 Copy and complete the missing factors:
   a $12b = \dots \times 3b$　　　**b** $6xy = \dots \times 2$　　　**c** $x^2 = x \times \dots$

9 List the common factors of the expressions:
   a $15xy$ and $20x$　　　　**b** $8x^2$ and $4xy$

10 State the highest common factor of:
   a $16a$ and 24　　　　　**b** $27x^2$ and $9x$

11 Factorise each expression:
   a $3w - 6$　　　　　　**b** $2p + 4q$　　　　　**c** $16ab - 2$

12 Factorise fully:
   a $6a + 18b$　　　　　**b** $12 - 8x$　　　　**c** $18x^2 - 6$
   d $am - an$　　　　　**e** $x^2 + x$　　　　　**f** $4ab - 6b^2$

6 Statistics – charts and tables

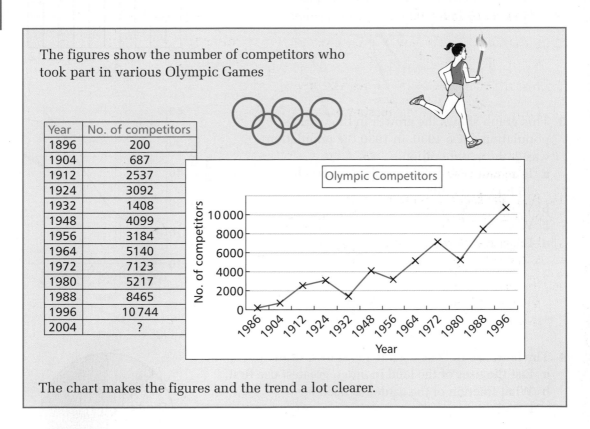

The figures show the number of competitors who took part in various Olympic Games

Year	No. of competitors
1896	200
1904	687
1912	2537
1924	3092
1932	1408
1948	4099
1956	3184
1964	5140
1972	7123
1980	5217
1988	8465
1996	10 744
2004	?

The chart makes the figures and the trend a lot clearer.

1 REVIEW

◀◀ Exercise 1.1

1 The students at Westway High School are asked whether they like cola, orange, tea or coffee best. Their choices are shown in the pictogram.
   a How many liked orange best?
   b Which drink had most votes?
   c How many students took part in the survey?

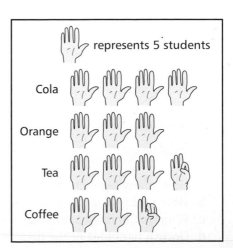

represents 5 students

Cola

Orange

Tea

Coffee

2 A group of pupils sat an exam on Information Handling.
It was scored out of 12.
The bar chart summarises the results.
  a What was the most common score?
  b How many students scored more than 10?
  c A student has to score at least 9 to pass. How many failed?

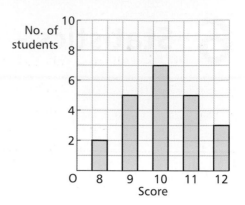

3 This graph shows the growth in the world's population since 1930. In 1930 the population was 21 hundred million.
  a In which year did the population reach 25 hundred million?
  b What was the population in 1960?
  c What was the *increase* from 1960 to 1980?
  d Describe the trend in world population.

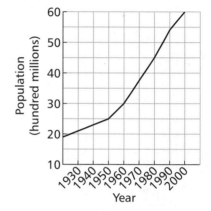

4 The land use in Peter's garden is shown in the pie chart.
  a List the uses of the land in order, greatest use first.
  b What fraction of the garden is used for
     i vegetables
     ii flowers
     iii other plants?

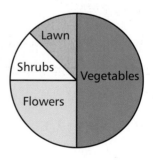

5 A confectioner makes boxes of chocolates.
On the lid it says there are approximately 25 chocolates in every box.
50 boxes are opened and the contents counted.

No. of chocolates	22	23	24	25	26	27	28
No. of boxes	3	8	4	9	13	10	3

  a How many boxes had less than the stated contents?
  b How many boxes had an even number of chocolates?
  c What is the most common number of chocolates in a box?
  d Draw a bar chart of the data.

2 Frequency tables

When data is originally collected it is usually unsorted.

The receptionist at a vet's surgery notes the types of animals as they are brought in.

dog	cat	bird	fish	dog	dog	cat
cat	cat	cat	dog	cat	bird	cat
bird	cat	cat	dog	dog	cat	bird
dog	dog	cat	cat	bird	fish	cat

She decides to sort the data into a table.

She makes a list of the types and starts to put tally marks against them as she goes through her notes. Here she has entered three columns of data.

Note that ⅻ stands for five tallies.

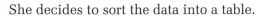

dog	cat	bird	fish	dog	dog	cat
cat	cat	cat	dog	cat	bird	cat
bird	cat	cat	dog	dog	cat	bird
dog	dog	cat	cat	bird	fish	cat

Type	Tally	Freq
dog	|||	
cat	ⅻ ||	
bird	||	
fish		

When this job is done she enters the number of tallies in a column headed **frequency**

What is the frequency of dog patients?

Type	Tally	Frequency
dog	ⅻ |||	8
cat	ⅻ ⅻ |||	13
bird	ⅻ	5
fish	||	2

Answer: There are 8 dog patients.

This kind of table is referred to as a **frequency table**

Exercise 2.1

1 Sort the following sets of data into frequency tables.
  a From which channel did you last record a movie?

BBC 1	BBC 2	ITV	Ch 4	Ch 5
BBC 1	BBC 2	Ch 5	BBC 2	Ch 5
BBC 2	Ch 4	ITV	BBC 1	Ch 4
BBC 1	Ch 5	ITV	Ch 4	BBC 1
ITV	BBC 2	BBC 1	Ch 4	BBC 2
Ch 4	ITV	BBC 2	BBC 1	Ch 4

Channel	Tally	Freq
BBC 1		
BBC 2		
ITV		
Ch 4		
Ch 5		

b How many wheels does each
vehicle have?

2	3	4	4	6
2	4	4	4	4
3	2	4	4	2
3	4	2	4	2
6	4	4	2	3
4	4	2	3	4

Wheels	Tally	Freq
2		
3		
4		
5		
6		

c Which club have you enrolled in?

golf	keep-fit	tennis	football
football	tennis	volleyball	keep-fit
football	football	keep-fit	golf
keep-fit	keep-fit	football	football
golf	tennis	golf	football
keep-fit	tennis	golf	football
golf	football	volleyball	keep-fit
tennis	golf		

Club	Tally	Freq
golf		
keep-fit		
tennis		
football		
volleyball		

2 Tracey is at the driving range. She pays for 50 golf balls.
For each shot she notes the last distance marker the ball reached.
Distances are in metres.

100	125	150	175	200	225	250	175	150	175
175	125	125	250	200	150	175	250	100	125
175	225	200	150	100	225	175	125	125	225
200	175	150	225	175	175	150	250	150	225
100	150	200	175	200	200	150	175	100	125

a How many different distance markers are used?
b Make a frequency table to sort out the data.
c How many shots:
  i reached the 250 m mark?
  ii reached the 150 m mark without getting past the 175 m mark?
  iii passed the 200 m mark? (Careful!)
d Copy and complete the bar graph.

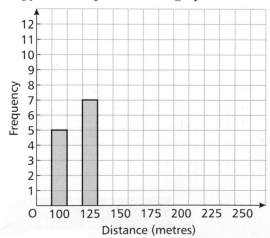

3 Simon was given a mobile phone for his Christmas.
He was told to keep a close watch on the lengths of calls he made.
He noted each call to the nearest 10 seconds.

90	80	110	80	90	110	100	90	100	100
60	100	70	100	110	90	100	110	90	100
100	70	90	70	90	110	80	90	100	80
120	100	100	110	70	100	70	100	80	100
120	120	100	110	120	80	100	80	90	80

a How many calls did he take a note of?
b How long is:
 i the shortest call **ii** the longest call?
c Make a frequency table of the data.
d How many calls lasted:
 i just 70 seconds **ii** just 100 seconds **iii** more than 100 seconds?
e Which length of call occurred most often?

Exercise 2.2

1 When trying to break a secret code, mathematicians will often make use of the fact that the letters of the alphabet occur with different frequencies It is known, for example, that in the English language the letter E is the most common.
When faced with a coded passage a count of the letters is done.
It is assumed that the most commonly occurring letter stands for E.
It is also assumed that the rest of the alphabet follows on. So if P represents E then Q represents F, R represents G and so on.

a Do a frequency count of the letters in the following passage.

Letter	A	B	C	D	E	F	G	H	I	J	K	L	M	N	O	P	Q	R	S	T	U	V	W	X	Y	Z
Frequency																										

```
f    r f s    j s y j w j i    f    x m t u    f s i
x u j s y    t s j    m f q k    t k    y m j
r t s j d    m j    m f i    b m j s    m j    h f r j
t z y    m j    m f i    y m j    x f r j    s z r g j w
t k    u j s s n j x    f x    m j    m f i
u t z s i x    b m j s    m j    b j s y    n s    f s i
m f q k    f x    r f s d    u t z s i x    f x    m j
m f i    u j s s n j x    b m j s    m j    b j s y
n s    m t b    r z h m    i n i    m j    m f a j
b m j s    m j    j s y j w j i
```

b The most frequent letter represents E.
Which letter represents E here?
c Decode the message.
d The message is a puzzle.
Can you solve it?

2 At a crossroads, a road engineer counts the direction taken by traffic coming from town.

left	right	left	ahead	ahead
left	left	ahead	ahead	ahead
left	ahead	left	left	ahead
left	ahead	ahead	right	right
ahead	ahead	ahead	left	right
ahead	right	ahead	right	right

a Make a frequency table of the data.

b One of the directions leads to a busy housing scheme. Which direction do you imagine that is?

c Of the two directions left, is the data enough for the engineer to say that one is busier than the other?

3 Drawing pie charts

The table shows the number of goals scored in 30 matches one Saturday.

Notice that:

$\frac{5}{30}$ of the matches had no score

$\frac{10}{30}$ of the matches had 1 goal

$\frac{8}{30}$ of the matches had 2 goals

$\frac{4}{30}$ of the matches had 3 goals

$\frac{3}{30}$ of the matches had 4 goals.

Goals scored	0	1	2	3	4
Number of games	5	10	8	4	3

If we let a circle represent all 30 matches, then the above fractions of a circle can represent the different outcomes in the matches. So:

$\frac{5}{30}$ of 360° = 60° will represent the matches which had no score

$\frac{10}{30}$ of 360° = 120° will represent the matches in which 1 goal was scored

$\frac{8}{30}$ of 360° = 96° will represent the matches in which 2 goals were scored

$\frac{4}{30}$ of 360° = 48° will represent the matches in which 3 goals were scored

$\frac{3}{30}$ of 360° = 36° will represent the matches in which 4 goals were scored.

 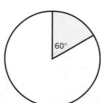 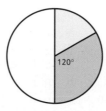 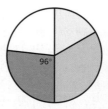 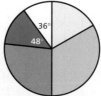

Draw a circle and a suitable radius at which to start.	Draw an arc with a 60° angle at the centre to show the games with 0 goals.	Draw a 120° angle at the centre to show the games with 1 goal.	Draw a 96° angle at the centre to show the games with 2 goals.	A 48° angle will show the games with 3 goals. The 36° angle left shows the games with 4 goals.

Complete your chart by adding a title and a key.

Goals scored in the matches on Saturday.

☐ 0 goals
☐ 1 goal
☐ 2 goals
■ 3 goals
☐ 4 goals

30 games played.

Exercise 3.1

1 Of 50 pupils asked, 10 thought a packed lunch was best, 20 preferred school dinners, 15 liked to go home and 5 went to the local baker's.
   a Write 10, 20, 15 and 5 each as a fraction of 50.
   b Calculate: **i** $\frac{10}{50}$ of 360°   **ii** $\frac{5}{50}$ of 360°
   c Draw a pie chart called 'School lunches' to show the pupils' preferences.

2 £3000 was collected by a school charity committee. £600 came from running a disco; £1000 came from the summer fête; £750 was raised at the fun run; and £650 came from various other sources.
   a What fraction of the money came from: **i** the disco   **ii** the fun run?
   b Calculate: **i** $\frac{1000}{3000}$ of 360°   **ii** $\frac{650}{3000}$ of 360°
   c Draw a pie chart to show how the charity fund was made up.

3 A survey was done to see in what format people preferred to buy their music. Of the 30 people asked, 2 said they still liked vinyl discs, 12 liked the convenience of tapes, 15 preferred CDs, and the rest couldn't make up their mind.
   a How many couldn't make up their minds?
   b Draw a pie chart to show the results of the survey.

Each of the questions above had convenient figures leading to exact angles for the pie charts. If this is not the case, then round the angles you find to the nearest degree.

Example   62% of rail travellers are satisfied with the service. 27% are unhappy and the rest are undecided. Show this in a pie chart.

Rail travellers

☐ Satisfied
☐ Unhappy
■ Don't know

62% of 360° = 0·62 × 360
          = 223·2° … use 223°
27% of 360° = 0·27 × 360
          = 97·2° … use 97°
11% of 360° = 0·11 × 360
          = 39·6° … use 40°

Exercise 3.2

1 The population of England is 78% of the population of the British Isles.

   The other 22% is made up of the populations of Scotland, Northern Ireland, Wales and the Republic of Ireland.

   a Show this in a pie chart.

   b The table shows the figures for the less populated nations.
   Draw a pie chart to represent the figures in the table.

	Pop. (millions)
Scotland	5
N. Ireland	1·5
Wales	3
Rep. Ireland	3·5

2 Scientists say that the Earth's crust is made of 47% oxygen, 23% silicon, 8% aluminium, 5% iron, 7% calcium/sodium, and the rest is small amounts of lots of things.

   a Draw a pie chart to show these figures.

   b They say that sea water has 85% oxygen, 10% hydrogen, 2% chlorine and the rest is made up of traces of other things.
   Show this as a pie chart also.

3 The 'silver' coins in your pocket are made from a mixture of metals: 55% copper, 27% zinc and 18% nickel.

   a Show this as a pie chart.

   b Before 1992 the 'copper' coins were a mixture of copper and tin.

   The make-up of a copper coin

   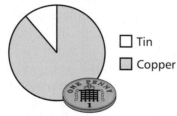

   ☐ Tin
   ☐ Copper

   The pie chart shows the proportions.

   i   What percentage is copper?

   ii What percentage is tin?

   c Copper coins made after 1992 can be picked up by a magnet.
   What does that suggest is in them?

4 There are 17 tracks on the Blueberries' latest CD.
   Of these, 3 are 2-minute tracks, 5 are 3-minute tracks, 7 are 4-minute tracks and the remainder are 5-minute tracks.

   a What percentage are

   i   2-minute tracks

   ii 4-minute tracks (to 1 d.p.)?

   b Draw a pie chart to illustrate these figures.

4 Good relations

We often graph one variable against another, for example traffic flow against the time of day, or the number of ice lollies sold and the outside temperature, or the age of a car and its value, to see if there is a connection between the variables.
The word **trend** is used to describe a general tendency for such a graph to rise or fall, especially when one variable is time.

This graph shows that, over a few weeks, the general trend is for the absentee figures to increase.

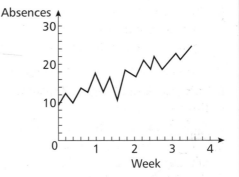

Similarly, you might find that scarf sales will generally fall as we head into summer.
Over a longer period of several years you might spot that scarf sales do indeed follow a seasonal trend.

Scatter diagrams can help us to spot connections between two things.

Example
The table shows the heights and shoe sizes of 14 students.

Height (m)	1·10	1·40	1·70	1·60	1·60	1·80	1·50	1·60	1·90	1·50	1·60	1·30	1·50	1·70
Shoe size	12	3	6	3	5	7	3	6	8	1	7	1	5	8

Is there a connection between height and shoe size?

Plotting each data pair on a graph gives us a scatter diagram like the one shown here.

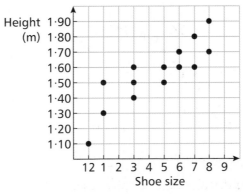

We can see a trend … the taller the person, the bigger the shoe.

When there is a simple connection like this it is called a **correlation**.
When both variables grow together, in this case height and shoe size, it is called a **positive** correlation.

As the temperature increases, the number of scarves sold will drop.
This is a **negative** correlation.

Exercise 4.1

1 Weather readings were taken every day during a two-week science project.
These scatter diagrams were produced.

   a What happened to the temperature as
   the wind rose?

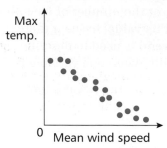

   b Was the rainfall affected by
   the wind speed?

   c What was the connection between the
   temperature and the hours of sunshine?

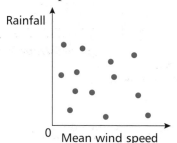

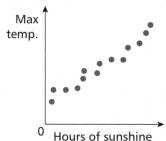

2 Here are four scatter diagrams.
Notice that the labels on the axes are missing.
Match up each graph with a pair of labels.

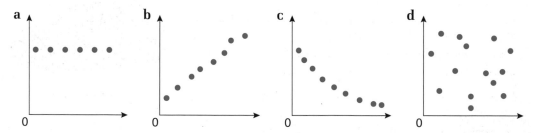

Labels:
   i   Age of driver, Age of car
   ii   Value of car, Age of car
   iii Number of rust spots, Age of car
   iv   Number of wheels, Age of car

3 Sketch the sort of scatter graph you would expect to see to show the connection
between students' exam marks and:
   a their heights
   b the time spent on revision
   c the number of lessons missed through absence.

Exercise 4.2

1 Several small bus companies have their fares sampled.
The table shows several journeys and their cost.

Length of journey (km)	3	7	5	7	5	6	8	8	6	6	4	5	7
Fare (pence)	40	75	60	65	45	60	80	75	70	55	55	65	60

a Draw a scatter diagram using a set
of axes like the ones shown.
b What kind of correlation is there between
length of journey and fare?

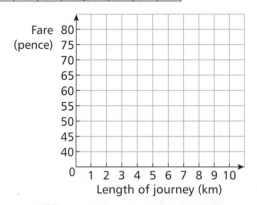

2 Sandra looked through the used car adverts in her local newspaper.
She noted the prices and the ages of the cars.

Age of car (years)	2	3·5	1	1·5	4·5	2·5	1·5	3·5	0·5
Price in paper (£1000)	3	2	6	7	1	4	5	3	7

a Draw suitable scales and make a scatter diagram of the data.
b Describe the correlation between the age of a car and its price
in the paper.
c From your graph, could you estimate:
   i   the age of a car estimated to be worth £3500
   ii the cost of a 4-year-old car?
d Sandra sees a 3-year-old car for £4250.
Is this reasonable in the above market?

3 Last term Mr Johnston tested the pupils in his group. He did it again this term.

Last term	5	3	6	7	5	6	5	3	6	5
This term	14	4	12	18	8	14	12	2	18	10

a Draw a scatter diagram to help you compare the two exams.
b Describe the relation between the two sets of results.
c This term someone was absent for the test. They scored 4 in the last test.
Suggest a reasonable estimate mark for them for this term's test.
d If someone scored 16 this time, what would you estimate his last term exam result
to be?
e What was the average result:
   i   last term   **ii**   this term?
f Use the results in part **e** to plot another data point on your diagram.

5 Line of best fit

The last two questions of the previous exercise asked you to spot a connection and then use it to estimate various values of the variables. This task is made easier by drawing a straight line that runs through the 'cloud' of points, representing its trend and leaving roughly half of the points on one side of the line and half on the other. We call such a line **the line of best fit**.

Letting the line run through the 'average' point can speed up your decision about where the line is.

Example   A shopkeeper notes the noon temperature and the number of sales made on the same day.

Temperature (°C)	20	16	12	11	14	10	11	8	9	4	2	1	9·83
Glove sales	0	2	5	6	7	8	10	12	13	17	18	20	9·83

The figures in the last column are the mean values of temperature and sales.

A scatter diagram is made from this.

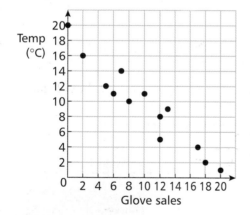 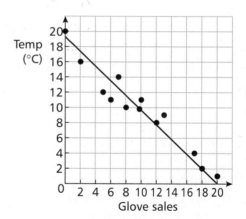

The average point is plotted and a line is drawn passing through it, following the trend in the points, and leaving 6 points above and 4 points below.

This is the line of best fit.

Using this line we can now estimate:
i   the temperature at which ten glove sales will be made (10 °C)
ii   the number of glove sales when the temperature is 6 °C (14 sales).

Exercise 5.1

1 Use the line of best fit in the above graph to help you estimate:
   a the glove sales expected at 0 °C
   b the temperature at which 4 glove sales are made.

2 Marie records the distances her friends are from school and the times it takes them to get there.

Distance (km)	29	20	4	10	24	15	8	24	12	14
Time (min)	70	50	10	25	60	40	16	55	30	44

The mean distance is 16 km, and the mean time is 40 minutes.
She plots the mean point M(16, 40).

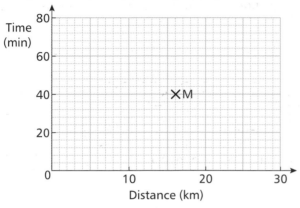

a Copy the axes on squared paper, and plot M.
b Draw a scatter diagram, and a line of best fit through M.
c Marjorie lives 18 km from school. Estimate her travel time.

3 Carol and her friends note the number of newspapers they deliver, and the time they take.

Time (min)	50	45	40	40	30	25	20	30	35	28
Newspapers	60	50	45	48	44	36	30	34	43	38

a Calculate:
   i   the mean time
   ii the mean number of newspapers.
b Draw axes on squared paper, and plot the mean point M.
c Draw a scatter diagram, and a line of best fit through M.
d Estimate the time Jason takes to deliver 55 papers.

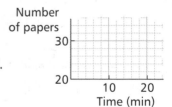

4 Mal wants to find out if there is any link between a poor defence, in soccer, and the number of points the team has. He chooses ten teams.

Goals against	9	28	19	10	13	20	14	24	16	22
Number of points	25	5	11	24	17	9	16	7	12	6

a Calculate each mean, and plot M on squared paper, as before.
b Draw a scatter diagram, and a line of best fit through M.
c Describe the link between goals against and points.
d A team has 20 points. Estimate the number of goals scored against it.

6 Stem-and-leaf diagrams

People were asked their age as they entered a health centre.
Their ages were 25, 28, 21, 17, 33, 15, 26, 31, 20, 21, 18.

The data can be shown in a **stem-and-leaf diagram**, also referred to as a **stem plot**.

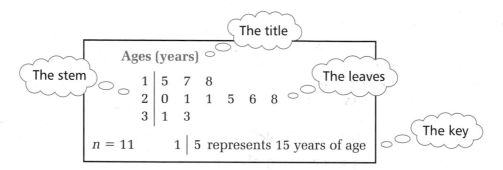

The title

The stem

The leaves

The key

Ages (years)

```
1 | 5  7  8
2 | 0  1  1  5  6  8
3 | 1  3
```

$n = 11$ 1 | 5 represents 15 years of age

- The figures on the left of the line form the stem.
- Each figure on the right is called a leaf.
- The leaves increase in value outwards from the stem.
- Each row is called a level.
- A title is needed at the top.
- A key is needed at the bottom. The key includes the size of the group, n, and an example of how to read the figures. The '1' level should be read as 15, 17, 18.

Exercise 6.1

1 This stem-and-leaf diagram shows how many houses have gas central heating in a sample of 11 streets.

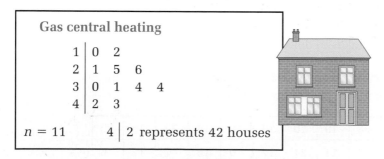

Gas central heating

```
1 | 0  2
2 | 1  5  6
3 | 0  1  4  4
4 | 2  3
```

$n = 11$ 4 | 2 represents 42 houses

a The 1 level should be read as 10 and 12 houses.
Write out the 2 level in the same way.

b What is the greatest number of houses recorded in the diagram?

c How many houses are recorded?

2 The number of visitors going into a theme park is recorded hourly.
The stem-and-leaf diagram shows the data collected.

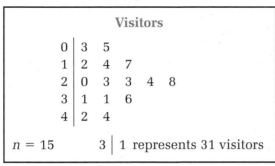

Visitors

```
0 | 3  5
1 | 2  4  7
2 | 0  3  3  4  8
3 | 1  1  6
4 | 2  4
```

$n = 15$ 3 | 1 represents 31 visitors

  a The 0 level can be read as 03 visitors and 05 visitors (3 and 5 visitors).
  List the 1 level in the same way.
  b List all the recordings in order of size.
  c For how many hours were records made?

3 A garden centre is testing a new variety of lettuce.
Heights are measured in centimetres. The stem plot shows the results.

Height of lettuce

```
 6 | 2  3
 7 | 5  7  9
 8 | 3  4  6  6  7
 9 | 2  6  7
10 | 1
```

$n = 14$ 6 | 2 represents 6·2 cm

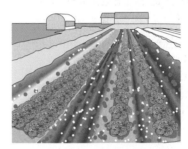

  a What is   **i**   the tallest   **ii**   the shortest height?
  b Which level has the most data?
  c Which height occurred most often?
  d What is the height of the seventh tallest plant?

4 The cost of putting an extension on a house is investigated.
The stem-and-leaf diagram shows the figures.

Quoted price of extension

```
10 | 3  6  7  9
11 | 0  4  8  8  9
12 | 1  6  7
13 | 5
14 | 0
```

$n = 14$ 10 | 3 represents £10 300

  a What is   **i**   the cheapest   **ii**   the dearest estimate?
  b Which level has the most data?
  c Write out level 12 in full.

5 Sales at a corner shop are recorded over one hour.

```
┌─────────────────────────────────────┐
│           Money spent                │
│                                      │
│      3 │ 6  8                         │
│      4 │ 0  2  2  5  7  9  9          │
│      5 │ 3  4  6  8  8  9             │
│      6 │ 0  2  5  7                   │
│      7 │ 1                            │
│                                      │
│  n = 20        3 │ 6 = £3·60          │
└─────────────────────────────────────┘
```

  a List the sales in order of size, least first.

  b The shopkeeper considers that £5·50 is a typical sale.
     How many customers bought goods worth more than that?

  c How many customers did the shop have in that hour?

One of the main uses of the stem-and-leaf diagram is in sorting a jumble of figures into order. This is usually a two-step process.

Example

Here are the strengths of earth tremors measured over 25 incidents.

3·0	1·7	0·3	1·0	3·7
3·6	2·5	3·6	4·9	0·1
0·2	2·9	0·7	2·6	1·2
4·0	1·1	3·8	2·1	4·3
0·9	2·8	3·3	0·7	3·7

The first step in putting them in order is to order the stem, adding the leaves as they occur in the table …

```
0 │ 3  1  2  7  9  7
1 │ 7  0  2  1
2 │ 5  9  6  1  8
3 │ 0  7  6  6  8  3  7
4 │ 9  0  3
```

then the leaves are sorted

```
0 │ 1  2  3  7  7  9
1 │ 0  1  2  7
2 │ 1  5  6  8  9
3 │ 0  3  6  6  7  7  8
4 │ 0  3  9
```

Exercise 6.2

1 This list gives the number of Christmas cards received by pupils in a class:

     22, 40, 15, 14, 35, 31, 23, 19, 18,
     22, 27, 33, 41, 26, 21, 20, 16, 46.

Make a stem-and-leaf diagram to help you sort the list in order.

2 Tariz looks up interest rates in some banks in the High Street.
  This is a list of the percentage rates he finds:

     4·8, 6·2, 7·1, 5·6, 4·9, 5·2, 6·4, 7·5, 4·3, 5·4,
     6·7, 7·6, 4·2, 5·5, 4·2, 4·5, 5·2, 6·0, 4·8, 5·0.

Make a stem-and-leaf diagram.

3 A travel agent wishes to sort this list of prices of foreign holidays:

£127, £149, £231, £437, £312, £556, £159, £199,
£218, £223, £264, £416, £127, £394, £195.

a Round all the prices to the nearest £10.
b Use these rounded figures to help you complete a stem-and-leaf diagram.

4 The length of time between one programme finishing and the next one starting is the subject of a survey. Twenty of these gaps are measured:

1·25, 2·35, 5·71, 4·74, 3·12, 5·10, 1·23, 3·61, 3·77, 2·79,
3·25, 1·45, 3·29, 4·88, 2·62, 4·16, 5·02, 1·94, 2·00, 4·77.

The times are in minutes.
a Round these times to 1 decimal place.
b Make a stem-and-leaf diagram of the rounded data.

7 Back-to-back stem-and-leaf diagrams

Sometimes you want to compare one set of figures with another.
A back-to-back stem-and-leaf diagram is useful for this.

Books borrowed from library

last week			this week
3	2	0	1
4 1	3	1	5 6
7 4 4 3	4	0	4 5
1 0	5	2	
1	6	3	

$n = 10$ $n = 10$

2 | 0 represents 20 books

Note that the leaves still increase in size away from the stem.
The 2 level can be read as:
'Last week there was an opening when 23 books were borrowed;
this week there were openings with 20 and 21 books borrowed.'
The library opens 10 times a week.

Exercise 7.1

1 Use the diagram above to answer this question.
 a What is the total number of books borrowed shown in the 3 level
  i this week
  ii last week?
 b A campaign to encourage the use of the library was started at the end of last week.
  Do you think it was successful? Comment.

2 Twelve pupils from two classes are asked how much they spend a week on essentials.

  a The 5 level can be read as
    '3rd year class: £5·20, £5·70;
    4th year class: £5·20, £5·30'.
    Write out the 6 level in the same way.

  b i What is the largest amount recorded?
    ii In which class is it?

Weekly expenditure		
3rd year class		**4th year class**
7 2	5	2 3
6 5 0	6	5
9 8 3 3	7	0 2 2 7
7 5 1	8	3 3 6
	9	4 8
$n = 12$		$n = 12$

5 | 2 represents £5·20

3 Trials are carried out to see if a new plant feed works.
Some plants are given the feed and some are not. After a while the heights of the plants are measured in centimetres. The results are shown below.

With feed

8·0	13·1	9·4	12·3	11·5	9·3	10·2
9·5	8·1	10·3	12·6	10·9	11·4	8·1
12·0	10·7	13·2	10·7	11·0	11·5	

Without feed

8·0	9·9	11·0	10·8	12·5	13·4	8·4
10·8	8·4	9·3	11·2	8·4	10·3	11·4
8·8	12·6	12·3	9·5	9·6	10·3	

  a Make a back-to-back stem plot to show these results.
  b Does the feed work? Comment.

4 Two types of light bulbs are being compared.
Fifteen bulbs of each type are tested to destruction. Here are the results of the tests. The figures give the lifetime, in months, of each bulb.

Brighter Bulbs: 14, 23, 09, 15, 26, 11, 31, 18, 23, 06, 17, 26, 33, 14, 09.
Luminous Lamps: 14, 28, 30, 22, 41, 33, 15, 22, 27, 19, 20, 35, 40, 19, 37.

  a Draw a back-to-back stem-and-leaf diagram.
  b Which bulb, if either, lasts longer?

◄◄ RECAP

Frequency tables are used to help sort raw data.

Example   The ages of the 25 members of the pupil council are noted …

15 15 14 13 15
12 15 12 17 12
12 14 12 12 14
17 14 12 14 15
14 16 12 17 14

and then sorted, with the
help of tally marks.

Age	Tally	Frequency
12	ЖЖ |||	8
13			1
14	ЖЖ ||	7
15	ЖЖ	5
16			1
17					3

A **pie chart** is useful for displaying the fraction of the group that fits each category.

Example

$\frac{8}{25}$ of the group are 12 years old … $\frac{8}{25}$ of circle = $\frac{8}{25} \times 360 = 115°$ (to nearest degree)

$\frac{1}{25}$ are 13 years old … $\frac{1}{25} \times 360 = 14°$ (to nearest degree)

$\frac{7}{25}$ are 14 years old … $\frac{7}{25} \times 360 = 101°$ (to nearest degree)

$\frac{5}{25}$ are 15 years old … $\frac{5}{25} \times 360 = 72°$

$\frac{1}{25}$ are 16 years old … $\frac{1}{25} \times 360 = 14°$ (to nearest degree)

$\frac{3}{25}$ are 17 years old … $\frac{3}{25} \times 360 = 43°$ (to nearest degree)

… leading to the chart:

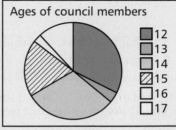

Ages of council members
12 13 14 15 16 17

A **scatter graph** is useful for looking at the relation between two variables.
Adding **a line of best fit** will allow you to estimate values of one variable when
given values of the other.

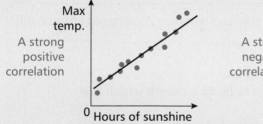

A strong positive correlation — Max temp. / Hours of sunshine

A strong negative correlation — Max temp. / Mean wind speed

A **stem-and-leaf diagram**, or **stem plot**, is useful for putting data in numerical order.

Example

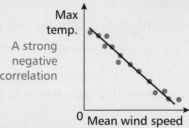

```
                Ages (years)
        1 | 5  7  8
        2 | 0  1  1  5  6  8
        3 | 1  3
n = 11   1 | 5 represents 15 years of age
```

1 Danny went to school by bike. Each day he passed a set of traffic lights.
Every day for a month he noted the colour as he passed by.

green	green	amber	amber	green
green	green	green	green	amber
green	amber	green	red	red
red	amber	green	amber	red

  a Sort the data out into a frequency table.

  b What colour occurred   **i** most often   **ii** least often?

2 A short survey is done with radio listeners.
Each is asked 'What station do you listen to most often?'
The results are shown in the frequency table.

Station	Listeners
Radio 1	20
Radio 2	10
Radio 3	6
Radio 4	18
Classic FM	6

  a What was the total number of listeners asked?

  b What fraction said   **i** Radio 1   **ii** Classic FM?

  c Draw a pie chart to display the figures.

3 The Transport Museum is very popular all the year round. Its museum shop is always
busy. The table shows the monthly figures for a year.

No. of visitors (1000s)	6	8	5	9	8	6	8	7	8	9	6	9
Sales at shop (£100s)	1	9	2	9	8	5	7	7	10	11	3	10

  a Make a scatter diagram to highlight the relation between *Number of visitors* and
Sales at the shop.

  b Describe this relation in words.

  c Draw a line of best fit on your scatter diagram.

  d What would you estimate the sales figures to be on a month which saw
6500 visitors?

  e How many visitors would you estimate attended when the sales figures
were £600?

4 Twenty people in the audience at a local pantomime
were asked their age.
The table shows the responses.

  a Make a stem-and-leaf diagram to help you sort the list.

  b What is the most common age group?

15	17	7	16
26	18	14	44
26	24	11	16
8	8	13	20
3	45	30	44

5 A pet food manufacturer runs an advertising campaign to promote Clifford's Canine Candies. Before the campaign, sales from 20 outlets were recorded.
They can be seen in the partially completed back-to-back stem-and-leaf diagram.

Sales of Clifford's Canine Candies

After		Before
	0	1 3 6 8
	1	0 1 3 3 7
	2	2 4 6 8 8 9
	3	0 5 5 7
	4	0

$n = 20$ $n = 20$

2 | 3 represents 23 sales

a How many outlets sold fewer than 20 cans of Canine Candies?

b After the campaign, sales were again recorded at the 20 outlets.

6	30	24	15	34	23	47	34	27	2
36	26	13	29	15	45	24	42	37	23

Use these figures to help you copy and complete the back-to-back stem-and-leaf diagram.

c Do you think there was an improvement in the sales?

7 Proportion and variation

The Scottish parliament is based on **Proportional** Representation (PR).

PR is a system of voting designed so that the number of MPs elected from each party reflects the share of votes cast for each party.

1 REVIEW

◀◀ **Exercise 1.1**

1 How many minutes are there in:
  a 2 hours   **b** 10 hours   **c** 0·5 hour?

2 Calculate:
  a £1·50 × 4   **b** £120 × 3   **c** £9·99 × 6
  d £1·20 ÷ 5   **e** £584 ÷ 4   **f** £74·40 ÷ 8

3 A pair of socks cost £1·99.
  Sharda buys three pairs. How much does she pay?

4 A 5 litre tin of undercoat will cover 85 m².
  What area will 1 litre cover?

5 A van costs £26 a day to hire. What is the cost of hiring the van for:
  a 2   **b** 4   **c** 8   **d** 16 days?

6 **a** If the distance of a walk is increased, does the time taken to complete it
    i increase   **ii** decrease   **iii** stay the same?
  b If the number of painters on a job is increased, does the time taken to complete it
    i increase   **ii** decrease   **iii** stay the same?

7 **a** $D = 5t$. Calculate D when $t = 7$.
  b $V = 0·3W$. Calculate V when $W = 20$.

8 Write these ratios in their simplest form:
   a 6 : 2   **b** 3 : 12   **c** 5 : 30   **d** 12 : 16

9 Michelle walks at 6 km/h. She runs at 15 km/h.
   Write the ratio of her walking speed to her running speed as a ratio in its simplest form.

10 The table shows the cost of parking a car at the Silver Shopping Centre.

Time (hours)	1	2	3	4	5
Cost (£)	0·50	1·00	1·50	2·00	2·50

Draw a graph to illustrate the data.

2 Direct proportion

Donna's garage charges £60 for 2 hours of labour.
For 3 hours' labour the garage charges £90.
Ratio of hours = 2 : 3
Ratio of charges = 60 : 90 = 2 : 3
The ratios are the same. We say the charges are **directly proportional** to the hours.

Example 1   A pipeline delivers 80 litres of water in 4 minutes.
               The volume delivered is directly proportional to the time it takes.
               How much will the pipeline deliver in: **a** 1 minute   **b** 5 minutes?

               4 minutes ... 80 litres
               1 minute   ... 80 ÷ 4 = 20 litres
               5 minutes ... 20 × 5 = 100 litres

Exercise 2.1

1 Sam sells his special compost at £0·45 per kilogram.
   Copy and complete the table of prices.

Weight (kg)	1	2	3	4	5	6	7	8	9
Cost (£)	0·45	0·90							

2 Which of these pairs of ratios are equal?
   a 1 : 2 and 2 : 4   **b** 3 : 1 and 9 : 3   **c** 1 : 5 and 3 : 12
   d 4 : 1 and 2 : 8   **e** 3 : 2 and 6 : 4

3 One volume of an encyclopedia weighs 4 kg. Five volumes weigh a total of 20 kg.
   a Is the ratio of number of volumes equal to the ratio of total weights?
   b Assuming the weight is directly proportional to the number of volumes, what is
       the weight of seven volumes?

4 Two postcards cost 40p. Three postcards cost 60p.
   a Is the ratio of the number of cards equal to the ratio of total costs?
   b Assuming the cost of the cards is directly proportional to the number of cards,
       how much will 12 cards cost?

5 Which of these pairs of prices could be examples of direct proportion?
   a 2 apples for 36p   4 apples for 72p
   b 5 pears for £1   7 pears for £1·40
   c 6 bananas for £1·80   2 bananas for 60p
   d 4 grapefruits for £3   3 grapefruits for £4

6 Two rides on the Big Dipper cost £10.
   How much does:
   a one ride
   b three rides cost?

7 It takes Jan 15 minutes to iron five shirts.
   Assuming she takes the same time to iron each shirt,
   a how long does it take her to iron a shirt?
   b how long would it take her to iron eight shirts?

8 Tania has three films processed. It costs her £12.
   a How much does it cost to process one film?
   b Tammy has four films processed at the same price per film as Tania.
      How much does Tammy pay?

9 Six copies of *The News On Sunday* weigh 2400 g.
   Calculate the weight of:
   a one copy   **b** eight copies.

10 Marie's mobile phone company charges the same amount for
   each minute.
   A 7 minute call costs £2·10. How much would:
   a 1 minute   **b** 9 minutes cost?

11 10 cm³ of silver weigh 105 g.
   Calculate the weight of 100 cm³ of silver.

12 Linda buys 10 litres of 2-star petrol at a garage. She pays £8·29.
   Next day she buys 20 litres at the same price per litre.
   Calculate the cost.

Example 2   A 20 cm³ gold nugget weighs 386 g.
              Calculate: **a** the weight of a 28 cm³ nugget
                           b the volume of a nugget that weighs 617·6 g.

   a A 20 cm³ nugget weighs 386 g
      so 1 cm³ weighs 386 g ÷ 20
      A 28 cm³ nugget weighs 386 ÷ 20 × 28 = 540·4 g
   b A 386 g nugget has a volume of 20 cm³
      so 1 g has a volume of 20 cm³ ÷ 386
      A 617·6 g nugget has a volume of 20 ÷ 386 × 617·6 = 32 cm³

Exercise 2.2

1 Four blank tapes cost £12. How much will five tapes cost?
  (Hint: find the cost of one first.)

2 Seven lines of advertising cost £28. How much would eleven lines cost?

3 Twelve eggs cost £1·80. How much do ten cost?

4 Henry cooks a 1·5 kg chicken for 75 minutes.
  How long should a 2 kg chicken take to cook?

5 A tree's shadow is proportional to its height.
  The taller tree is 12 m tall and casts a shadow
  of 18 m.
  The shorter tree is 10 m tall. Calculate the length
  of its shadow.

6 Yvonne walks at a constant speed for 5 hours and covers 30 km.
  a If she had walked on for an extra hour at the same speed, how far would she
    have gone in total?
  b If, however, she had walked for an hour less, how far would she have gone?

7 Ron reckons that if he cycles on his exercise bike for 10 minutes he uses 60 calories.
  Assuming direct proportion:
  a how many calories will he use when he cycles for 45 minutes?
  b how long has he cycled for if he uses 288 calories in a session?

8 A 600 cm² pane of toughened glass costs £25.
  a What area of glass costs £52?
  b Calculate the cost of a pane of glass of area 750 cm².

9 300 cm³ of lead weigh 3390 g. Calculate:
  a the weight of 500 g of lead.
  b the volume of lead that weighs 5085 g.

10 A 250 ml tin of varnish will cover 4·5 m².
  a What area will a 450 ml tin cover?
  b Calculate the volume of varnish needed to cover an area of 3·6 m².

11 A 50 g portion of porridge oats contains 180 calories.
  a How many calories are in an 80 g portion?
  b What weight of oats contains 234 calories?

12 Barbara reckons that it costs her 1·6p to run a 100 watt light
  bulb for 2 hours.
  a Calculate the cost of running a 250 watt bulb for 2 hours
    (assuming the wattage is directly proportional to the cost).
  b What is the cost of running a 100 watt bulb for 5 hours
    (assuming the time is directly proportional to the cost)?

13 On holiday in Europe, Holly is about to exchange £400 for €560 (euro).
 a If she changes an extra £180, how much would she get altogether?
 b If she wants another €70 more than €560, how much in pounds
   should she change altogether?

Brainstormer

a For which pair of the three bottles of
 perfume is the cost proportional to
 the volume?
b What price should the third bottle be
 so that its cost is proportional to the
 others?

---

3 Direct proportion and recipes

Example   These ingredients make 6 portions of chocolate ice cream:

    300 ml whipped cream
    60 g chocolate
    30 g sugar

List the ingredients needed for 10 portions.

Ingredients for 1 portion		for 10 portions
whipped cream	$300 \div 6 = 50$ ml	$50 \times 10 = 500$ ml
chocolate	$60 \div 6 = 10$ g	$10 \times 10 = 100$ g
sugar	$30 \div 6 = 5$ g	$5 \times 10 = 50$ g

Exercise 3.1

1 Lemonade (4 glasses)
 4 lemons
 100 g sugar
 1000 ml boiling water

 List the ingredients for:
 a 1 glass   **b** 6 glasses of lemonade.

2 Flapjacks (8)
 80 g butter
 40 ml syrup
 160 g oats

 List the ingredients needed for:
 a 1 flapjack   **b** 10 flapjacks.

3 Rice pudding (5 portions)
 150 g rice
 1000 ml milk
 85 g sugar
 5 ml vanilla

 List the ingredients needed for 4 portions.

4 Treacle toffee (800 g)
 450 g soft brown sugar
 230 g black treacle
 110 g unsalted butter
 2 tbsp water
 1 tbsp white vinegar

 List the ingredients needed to make
 1200 g of treacle toffee.

4 Inverse proportion

'Many hands make light work' is an old saying.
If the number of people sharing a task is doubled, then the time to complete the task is halved.
Supplies that would last four men 6 days would only last eight men for 3 days.
If the number of winners doubles, the lottery payout to each winner is halved.

These are all examples of **inverse proportion**

Example 1   Three people volunteer to keep watch on a rare bird's nest.
Each of them will keep guard for 8 hours.
If, instead, four volunteers shared the work, how many hours would each one keep watch?

3 people spend 8 hours each
1 person would spend 8 × 3 = 24 hours
4 people spend 24 ÷ 4 = 6 hours each

Exercise 4.1

1 Five winners share a prize equally. Each of them receives £12.
If, instead, there were six winners sharing the prize, how much would each one get?
Copy and complete:
5 winners would get £12 each
1 winner would get £12 × 5 = £...
6 winners would get £... ÷ 6 = £... each.

2 A supermarket receives a delivery of eggs.
They are packed into trays which hold 6 eggs each.
There are enough eggs to fill 100 trays.
If the eggs are repacked into trays which hold 10 eggs, how many trays would there be?

3 Two people take 6 hours each to deliver a batch of leaflets.
Working at the same rate, how long would:
a one person   **b** three people take?

4 A jar of sweets is shared out equally among eight children.
They each receive nine sweets.
a How many sweets were in the jar?
b If there were only six children, how many sweets would each one get?

5 At Golden Valley Orchard the apples are ripe for picking.
It will take six people 15 hours each to pick the whole crop.
Working at the same rate, how many hours would:
a just one person
b ten people take?

6 Amy has just enough money to buy eight choc ices at 60p each.
  a How much money has she got?
  b She could buy six cones instead (no change).
    How much does a cone cost?

7 A piano teacher visits a school for 4 hours to
give personal tuition to pupils.
Each pupil gets an equal share of her time.
How much time can she give to each pupil if
there are:
  a 2
  b 4
  c 6
  d 8 pupils to teach?

8 Darren can travel three times quicker on his bike than walking.
If he cycles to the youth club it takes him 12 minutes.
How long does it take him when he walks?

9 Nine teams each of four pupils enter a quiz.
They are reorganised into six teams.
How many will be in each team now?

10 At Highmoor School there are 8 lessons of 35 minutes each day.
They change to a new timetable of 7 lessons a day.
The total teaching time remains the same.
How long is each lesson with the new timetable?

Example 2   Helen takes 25 minutes at an average speed of 40 miles per hour to
drive to work.
How fast would she need to drive to cut her time by 5 minutes?

25 minutes ...   40 mph
1 minute   ... $25 \times 40 = 1000$ mph
20 minutes ... $1000 \div 20 = 50$ mph

Exercise 4.2

1 Comfy Coaches have two sizes of coach. The larger has 72 seats and the smaller 48.
To take fans to an away match they reckon they need exactly eight of the larger
coaches.
How many small coaches would be needed to take the same number of fans?

2 A piece of land can be divided into 20 individual allotments each with an area of
120 m². It is decided to increase the number of allotments to 24.
Calculate the area of each of these allotments.

3 Five lottery winners each received £840 000.
If the same amount was shared between seven winners, how much would each person receive?

4 Eight friends rent a caravan for a fortnight's holiday.
They each agree to pay £73·50.
One of them has to drop out, leaving seven of them to share the bill.
How much does each of them have to pay?

5 A store sells cooking oil in three sizes.

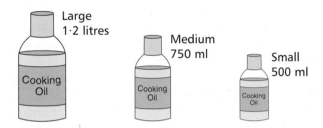

A container of oil will fill 24 medium size bottles.
Using the same container, how many:
a large
b small bottles could be filled?

6 Sarfraz and four friends take 4·5 hours each to weed and dig his garden.
How much time would each of them have saved if they'd had one more person to share the work?

7 Billy plants 20 cabbages in a vegetable patch. Each cabbage has 0·24 m² of ground.
a If he planted 16 cabbages on the same patch, how much ground would each one have?
b If each cabbage had 0·2 m² of ground, how many could he plant?

8 A census of every home in a town is planned. The council decide to employ a team of 80 people. Each of these will visit an average of 225 homes.
a If ten more people are employed how many homes, on average, will each person have to visit?
b How many people will need to be employed to get the average down to 150 homes?

Investigation

For one week find out the number of winners in the National Lottery and how much they each receive. Calculate how much each winner would have received for between one and ten winners.

5 Direct and inverse proportion: mixed examples

Example 1 5 kg = 11 pounds

Convert: **a** 8 kg to pounds   **b** 16·5 pounds to kilograms

a 5 kg = 11 pounds
1 kg = 11 pounds ÷ 5
8 kg = 11 ÷ 5 × 8 = 17·6 pounds

b 11 pounds = 5 kg
1 pound = 5 kg ÷ 11
16·5 pounds = 5 ÷ 11 × 16·5 = 7·5 kg

> If I double the number of kilograms, I double the number of pounds ... direct proportion.

Example 2 A farmer has enough hay to feed 10 cows for 8 days.
How long would this amount feed 16 cows?
10 cows ... 8 days
1 cow ... 10 × 8 = 80 days
16 cows ... 80 ÷ 16 = 5 days

> If I double the number of cows, I halve the number of days... inverse proportion.

Be careful, not everything is direct or inverse proportion.
- It takes one man 10 minutes to clean out a telephone box.
  How long would it take 20 men?
- It takes 3 minutes to boil an egg. How long does it take to boil 3 eggs?

Exercise 5.1

1 Say whether each is an example of direct or inverse proportion:
   a the time taken for a journey and the speed travelled
   b the total cost and the number of lottery tickets bought
   c the number of cups of tea that can be poured from a teapot and the size of the cup
   d the amount of wheat grown and the area of the field it's planted in.

2 The number of people delivering free newspapers to a housing estate is doubled.
   What happens to the time taken to deliver the papers?

3 The number of spectators at Town's home games is trebled.
   What happens to the amount of money taken?

4 Four loaves of bread cost a total of £2·40.
   How much will six loaves cost?

5 Three cleaners can do an office block in eight hours.
   How long would four cleaners take?

6 The label on a tin of baked beans says that 100 g contain 86 calories.
   How many calories are in a 475 g tin?

7 Main Street High School holds a monthly lottery for charity.
   In January two winners each receive £450.
   In February the total prize money is the same.
   There are three winners. How much does each one win?

8 Mike takes on the challenge of walking from
John O'Groats to Land's End.
His target is to average 20 miles a day and that
will mean a total walk of 42 days.
If he averaged 24 miles a day, how many days
would it take?

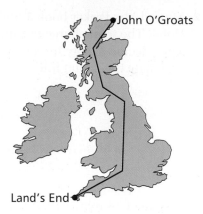

9 When Liz runs for 8 minutes she uses 88 calories.
   a How many calories does she use when she runs for 20 minutes?
   b How long should she run for to use 55 calories?

10 800 cm³ of aluminium weigh 2160 g.
   a Calculate the weight of 300 cm³.
   b What volume of aluminium will weigh 5400 g?

11 5 miles are equal to 8 km. Convert:
   a 20 miles to kilometres
   b 48 miles to kilometres
   c 48 km to miles
   d 20 km to miles

Example 3   Eight winners of a weekly lottery each receive £4500.
The following week ten winners share the same total prize money.
   a How much does each winner receive?
   b The week after this each winner receives £7200.
     The total prize is unchanged.
     How many winners are there?

   a 8 winners   ... £4500 each
     1 winner   ... £4500 × 8 = £36 000
     10 winners ... £36 000 ÷ 10 = £3600 each
   b £4500   ... 8 winners
     Total = £4500 × 8 = £36 000
     £36 000 ÷ £7200 = 5 winners

Exercise 5.2

1 Say whether each of these pairs is in direct or inverse proportion:
   a 4 hours of boat hire for £10; 6 hours for £15
   b 10 minutes to walk to the shops at 6 km/h; 15 minutes at 4 km/h
   c 5 prizes of £40; 8 prizes of £25
   d 36 g of fat in 100 g of cheese; 45 g of fat in 125 g of cheese.

2 Mr and Mrs Parker book 5 nights at the Highland Hotel. The total charge is £300.
They decide to stay for an extra night.
Calculate their total bill.

3 A team of 14 relay runners plans to run between Glasgow and Fort William.
Each of them will run 20 km.
They recruit two more runners to share the distance.
How far will each member run now?

4 Trendy Textiles Plc give the workforce of 60 employees a Christmas bonus of £250 each.
The following year the total bonus remains the same but there are ten fewer employees.
How much is each worker given?

5 Gill has enough food to last her five horses for 12 days.
How many days will the food last if the number of horses is:

a increased by one

b decreased by one?

6 Malcolm is paid on an hourly rate.
On Monday he earns £54 for a 7·5 hour day.
How much does he earn on:

a Tuesday when he works 30 minutes less than Monday

b Wednesday when he works 30 minutes more than Monday?

7 Sue uses a 4 m ladder to reach a window 3·2 m above the ground.

a What length of ladder should she use to reach a window which is 6 m high? (Assume proportion.)

b What height will a 7 m ladder reach?

8 A metallurgist makes brass by mixing copper and zinc.
For one cast he uses 2·5 kg of zinc and 3·75 kg of copper.
Keeping the same ratio of zinc to copper, what weight of:

a copper should be used with 5·6 kg of zinc

b zinc should be used with 18·3 kg of copper?

6 Finding a formula (direct variation)

Another word for proportion is **variation**.

Mathematicians use the symbol $\propto$ which is read as 'varies directly as'.

'Varies directly as' means the same as 'directly proportional to'.

Example 1   The number of calories (C) in jam varies directly as the weight (W g) of jam. We write $C \propto W$.

This means that $C = k \times W$ or $C = kW$ where k is a constant.

The label on a jar of jam tells us that there are 250 calories in 100 g.
We can use these values to calculate k.
When $C = 250$ we have $W = 100$.
$250 = k \times 100$
$\Rightarrow k = 250 \div 100 = 2{\cdot}5$
$\Rightarrow C = 2{\cdot}5W$ is the formula connecting C and W.

Example 2 $X \propto y$ and when $X = 36$, $y = 3$.
  a Find a formula for X in terms of y.
  b Calculate the value of X when $y = 7$.

  a $X \propto y \Rightarrow X = ky$
    When $X = 36$, $y = 3$
    $\Rightarrow 36 = k \times 3$
    $\Rightarrow k = 36 \div 3 = 12$
    $\Rightarrow X = 12y$
  b When $y = 7$
    $X = 12 \times 7 = 84$

Exercise 6.1

1 In which of the following does direct variation apply?
  Where it does, write it in the form $C \propto W$.
  a The thickness of a book (T) and the number of pages (n)
  b The distance walked (D) and the number of paces (n)
  c The height of a person (H) and their weight (W)
  d The distance cycled (D) and the time taken (t)
  e The mark in a maths test (M) and the hours spent revising (h)

2 $A = kB$. When $A = 20$, $B = 4$.
  a Calculate the value of k.
  b Write down a formula for A in terms of B.

3 $P \propto Q$. When $P = 5$, $Q = 10$.
  a Calculate k.
  b Write down a formula for P in terms of Q.

4 The formula connecting centimetres (C) and inches (i) is $C = 2{\cdot}54i$.
  Calculate C when:
  a $i = 2$ **b** $i = 10$.

5 The formula connecting the amount of pounds (P) exchanged for euro (E) is
$P = 0·7E$.
Calculate P when:
a $E = 4$　　　　　　　　　**b** $E = 20$.

6 Kev's mobile phone costs (C pence) vary directly with the time (t min).
A 4 minute call costs him 140p.
a Find a formula for C in terms of t.
b Calculate the cost of a 7 minute call.

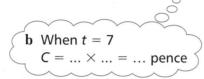

> **b** When $t = 7$
> $C = ... \times ... = ...$ pence

> **a** Copy and complete:
> $C \propto t$
> $\Rightarrow$ $C = k...$
> When $C = 140$, $t = 4$
> $140 = k \times ...$
> $\Rightarrow$ $k = 140 \div ... = ...$
> $\Rightarrow$ $C = ...t$

7 The distance (D metres) Mel travels on her bike
varies directly as the number of turns (n) of the wheels.
For ten turns she travels 20 m (when $D = 20$, $n = 10$).
a Find a formula for D in terms of n.
b Calculate D when $n = 25$.

8 $F \propto w$. When $F = 64$, $w = 2$.
a Find a formula for F in terms of w. (Hint: $F = kw$)
b Calculate F when $w = 5$.

9 The wage (£W) Danny earns varies directly with the number of hours worked (n).
$W \propto n$. When $W = 54$, $n = 6$.
a Find a formula for W in terms of n.　　**b** Calculate W when $n = 8$.

10 The distance (D m) Louise drives varies directly with
the speed (s m/s).
$D \propto s$. When $D = 150$, $s = 5$.
a Find a formula for D in terms of s.
b Calculate D when $s = 7$.

Example 3　　The weight (W g) of sand varies directly with the volume (V cm³).
40 cm³ of sand weigh 104 g.
a Find a formula for W in terms of V.
b Calculate the weight of 55 cm³ of sand.

a $W \propto V$
$\Rightarrow W = kV$
When $V = 40$, $W = 104$
$\Rightarrow 104 = k \times 40$
$\Rightarrow k = 104 \div 40 = 2·6$
$W = 2·6V$
b When $V = 55$
$W = 2·6 \times 55 = 143$ g

Exercise 6.2

1 The distance (D metres) Amy runs varies directly with the time (t seconds).
When $D = 56$, $t = 8$.
  a Find a formula for D in terms of t.
  b Calculate the distance (D) run after 20 seconds ($t = 20$).

2 The depth of water (W cm) in a tank varies directly with the time (t seconds).
When $W = 80$, $t = 320$.
  a Find a formula for W in terms of t.
  b Calculate the depth of water (W) after 44 seconds ($t = 44$).

3 The weight (W g) of sugar varies directly with the
volume (V cm^3). 60 cm^3 of sugar weigh 90 g.
  a Find a formula for W in terms of V.
  b Calculate the weight of 300 cm^3 of sugar.

4 Julie's taxi fare (£T) varies directly with the distance travelled (d miles).
A trip of 3 miles costs £8·40.
  a Find a formula for T in terms of d.
  b Calculate the fare for a trip of 6·5 miles.

5 The cost (C pence) of Val's electricity units varies directly with the number (n) used.
240 units cost her 1104 pence.
  a Find a formula for C in terms of n.
  b Calculate the cost of 350 units.

6 The voltage (V volts) in an electrical circuit varies directly with the current (I amps).
When $V = 5$, $I = 8$.
  a Find a formula for V in terms of I.
  b Calculate V when $I = 20$.

7 In silver plating the weight of silver deposited (S g) varies directly with the time
(t minutes). 6 g of silver are deposited in 60 minutes.
  a Find the formula connecting S and t.
  b Calculate the weight of silver deposited in 85 minutes.

Investigation

Investigate mobile phone costs. Find some where the cost (C p)
varies directly with the time (t s).
Write the formulae in the form $C = kt$.

7 Graphs and direct variation

Example 1

The volume of water flowing out of a tap is measured and recorded in a table.

Time (min)	1	2	3	4	5	6
Volume (litres)	3·5	7	10·5	14	17·5	21

A graph of volume against time is drawn.

The graph is a straight line and it passes through $(0, 0)$.
In 0 minutes, 0 litres have flowed.

This shows that the volume is directly proportional to the time or that the volume (V) varies directly as the time (t).
$V \propto t \Rightarrow V = kt$ where k is a constant.

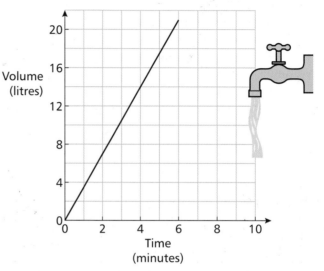

By using a pair of values from the table we can calculate k.
For example, when $t = 2$, $V = 7$
$\Rightarrow 7 = 2 \times k$
$\Rightarrow k = 7 \div 2 = 3·5$
$\Rightarrow V = 3·5t$ is the formula for V in terms of t.

Exercise 7.1

1 The graph shows how the angle the minute hand turns through (A) varies with time (t).
   a Explain how the graph shows $A \propto t$.
   b Through what angle has the hand turned after 10 minutes?
   c $A = kt$. Use your answer to **b** to calculate k.
   d Write down the formula connecting A and t.

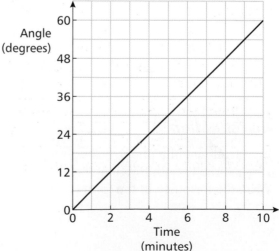

2 The table shows the cost of Tony's off-peak local calls.

Time (min)	0	1	2	3	4	5	6
Cost (pence)	0	1·5	3·0	4·5	6·0	7·5	9·0

A graph of cost against time is drawn.
a How does the graph show that the cost varies directly as the time?
(Give two features of the graph.)
b $C \propto t \Rightarrow C = kt$
From the table when $C = 3$, $t = 2$.
Calculate the value of k and hence find a formula for C in terms of t.

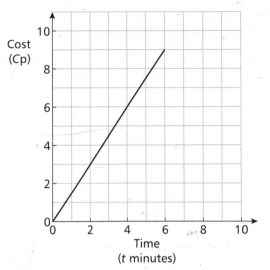

Cost (C p)

Time (*t* minutes)

3 Carla sells Christmas trees.
The table gives the prices of trees of varying heights.

Height (*h* feet)	3	4	5	6	7	8
Cost (£C)	9	12	15	18	21	24

a Draw a graph to illustrate the table, labelling the horizontal axis Height (feet) and the vertical axis Cost (£).
b Check that the graph is a straight line passing through (0, 0). What does this show?
c Find a formula for C in terms of h. (Hint: $C = kh$)

4 The graph shows the distance (D metres) Alice goes on her roller blades and the time taken (t seconds).
a Explain how the graph shows that distance varies directly with the time.
b Copy and complete the table.

Time (*t* s)	0	10	20	30	40	50
Distance (*D* m)						400

c Find a formula connecting D and t.

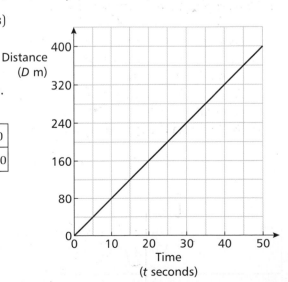

Distance (*D* m)

Time (*t* seconds)

5 A car company records the petrol its latest model consumes as it travels a distance.

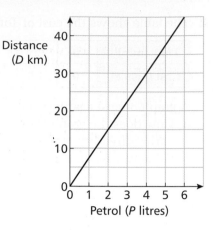

a What does the graph tell us about the amount of petrol used and the distance travelled?

b Copy and complete the table.

Petrol (P litres)	1	2	3	4	5	6
Distance (D km)						45

c Find a formula for the distance (D) in terms of the petrol used (P).

Example 2   In an experiment, different weights are loaded on to a spring. The amount the spring extends and the load are recorded in a table.

Weight (W g)	10	20	30	40	50
Extension (E mm)	4	8	12	16	20

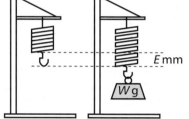

a Draw a graph to illustrate the table.

b How does the graph show that the extension varies directly as the weight?

c Find a formula for E in terms of W.

d Calculate E when W = 65.

a

(graph: Extension (E mm) against Weight (W g))

b The graph is a straight line through (0, 0) so $E \propto W$

c $\Rightarrow E = kW$

When $E = 4$, $W = 10$

$\Rightarrow 4 = k \times 10$

$\Rightarrow k = 4 \div 10 = 0{\cdot}4$

$\Rightarrow E = 0{\cdot}4W$ is the formula

d When $W = 65$, $E = 0{\cdot}4 \times 65 = 26$

A 65 g weight gives an extension of 26 mm.

Exercise 7.2

1   Phil is downloading data from the internet.
    The graph shows the amount of data downloaded,
    in kilobytes, against time in seconds.
    a What does the graph show about the
      amount of data and time?
    b Copy and complete the table.

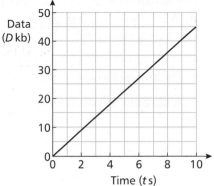

Time (*t* s)	0	2	4	6	8	10
Amount of data (*D* kb)						

   c Find a formula for *D* in terms of *t*.
   d Calculate the amount of data downloaded in 15 seconds.

2   In an electricity experiment, Erica records the current flowing in a circuit (*I* amps) for
    different voltages (*V* volts).

Voltage (*V* volts)	5	10	15	20	25
Current (*I* amps)	0·6	1·2	1·8	2·4	3·0

   a Draw a graph to illustrate the table.
   b How does the graph show that current varies directly as voltage?
   c Find a formula for *I* in terms of *V*.
   d Calculate *I* when $V = 35$.

3   The table shows the output voltage and the input
    voltage of a transformer.

Input voltage (*v* volts)	0	3	6	9	12
Output voltage (*V* volts)	0	60	120	180	240

   a Draw a graph to illustrate the table.
   b How does the graph show that output voltage (*V*)
     varies directly as the input voltage (*v*)?
   c Find a formula for *V* in terms of *v*.
   d Calculate *V* when $v = 8·5$.

4   On holiday, Ricky wants to hire a mountain bike.
    He compares the charges of Freewheelers with Beta Bikes.

Freewheelers

No. of days (*d*)	1	2	3	4	5	6
Cost (£*C*)	6	12	18	24	30	36

Beta Bikes

No. of days (*d*)	1	2	3	4	5	6
Cost (£*C*)	9	13	17	21	27	31

   a On the same axes, draw graphs to illustrate both tables.
   b Which company's charges are in direct proportion to the
     number of days hired?
     Find a formula for *C* in terms of *d* for this company.
   c How much would each company charge for one week's hire?

◀◀ **RECAP**

Direct and inverse proportion

You should be able to recognise direct and inverse proportion.

- With direct proportion, if one quantity is doubled so is the other.
- With inverse proportion, if one quantity is doubled the other is halved.

Calculations involving direct proportion

Example   2 batteries cost 70p. Find the cost of 5 batteries.

If we double the number of batteries we would expect the cost to double (direct proportion).

2 batteries   cost   70p
$\Rightarrow$ 1 battery   costs   70p $\div$ 2 = 35p
$\Rightarrow$ 5 batteries   cost   35p $\times$ 5 = 175p

Calculations involving inverse proportion

Example   The journey to school takes 36 minutes at 5 km/h. How long will it take at 6 km/h?

If we double the speed we would expect the time taken to halve (inverse proportion).

5 km/h   ...   36 min
$\Rightarrow$ 1 km/h   ...   36 min $\times$ 5
$\Rightarrow$ 6 km/h   ...   36 $\times$ 5 $\div$ 6 = 30 min

Finding a formula (direct variation)

Example   The number of litres (L) varies directly as the number of gallons (G). When $L = 18 \cdot 2$, $G = 4$. Find a formula for L in terms of G.

$L \propto G \Rightarrow L = kG$
When $L = 18 \cdot 2$, $G = 4 \Rightarrow 18 \cdot 2 = k \times 4$
$\Rightarrow k = 18 \cdot 2 \div 4 = 4 \cdot 55$
$\Rightarrow L = 4 \cdot 55G$

Direct variation and graphs

When a graph of two variables in direct proportion is drawn, a straight line which passes through the origin (0, 0) is produced.

1 Paul buys six oranges for 90p. Paula pays 75p for five oranges.
Is the cost of the oranges in direct proportion to the number bought?

2 Say whether each of these pairs could be an example of direct or inverse proportion.
  a 4 hours of work for £26; 7 hours for £45·50
  b forming 4 teams of 6 players from a class; forming 3 teams of 8 players
  c sailing 160 km in 4 days; sailing 240 km in 6 days
  d six people receiving a bonus of £80 each; ten people getting a bonus of £48 each

3 Eight bricks weigh 24 kg. What would 12 bricks weigh?

4 A florist prepares 30 bunches of 12 daffodils.
If they were arranged so that there were nine daffodils in
each bunch, how many bunches would there be?

5
> Scrambled eggs (2 portions)
> 2 eggs
> 10 g butter
> 50 ml milk

How much of each is needed for 5 portions?

6 Ron calculates that the cost of running his shower for 5 minutes is 4p.
  a How much would a 3 minute shower cost?
  b How long would he get for 6·4p?

7 $M \propto n$. When $M = 4·8$, $n = 8$.
  a Find a formula for M in terms of n.
  b Calculate the value of M when $n = 20$.

8 The amount of fat (F g) in a loaf of wholemeal bread varies directly with the total
weight (w g). There are 2·8 g of fat in 100 g of wholemeal bread.
  a Find a formula for F in terms of w.
  b Calculate the amount of fat in a loaf weighing 450 g.

9 A garage records the amount of fuel (F litres) delivered by its pumps and the time
taken (t s).

Time (s)	0	20	40	60	80	100	120
Fuel (litres)	0	8	16	24	32	40	48

  a Draw a graph to illustrate the table.
  b How does the graph show that fuel varies directly with time?
  c Find a formula for F in terms of t.
  d Calculate F when $t = 45$ s.

REVISE

8 Pythagoras

Pythagoras was born on the Greek island of Samos around 570 BC.
He later lived in the south of Italy where he formed a school of Mathematics.
He is famous, amongst other things, for proving a connection between the sides of any right-angled triangle.

1 REVIEW

◀◀ **Exercise 1.1**

1 a Without using a calculator, find:
   i 3^2 **ii** 5^2 **iii** 8^2 **iv** 10^2

   b With the aid of a calculator, find:
   i 4^2 **ii** 17^2 **iii** 25^2 **iv** 100^2

   c Use the (√) key on your calculator to find:
   i $\sqrt{49}$ **ii** $\sqrt{81}$ **iii** $\sqrt{121}$ **iv** $\sqrt{225}$

   d Evaluate:
   i $\sqrt{16}$ **ii** $\sqrt{64}$ **iii** $\sqrt{169}$ **iv** $\sqrt{625}$

2 Calculate the area of each square.

a
9 cm
9 cm

b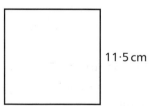
11·5 cm

3 Calculate the length of side of each square.

a
289 cm²

b
1369 cm²

4 Copy and complete the following:
  a 5 is the square root of 25, so 25 is the square of …
  b 7 is the square root of …, so … is the square of … (careful)
  c $6^2 = 36, \Rightarrow \sqrt{36} = \ldots$
  d $\sqrt{64} = \ldots \Rightarrow \ldots^2 = \ldots$

5 Use your calculator to help you evaluate:
  a $5^2 + 9^2$ **b** $7^2 + 15^2$ **c** $17^2 + 21^2$

6 Sketch each shape and mark all the right angles.
  a An isosceles triangle   **b** A kite   **c** A rhombus

 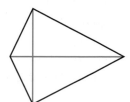 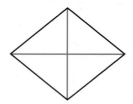

2 Pythagoras' theorem

The longest side in a right-angled triangle is always opposite the right angle and it is called the **hypotenuse**. This comes from an ancient Greek word meaning 'stretched under'.

In the diagram you can see that four identical right-angled triangles can be arranged in two different ways to form a square whose side is $(b + c)$ units.

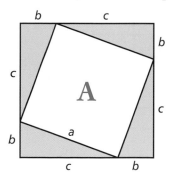 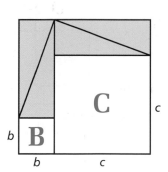

Removing the four triangles, we see that the area of the square A is equal to the sum of the squares B and C.

Area A = Area B + Area C
$$a^2 = b^2 + c^2$$

This is what Pythagoras proved and it is known as **Pythagoras' theorem**

> In any right-angled triangle, the square on the hypotenuse is equal to the sum of the squares on the two shorter sides.

Exercise 2.1

1 Name the hypotenuse in each right-angled triangle.

a 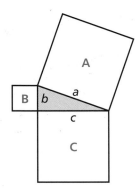   **b** 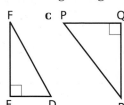   **c** 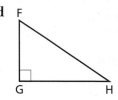   **d**   **e**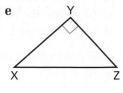

2

Area A = Area B + Area C

Check this is true for the triangle shown on this Greek postage stamp which was issued to commemorate Pythagoras.

3 i Find the area of the square on the hypotenuse in these right-angled triangles.

   ii Calculate the length of each hypotenuse using the √ button on your calculator.

a 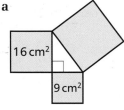   **b** 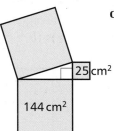   **c** 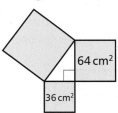   **d**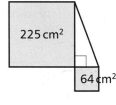

16 cm²   9 cm²

144 cm²   25 cm²

64 cm²   36 cm²

225 cm²   64 cm²

---

3 Calculating the hypotenuse

Example Calculate the value of x in this triangle.

The triangle is right-angled so we can use Pythagoras' theorem.

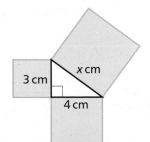

By Pythagoras' theorem,

$$x^2 = 3^2 + 4^2$$
$$\Rightarrow x^2 = 9 + 16$$
$$\Rightarrow x^2 = 25$$
$$\Rightarrow x = \sqrt{25}$$
$$\Rightarrow x = 5$$

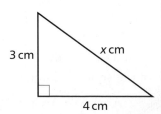

Exercise 3.1

1 Copy and complete the working to calculate x in this right-angled triangle.

By Pythagoras' theorem,

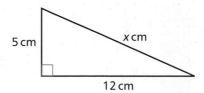

$$x^2 = 5^2 + \ldots^2$$
$$\Rightarrow x^2 = \ldots + \ldots$$
$$\Rightarrow x^2 = \ldots$$
$$\Rightarrow x = \sqrt{\ldots}$$
$$\Rightarrow x = \ldots$$

2 Calculate the length of the hypotenuse in each of these right-angled triangles.
(All lengths are in centimetres.)

a    b   c 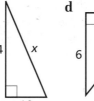   d 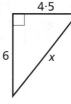   e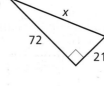

3 Calculate h in these right-angled triangles.
(All lengths are in centimetres.)

a    b 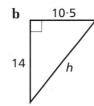   c   d   e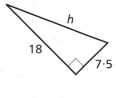

4 Calculate z in each triangle.
Give your answer correct to 1 decimal place.

a 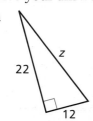   b 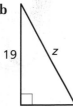   c   d 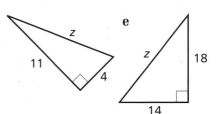   e

5 Calculate the length of the hypotenuse, correct to 1 d.p., in a right-angled triangle whose shorter sides are:
   a 14 cm and 17 cm   b 27 cm and 29 cm
   c 7 cm and 7 cm   d 8·5 cm and 5 cm
   e 12 cm and 9·7 cm   f 1 cm and 8 cm

Exercise 3.2

1 Calculate the length of the ladder.

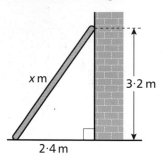

2 Calculate the length of the ramp.

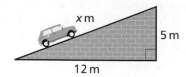

3 Calculate the length of the wire.

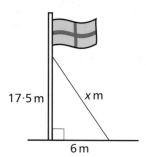

4 Calculate the length of the sloping edge.

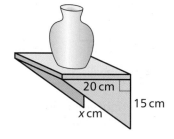

5 Calculate the distance (x m) Ewan runs along the ground to the foot of the steps for another turn on the slide.

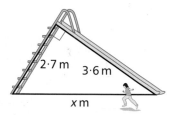

6 Calculate the length of Channel Street.

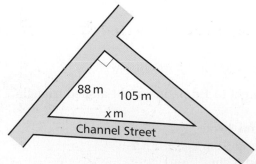

4 Calculating a shorter side

Example   A ladder 6·5 m long is set up with its foot 2·5 m from the base of a wall.
How far up the wall will the ladder reach?

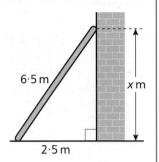

The triangle is right-angled

$\Rightarrow \quad 6{\cdot}5^2 = 2{\cdot}5^2 + x^2$

$\Rightarrow \quad x^2 = 6{\cdot}5^2 - 2{\cdot}5^2$

$\Rightarrow \quad x^2 = 42{\cdot}25 - 6{\cdot}25$

$\Rightarrow \quad x^2 = 36$

$\Rightarrow \quad x = \sqrt{36} = 6$

The ladder will reach 6 m up the wall.

Exercise 4.1

1 Copy and complete the working to calculate x in this right-angled triangle.

The triangle is right-angled

$\Rightarrow \quad 15^2 = 9^2 + \ldots^2$

$\Rightarrow \quad x^2 = 15^2 - \ldots^2$

$\Rightarrow \quad x^2 = \ldots - \ldots$

$\Rightarrow \quad x^2 = \ldots$

$\Rightarrow \quad x = \sqrt{\ldots} = \ldots$

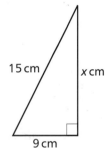

2 Calculate the value of x in each right-angled triangle.
Give your answers to **c–e** correct to 1 d.p.
(All measurements are in centimetres.)

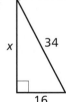
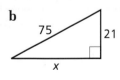
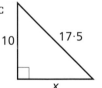

3 Calculate the missing side in each right-angled triangle, correct to 1 d.p.
(All measurements are in centimetres.)

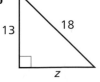

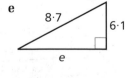

Exercise 4.2

1 Calculate the length of the vertical cable.

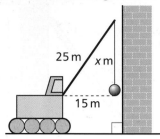

2 Calculate the height of the back of the shelf.

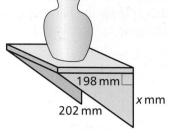

3 Calculate the distance d m between the struts on the clothes dryer.

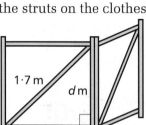

4 Calculate the length of: **a** AB   **b** DC.

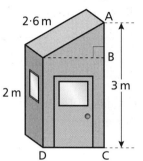

5 By spotting suitable triangles, calculate the lengths indicated. (All measurements are in centimetres.)

a rectangle

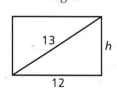

b parallelogram

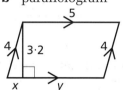

c rhombus

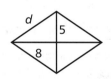

d kite

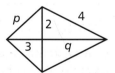

---

5 Hypotenuse or shorter side?

Before you tackle a question, ask yourself if it's the hypotenuse or a shorter side that is required.

Exercise 5.1

1 Calculate the value of the letter in each diagram, correct to 1 d.p.

a

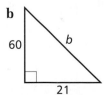

b

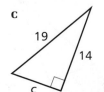

c

d

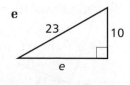

e

2 A 3·5 metre ladder reaches the top of a wall which is 3·3 metres high.
   a Draw a diagram of the situation, highlighting the right-angled triangle.
   b How far is the foot of the ladder from the foot of the wall? Give your answer to 1 d.p.

3 A fishing trawler leaves port and sails 120 km east and then 55 km north.
The skipper of the ship then decides to sail straight back to port.
   a Draw a diagram of the situation.
   b What distance is this return journey, to the nearest kilometre?

Round your answers to questions **4–6** to 2 d.p.

4 A support wire must be attached 2 metres up a tree.
The wire is 2·25 metres long.
   a Illustrate the situation with a sketch.
   b How far from the base of the tree will the wire be fixed to the ground?

5 A gate is rectangular with a length of 3·6 m and a breadth of 1·2 m.
How long is the diagonal of the gate?

6 This elevator is 10 metres long and the bottom is 4 metres
from the foot of the support.
How high is the support?

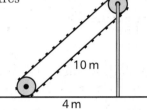

Finding the right-angled triangle

Many geometric shapes contain right angles and right-angled triangles.
You may find it helpful to sketch the right-angled triangle being used.

Example   Find the length of side of a rhombus whose diagonals are 10 cm
and 16 cm.

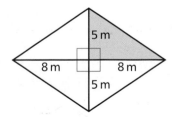
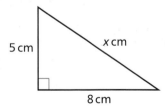

A right-angled triangle has been identified by a sketch.
By Pythagoras' theorem:
$$x^2 = 5^2 + 8^2$$
$$\Rightarrow \quad x^2 = 25 + 64$$
$$\Rightarrow \quad x^2 = 89$$
$$\Rightarrow \quad x = \sqrt{89} = 9\cdot4 \text{ (to 1 d.p.)}$$

Exercise 5.2

1 Name all the right-angled triangles you can find in these diagrams.

a isosceles triangle with altitute BD **b** rhombus **c** kite **d** rectangle

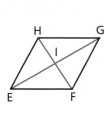

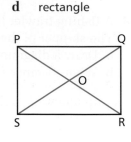

2 Find the value (to 1 d.p.) of the letters in these diagrams. (All lengths are in centimetres.)

rhombus rectangle kite square

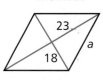

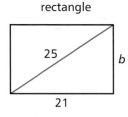

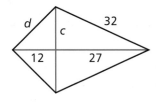

3 A TV mast is supported by two wires secured to the ground at the same point.
This point is 26 metres from the foot of the mast.
One support wire is 34 metres long.
The other is 52 metres long.
  a Find the height at which each wire is attached to the mast (x m and y m).
  b Find the distance between these two points.
  Round your answers to 1 d.p.

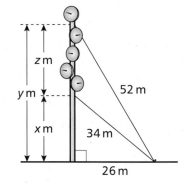

4 Calculate the length of the marked edges of the sails on this yacht.
(All lengths are in metres.)
Give your answers correct to 2 d.p.

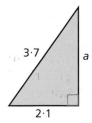

5 An earring is made in the shape of a kite.
(All lengths are in millimetres.)
  a Calculate the value of x and y.
  b What is the length of the long diagonal?
  c What is the perimeter of the earring?

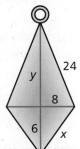

6 Calculate the length, w cm, of the leading edge
of the wing of the paper aeroplane.
Give your answer correct to 2 d.p.

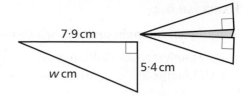

7 a Find the value of x. (All lengths are in metres.)
b Calculate y m, the width of the chimney stack, to 2 d.p.

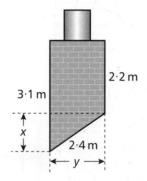

6 Adding lines to the diagram

In some problems it is necessary to add a line or lines to the diagram.

Example   Calculate the vertical height of this isosceles triangle.

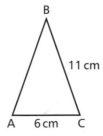

Add the axis of symmetry, BD, to the diagram.
This creates a right-angled triangle to work with.
Also, in an isosceles triangle, this added line is the
required height.
By Pythagoras' theorem,

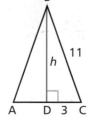

$$11^2 = h^2 + 3^2$$
$$\Rightarrow h^2 = 11^2 - 3^2$$
$$\Rightarrow h^2 = 121 - 9$$
$$\Rightarrow h^2 = 112$$
$$\Rightarrow h = \sqrt{112} = 10{\cdot}6 \text{ (to 1 d.p.)}$$

So the height of the isosceles triangle is 10·6 cm to 1 d.p.

Exercise 6.1

Round your answers to 1 d.p. where necessary.

1 Calculate the labelled length in each of these isosceles triangles.
(All lengths are in centimetres.)

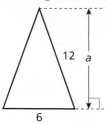 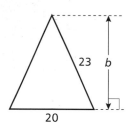 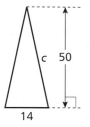 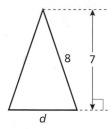

2 Calculate the length of the base of the isosceles triangle which has a vertical height of 12 m and equal sides of length 20 m.

3 Calculate the length of the diagonal of a rectangle which is:
   a 2·6 cm by 7 cm   **b** 3·8 cm by 9·4 cm.

4 a Calculate the value of y in this trapezium.
    (Hint: create a right-angled triangle.)

   b A swimming pool has a cross-section as shown.
    What is the length, x m, of the pool?

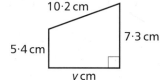

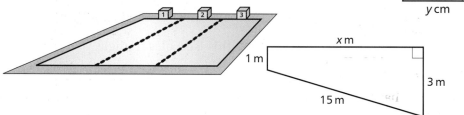

5 The side of a house is in the shape of an isosceles triangle on top of a rectangle.
What is the length of the sloping edge of the roof of this house?

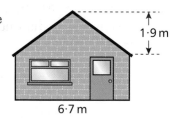

6 The front of a tent is an isosceles triangle with a base of 3 m. The tent ridge is 2 m high. Calculate the length of the sloping edge of the tent.

7 Each face of the pyramid is an isosceles triangle.
The entrance is at the centre, B, of the base.
   a Sketch △TAC, with TA = TC.
   b Draw TB, and calculate its length.

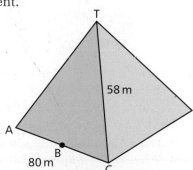

Exercise 6.2

1 Find the height of this church spire, to 1 d.p.

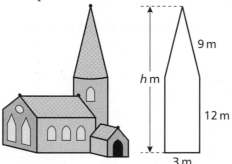

2 How long is the base of the window box?

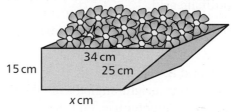

3 The edge of this label is gold leaf. Calculate:
  a x
  b the perimeter of the label.

4 Calculate the length of the sloping edge of this writing bureau.
(All lengths are in centimetres.)

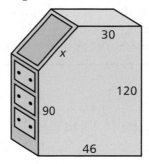

5 The fire engine has an extension ladder. Calculate:
  a the distance, AB, from A to the wall
  b the length of ladder needed to reach from A to D.

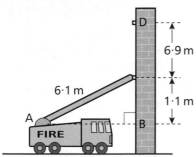

6 How far is it, to the nearest yard, from the corner flag A to:
  a player X
  b player Y?

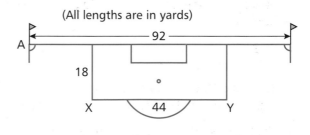

7 A club has designed a badge which consists of a square, a circle and a line.
The line is a diagonal of the square.
The side of the square is 6 cm long.
  a What is the length of the diagonal of the square (to 1 d.p.)?
  b What is the length of the radius of the circle (to 2 d.p.)?

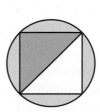

7 Pythagoras and coordinates

We can use Pythagoras to calculate the distance between any two points on a coordinate grid.

Example   Find the distance between the points A(2, 1) and B(8, 4) correct to 1 decimal place.

Plot A and B.
We can draw a right-angled triangle ABC, with AB as hypotenuse, and the two shorter sides parallel to the axes.
We can read off the lengths of the shorter sides.
AC = 6 units; BC = 3 units.
By Pythagoras' theorem:

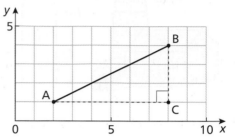

$$AB^2 = 6^2 + 3^2$$
$$\Rightarrow AB^2 = 36 + 9$$
$$\Rightarrow AB^2 = 45$$
$$\Rightarrow AB = \sqrt{45} = 6{\cdot}7 \text{ (to 1 d.p.)}$$

So the distance from A to B is 6·7 cm to 1 d.p.

Exercise 7.1

1 Find the length of AB in the following coordinate diagrams.

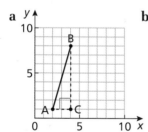
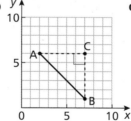
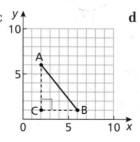
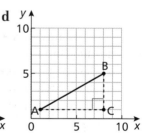

2 Find the distance between the following pairs of points.
    a A(3, 4) and B(6, 8)   **b** M(2, 4) and N(14, 9)   **c** P(5, 2) and Q(7, 9)

3 Two plant pots stand on a patio made of square slabs of side 1 metre.
Use Pythagoras' theorem to work out the distance between the pots.

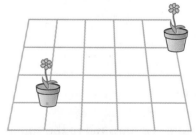

4 Plot these sets of points on coordinate diagrams and join them up.
Calculate the hypotenuse of each right-angled triangle.
    a A(1, 2), B(6, 2), C(6, 5)   **b** P(1, 7), Q(1, 3), R(7, 3)   **c** X(0, 6), Y(0, 1), Z(6, 6)

5 Two young ospreys (called Oscar and Oliver) are fitted with tracker devices before they leave the nest.
Their position is monitored closely on a map of the area.

Each square has a side of 1 km. Which osprey is further from the nest and by how far?

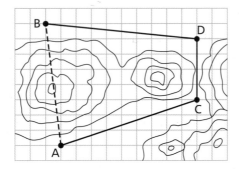

6 a Plot the points P(1, 1), Q(2, 5) and R(6, 4).
  b Calculate the length of PQ and QR.
  c What kind of triangle is PQR?

7 The only way to get from A to B in a mountainous country is to go by the pass CD.
The dotted line AB shows the route of a proposed tunnel.
The side of each square is 1 km long.

Calculate:
  a the length of the tunnel route, AB
  b the length of the road route A → C → D → B
  c the saving in distance by the tunnel.

◀◀ RECAP

Pythagoras' theorem states that:
the square on the hypotenuse of a right-angled triangle is equal to the sum of the squares on the two shorter sides.

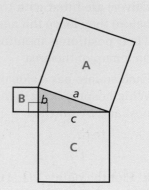

Area A = Area B + Area C
$$\Rightarrow a^2 = b^2 + c^2$$

Calculating the hypotenuse
The triangle is right-angled.
By Pythagoras' theorem:

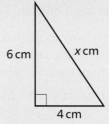

$$x^2 = 6^2 + 4^2$$
$$\Rightarrow x^2 = 36 + 16$$
$$\Rightarrow x^2 = 52$$
$$\Rightarrow x = \sqrt{52} = 7 \cdot 2 \text{ (to 1 d.p.)}$$

The hypotenuse is 7·2 cm.

Calculating a shorter side
The triangle is right-angled.
By Pythagoras' theorem:

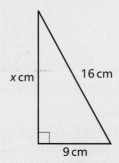

$$16^2 = x^2 + 9^2$$
$$\Rightarrow x^2 = 16^2 - 9^2$$
$$\Rightarrow x^2 = 256 - 81 = 175$$
$$\Rightarrow x = \sqrt{175} = 13 \cdot 2 \text{ (to 1 d.p.)}$$

Calculating the distance between two points
When working out the distance between two points, plot the points and form a right-angled triangle using the line joining the points as the hypotenuse.

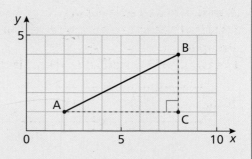

1 Name the hypotenuse in each of these right-angled triangles.

a

b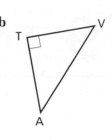

2 Calculate the missing side in each of these right-angled triangles.

a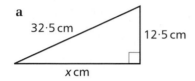

b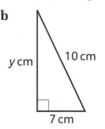

c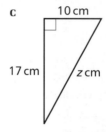

3 A cable car drops 0·8 km over a distance of 4 km. What is the length of the cable?

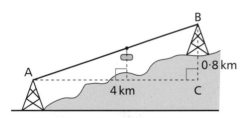

4 What is the vertical height of an isosceles triangle whose base is 1·2 m and whose equal sides are 7·2 m long?

5 How far apart are the points (3, 7) and (7, 11), correct to 1 decimal place?

6 A garden centre sells edging for paths in 3·6 m sections.
Wire is attached to the frame at regular intervals forming isosceles triangles for strength.
How much wire, marked in green, is needed for each section?

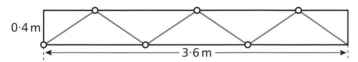

REVISE

9 Time, distance and speed

The greatest speed at which a human has travelled is 39 897 km/h and that was by the crew of *Apollo 10* in 1969.

At this speed you could go from Edinburgh to Glasgow in 6 seconds.

I do not *believe* it!

1 REVIEW

◄◄ **Exercise 1.1**

1 What time is shown on the clock?

2 **a** What speed is shown here in miles per hour?
   b Estimate this speed in kilometres per hour.
   c How many miles has the vehicle travelled?

3 **a** How many minutes are there in:
   i 1 hour   **ii** $\frac{1}{2}$ hour   **iii** $\frac{1}{4}$ hour   **iv** $2\frac{1}{2}$ hours?
   b What fraction of an hour is:
   i 30 minutes   **ii** 15 minutes   **iii** 45 minutes
   iv 10 minutes   **v** 20 minutes?

4 Write in decimal form:
   a $\frac{1}{2}$ **b** $\frac{1}{4}$ **c** $\frac{3}{4}$ **d** $6\frac{1}{2}$ **e** $1\frac{3}{4}$ **f** $4\frac{1}{4}$

5 a Write down the distance from:
   i Miltown to Cooper
   ii Dunbeg to Miltown.
   b Which towns are furthest apart?

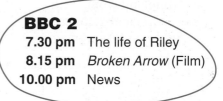

Miltown			Distances in miles
37	Redly		
47	65	Dunbeg	
19	51	40	Cooper

6 Martin has circled some programmes he wants to see in the paper.
   a What is the duration of 'The Life of Riley'?
   b For what length of time does the film run?
   c How long is it between the start of 'The Life of Riley' and the News?

BBC 2
7.30 pm   The life of Riley
8.15 pm   *Broken Arrow* (Film)
10.00 pm News

7 Gregor was training for a cross-country cycling competition. This graph shows his journey from home and back again.
   a How far from home was he after:
   i 1 hour
   ii 4 hours?
   b i When was he furthest from home?
   ii How far from home was this?

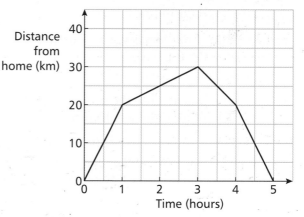

---

2 Using time

Calculating time intervals

Example 1   How long is it from 9.40 am to 4.10 pm?

Use a step-by-step approach:

From 9.40 am to the next hour (10.00 am)	= 20 minutes
From 10 till noon	= 2 hours
From noon till 4.10 pm	= 4 hours 10 minutes
Total time	= 6 hours 30 minutes

Example 2   How long is it from 22 05 to 06 15 (the next day)?

From 22 05 to the next hour (23 00)	= 55 minutes
From 23 00 till midnight	= 1 hour
From midnight till 06 15	= 6 hours 15 minutes
Total time	= 7 hours 70 minutes
	= 8 hours 10 minutes

Exercise 2.1

1 Write these times using 24-hour notation:
   a 11 am   **b** 5 am   **c** 2.30 pm   **d** 11.50 pm   **e** 12.10 am

2 Write these times in 12-hour notation (remember to include am or pm):
   a 07 30   **b** 14 00   **c** 19 57   **d** 11 15   **e** 12 20   **f** 00 35

3 Calculate the time between:
   a 4.30 am and 7 am   **b** 9.30 am and 11.45 am
   c 10 am and 5 pm   **d** 11.30 am and 3.10 pm
   e 9.25 am and 2.15 pm   **f** 7.30 am and 3.25 pm
   g 11 pm and 6 am (next day)   **h** 9.30 pm and 3 am (next day).

4 How long is it between these times?
   a 10 00 and 14 00   **b** 08 00 and 13 20
   c 11 45 and 14 30   **d** 08 50 and 23 30
   e 22 00 and 01 00 (next day)   **f** 22 30 and 04 00 (next day)
   g 20 15 and 08 40 (next day)

5 Lily set out from home at 10.35 am to walk to the shops.
   She arrived at the baker's at 11.17 am.
   For how long did she walk?

6 Tom put a lasagne into the oven at 6.55 pm.
   If it takes an hour and a half to cook, when will it be ready?

7 Sarah wants bread to be ready for breakfast at 8.30 am.
   The bread takes two and a quarter hours to make.
   What time should she set the timer on the breadmaker?

8 Nick set out from base at 23 00 to make a practice night-flight.
   He arrived back at base at 05 20 next day.
   For how long was he flying?

9 A bus set out from Crailing at 10.45 pm on Monday and arrived in Macduff at 3.10 am on Tuesday.
   How long did the journey take?

10 The timetable shows the times of a bus journey between Indio and Banning.
   a At what time did the bus leave Indio?
   b How long did it take to reach Thermal?
   c For how long did the bus stop in Nine Palms?
   d How long was the journey from Indio to Banning?
   e Write the time the bus arrives in Beaumont in 12-hour notation.
   f Aleta's watch said it was twenty-five to three. How long will it be before the bus reaches Banning?

TIMETABLE		
Indio		10 55
Thermal		11 30
Nine Palms	*arrive*	11 50
	depart	13 05
Beaumont		14 18
Banning		15 15

Exercise 2.2

1 Calculate the time between:
   a 10.20 am and 4.05 pm   **b** 5.15 am and 1.23 pm
   c 1.55 am and 3.38 pm   **d** 10.35 pm and 2.50 am (next day)
   e 11.11 pm and 6.14 am (next day)

2 Calculate the time between:
   a 09 35 and 13 55   **b** 04 30 and 16 10
   c 11 27 and 19 08   **d** 23 10 and 05 50 (next day)
   e 20 55 and 03 17 (next day)   **f** 19 56 and 02 04 (next day).

3 Use this train timetable to answer the questions.

Hillton	09 05	10 05	12 35	15 05	19 35	22 35
Berry	09 54	10 53	...	15 54	...	23 26
Dunmore	10 17	11 16	13 42	16 15	20 41	23 45
Little Don	10 45	11 43	14 10	16 45	21 10	00 12
Norseman	...	12 38	...	17 40	22 04	01 07
Camptown	12 01	13 00	15 24	18 01	22 24	01 30

   a At what time does:
      i the first train leave Hillton   **ii** the second train leave Little Don
      iii the last train leave Berry?
   b At which stations does the third train not stop?
   c How long does the last train take:
      i between Dunmore and Little Don   **ii** between Little Don and Norseman
      iii for the whole journey?
   d Write down the times, in 12-hour notation, that the last train is at each station.
   e **i** Which train takes the shortest time for the whole journey?
      ii How long is it?

3 Distance – how far?

Aiden hikes between camping sites. He walks at a steady
5 km per hour. The journey takes him 3 hours.
What is the distance between the camp sites?

In 1 hour he walks 5 kilometres   (given)
In 2 hours he walks 10 kilometres   (2×5 km)
In 3 hours he walks 15 kilometres   (3×5 km)

> **Distance travelled = speed × time**

A memory aid
$D = S \times T$

Note: units must be consistent.
If speed is measured in km/h then distance is measured in kilometres and time in hours.

Example   If you travelled at 25 km/h for 3 hours, how far would you go?
        $D = S \times T \Rightarrow D = 25 \times 3 = 75$ km.

Exercise 3.1

1 Calculate the distance you would travel in:
  a 4 hours at 8 km/h   **b** 6 hours at 10 km/h
  c 2 hours at 75 km/h   **d** 5 hours at 90 km/h

2 How far, in miles, you would travel if you were:
  a walking at 3 miles per hour (mph) for 4 hours
  b cycling at 12 mph for 3 hours
  c running at 7 mph for 2 hours
  d driving at 46 mph for 5 hours?

3 a Conor runs at a steady speed of 6 metres per second (m/s) for 30 seconds.
    How many metres has he run?
  b Nathan ran at 7 m/s for 25 seconds.
    How far did he run?

4 Find the length of all four journeys.

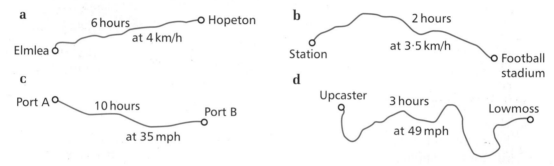

a Elmlea — 6 hours at 4 km/h — Hopeton

b Station — 2 hours at 3·5 km/h — Football stadium

c Port A — 10 hours at 35 mph — Port B

d Upcaster — 3 hours at 49 mph — Lowmoss

Exercise 3.2

1 Calculate the distances travelled on each journey.
  a 50 km/h for 6 hours   **b** 63 mph for 4 hours   **c** 12 m/s for 30 seconds
  d 44 km/h for 5 hours   **e** 120 mph for 2 hours   **f** 10 m/s for 8 seconds

2 a Neil jogs for two and a half hours
    He keeps up an average speed of 13 km/h.
    How far does he jog?
  b A car averages 68 mph on the motorway.
    How far will it travel in 5 hours?
  c A horse was trotting at 6 m/s.
    What distance would it cover in 55 seconds?
  d A racing car can average 246 km/h.
    How far would it travel in half an hour?

3 A migrating swallow can keep up an average speed of 20 mph for 45 hours without stopping.
  What total distance does it fly in this time?

4 Concorde, the supersonic aircraft, could fly at 2300 km/h.
  What distance could it cover in $3\frac{1}{2}$ hours?

5 Karen ran at 7 m/s for 3 minutes.
  a For how many seconds was she running?
  b How far did she run?

6 At an average speed of 55 km/h the *QE2* crossed the Atlantic in 5 days and 4 hours.
  What was the distance across the Atlantic?

7 Twins Matthew and Michael went cycling.
  Matthew cycled for 3 hours at a speed of 11 mph.
  Michael cycled at 13 mph for $2\frac{1}{2}$ hours.
  a Which twin cycled further?   **b** How much further did he cycle?

8 Jade left home at 11 30. She arrived at her gran's house at 13 00.
  a How long did the journey take her?
  b Jade travelled at 55 mph. How far is it from her house to her gran's?

9 a Calculate the distances
    between the towns.

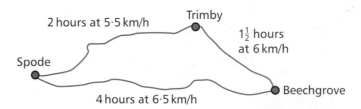

  b Copy the table and fill in the distances.

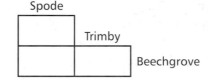

---

4 Average speed – how fast?

Carrie walked 12 km from Johnstone to Paisley in 4 hours.
What was her *average* speed?

Obviously her actual speed changed as she stopped to cross the road; as she speeded up going down hill; as she slowed down in the busy pavements.

However, we say that if she travelled 12 km in 3 hours then she averaged 4 km in each hour.
Her average speed = 12 ÷ 3 = 4 km/h.

$$\text{Average speed} = \frac{\text{distance travelled}}{\text{time taken}}$$

Example 1   Peter travelled 100 km in 5 hours.
          What was his average speed?

$$S = \frac{D}{T} = \frac{100}{5} = 100 \div 5 = 20 \text{ km/h}$$

Remember: units must be consistent.

Exercise 4.1

1 Calculate the average speed in km/h for each journey:
   a 100 km in 2 hours
   b 30 km in 6 hours
   c 350 km in 10 hours
   d 210 km in 3 hours.

2 Calculate these average speeds in miles per hour:
   a 12 miles in 2 hours   **b** 55 miles in 5 hours   **c** 360 miles in 4 hours

3 Calculate the average speeds for these journeys:
   a 100 metres in 10 seconds
   b 660 metres in 11 seconds
   c 900 metres in 45 seconds

4 Complete the last row of the table. (Remember the units for speed.)

	a	b	c	d	e
Distance	45 km	150 miles	200 metres	840 miles	27 metres
Time	5 hours	2 hours	20 seconds	12 hours	9 seconds
Speed					

5 Calculate the average speeds for these journeys.
   a Malcolm travelled from London to New York ... 5520 km in 3 hours.
   b Sarah went from Birmingham to Newcastle ... 332 km in 4 hours.

6 Harry cycled 25 km in two and a half hours.
   Calculate his average speed in kilometres per hour.
   (Remember to type the half as a decimal.)

7 Rachel took $3\frac{1}{2}$ hours to drive from Hawick to Liverpool, a distance of 175 miles.
   Calculate Rachel's average speed.

8 Megan set out from home at 11.30 am to drive to the city 69 km away.
   She arrived at 1 pm.
   a How long did the journey take, in hours?
   b Calculate her average speed.

Example 2   A hot air balloon travelled 52 km in 1 hour 18 minutes.
What was its average speed?

Note that 18 minutes = $\frac{18}{60}$ hours = 0·3 hour
⇒ 1 hour 18 minutes = 1·3 hours

$$S = \frac{D}{T} = \frac{52}{1·3} = 40 \text{ km/h}$$

Exercise 4.2

1 Write these times in decimal form:

   a $1\frac{1}{4}$ hours   **b** $3\frac{1}{2}$ hours   **c** $\frac{3}{4}$ hour   **d** $5\frac{1}{2}$ hours.

2 Write these times in hours only (i.e. change the minutes into decimal parts of an hour):

   a 1 hour 15 minutes   **b** 3 hours 30 minutes

   c 5 hours 45 minutes   **d** 2 hours 24 minutes

   e 4 hours 6 minutes   **f** 1 hour 9 minutes

   g 27 minutes   **h** 42 minutes

   i 2 hours 20 minutes (to 2 d.p.)

3 Using the times in decimal form, calculate each person's speed.

   a Winston took $2\frac{1}{2}$ hours to walk 10 km.

   b Eva took $1\frac{1}{2}$ hours to run 9 km.

   c Jacqui cycled 15 km in $1\frac{1}{4}$ hours.

   d Caitlin drove 143 km in $2\frac{3}{4}$ hours.

   e Sue sailed 7 km in half an hour.

4 Euan cycled 105 km in 3 hours 30 minutes. What was his average speed?

5 Rae took 2 hours 45 minutes to walk $16\frac{1}{2}$ km. Calculate her average speed.

6 **a** Mrs Hughes drives from Glasgow to Liverpool in 3 hours 30 minutes. Use the table to help you calculate her average speed.

   b Next morning she continues her journey and drives to Cardiff in 2 hours 45 minutes. Calculate her average speed for this part of her journey.

Glasgow				
343	Liverpool			Distances in km
341	56	Manchester		
595	264	277	Cardiff	
634	317	296	248	London

5 Time – how long?

Rory aimed to walk a distance of 10 km at an average speed of 5 km/h. How long would it take him?

Rory travels 5 km every hour.
There are two fives in 10 km ($10 \div 5 = 2$)
$\Rightarrow$ it will take 2 hours.

$$\boxed{\text{Time taken} = \frac{\text{Distance}}{\text{Speed}}}$$

Example   How long would it take to cover 175 km at 50 km/h?

$$T = \frac{D}{S} = \frac{175}{50} = 3 \cdot 5 \text{ hours (or 3 hours 30 minutes)}$$

Exercise 5.1

1 Calculate the time taken for each journey:
   a Aisha cycles 30 km at 15 km/h
   b Simon drives 195 km at 65 km/h
   c Erin walks 12 miles at 4 mph
   d Cara rides her horse for 9 miles at 6 mph

2 How long would each of these journeys take?
   a Walking 16 km at 8 km/h
   b Driving 240 miles at 40 mph
   c Running 400 m at 8 m/s
   d Skiing 600 m at 10 m/s
   e Driving at 25 mph for 125 miles
   f Crawling 8 cm at 2 cm/s
   g Running at 10 mph for 15 miles
   h Flying at 500 km/h for 1250 km

3 Arnie leaves home and drives 76 miles to work at an average speed of 38 mph.
   a How long will his journey take?
   b If he left home at 09 00, when would he arrive at his place of work?

4 A train left Hassendean at 14 30 to travel 50 km
   to Chapeltown.
   The average speed for the journey was 40 km/h.
   When did the train arrive at Chapeltown?

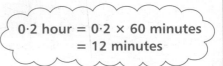

5 Use the mileage chart to find how long these
   journeys would take:
   a Sanday to Henley at 35 mph
   b Redchester to Henley at 27 mph
   c Sanday to Redchester at 18 mph

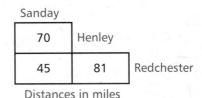

Sanday

70	Henley
45	81	Redchester

Distances in miles

Example   A bus travels 48 km at an average speed of 40 km/h.
   a How long will the journey take?
   b If the bus left at 13 50, when would it arrive at its destination?

   a $T = \dfrac{D}{S} = \dfrac{48}{40} = 1 \cdot 2$ hours

   $= 1$ hour 12 minutes

   > 0·2 hour = 0·2 × 60 minutes
   > = 12 minutes

   b The bus left at 13 50.
   One hour later it is 14 50.
   12 minutes later is 14 62 = 15 02.

   The bus arrives at 15 02.

Exercise 5.2

1 Calculate the time taken for each of these journeys:

    a 55 miles at 11 mph   **b** 135 miles at 27 mph   **c** 220 metres at 10 m/s

    d 144 km at 48 km/h   **e** 160 miles at 64 mph   **f** 77 metres at 14 m/s

2 Calculate the time, in hours and minutes, for each of these journeys:

    a 210 km at 60 km/h   **b** 462 km at 88 km/h   **c** 63 miles at 36 mph

    d at 118 mph for 531 miles   **e** at 56 km/h for 182 km

3 Usman drove 299 miles at an average speed of 52 mph.
How long, in hours and minutes, did his journey take?

4 Nathan set out at 14 40 to cycle the 13 miles to the sports centre.
His average speed was 4 mph.

    a How long did it take him to get there?

    b When did he arrive?

    c After his work-out he cycled home by a different route.
He cycled the 15 miles home at an average speed of 5 mph.
How long did it take him to get home?

5 a Find the time taken by the tour bus for each of the four journeys.

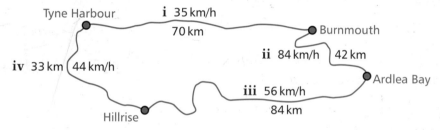

    b i Calculate the total time taken to do a complete circuit of the towns.

      ii A bus left Tyne Harbour at 10 15 to drive round the circuit of towns.
When would it arrive back in Tyne Harbour?

6 Calculate the time, in hours and minutes, taken to travel:

    a 143 km at 65 km/h   **b** 42 km at 30 km/h   **c** 408 km at 80 km/h

7 Mr Burchell, an oil-rig worker, leaves London at 8 am to drive to Aberdeen 780 km away.
He drives at an average speed of 65 km/h.
He stops for breaks which total 1 hour 25 minutes.
When will he reach Aberdeen?

8 The speed of sound is about 340 m/s.
John shouts to Lisa, who is 1156 metres away.
How long is it before Lisa hears John's voice?

9 The 12 20 train leaves Ashford and travels the 221 km to Leapbay at an average
speed of 85 km/h. When will it arrive at its destination?

10 Light travels at 186 000 miles per second.
How long does light from the sun take to reach us, 93 000 000 miles away?

6 Distance–time graphs

Graphs can help us understand situations.

Example 1

This is the graph of a tortoise moving about a lawn. Describe the main features.

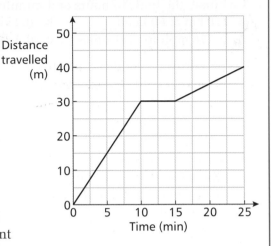

In the first 10 minutes the tortoise travelled 30 m
... a speed of 30 ÷ 10 = 3 m/min.

For the next 5 minutes it covered 0 m
... it didn't move.

In the last 10 minutes it travelled 10 m
... a speed of 10 ÷ 10 = 1 m/min.

Note that:

- the steeper the line, the faster the speed
- a horizontal line represents no movement
- from the start to the end of its journey the tortoise travelled 40 m in 25 min ... an average speed of 1·6 m/min.
- we don't know how far the tortoise is from its starting point. It could be travelling in circles.

Example 2

This graph represents a boy leaving home to go to the shops and back. Describe its main features.

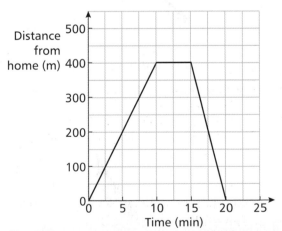

In the first 10 minutes he travelled 400 m ... a speed of 40 m/min.
For the next 5 minutes he stayed the same distance from home ... at the shops.

In the last 5 minutes he travelled 400 m back home ... a speed of 80 m/min.

Note that:

- in this case the line can go down as well as up
- from the start to the end of his journey the boy travelled 800 m in 20 min ... an average speed of 40 m/min.
- at all points we know how far the boy is from his home.

Exercise 6.1

1 Jenna sets out to walk to her friend's house.
She records how far she has walked after each minute and draws a graph of the journey.

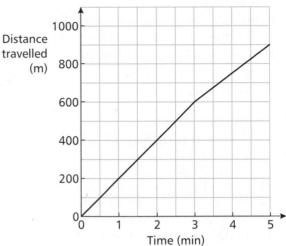

  a How far has she gone after
   i   2 minutes
   ii 3 minutes
   iii 5 minutes?
  b How far has she walked when she arrives at her friend's house?
  c How long did it take her to walk
   i   the first 200 metres
   ii the last 300 metres?
  d Estimate how far she had gone after $4\frac{1}{2}$ minutes.
  e i   Which part of the journey was faster?
   ii Is the graph steeper here?

2 This graph shows Ailidh's trip to the supermarket and back.

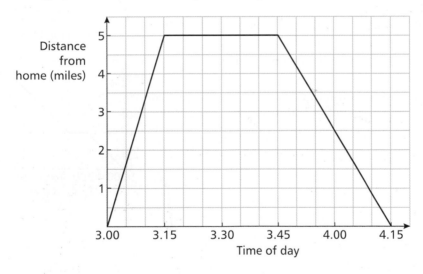

  a At what time did Ailidh leave for the supermarket?
  b How far is it from her home?
  c How long did it take her to get to the supermarket?
  d How long did she stay there?
  e When did she arrive home?
  f For how long was she away from home altogether?
  g How long was her whole journey?
  h At 4 o'clock how far was she from home?
  i Which was quicker, her journey to the supermarket or her journey back?

3 Anwar drives from one town to the next.
The graph shows the whole journey.

  a How far had he gone after
   i 10 minutes
   ii 15 minutes?
  b Estimate how far he had gone after
   6 minutes.
  c What distance did Anwar cover
   between the towns?
  d Estimate how long it took him to do
   i the first 5 km
   ii the last kilometre.
  e Which part of the journey was faster:
   the first or the last part?

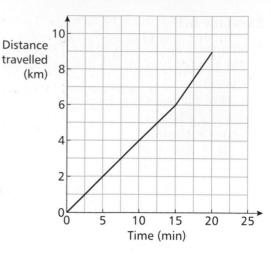

4 Owen set off from home to jog to the park.
On the way he met a friend and stopped for a chat.

  a How far had he run when he met his friend?
  b For how long did they chat?
  c How long did it take him to get 4 km from home?
  d How far from Owen's home is the park?
  e How long did it take him to get to the park?
  f Did he run faster before or after he stopped
   for a chat?

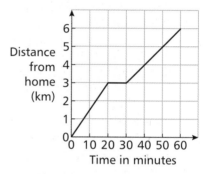

5 Michaela drove from home to the ferryport at the
start of her holiday.

  a How far from her home is the ferryport?
  b **i** How far had she gone before she stopped?
   ii Calculate her average speed for this part
    of her journey.
  c For how long did she stop?
  d How much further had she still to go?
  e Calculate her average speed for the last part of
   her journey.

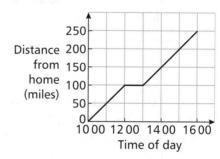

6 Steve drives a van for a company which
delivers vegetables to local stores.
He sets out from the depot to make his
deliveries and returns there when he
has finished.

  a When does Steve:
   i start out
   ii arrive back at the depot?
  b Steve made his first delivery at 10 00.
   How far had he gone?
  c **i** When did he make his second
    delivery?

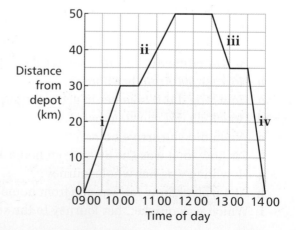

ii   How far from the depot is this store?

iii   For how long did he stop here?

d How far from the depot was he at 1 pm?

e Which part of the journey was the fastest?

f Calculate the average speed for each of the four parts of his journey.

Crossing paths

Example 3

Emma and Pat live 10 miles apart. The graph shows Emma going to Pat's house and Pat going to Emma's.

a What is important about the point where the lines cross?

b Who was travelling faster?

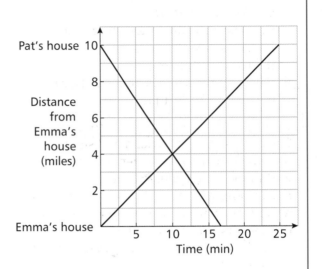

a The lines cross when the two girls are at the same distance from Emma's house at the same time.
Emma and Pat met 4 miles from Emma's house after 10 minutes travel.

b Pat's line is steeper, so she was the faster traveller.

Exercise 6.2

1 Bus A set out from Morseby to Hayton, a distance of 300 km.
Bus B goes from Hayton to Morseby.

a How long does Bus A take to make the journey?

b Calculate the average speed of Bus A.

c i   At what time did the two buses meet?

ii   How far from Morseby were they when they met?

d When did Bus B arrive in Morseby?

e How fast did Bus B do

i   the first part of the journey

ii   the second part of the journey?

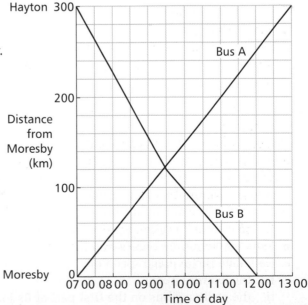

2 Two trains set out at the same time.
One train goes directly from Tynehead to Mossburn.
The other sets out from Mossburn, stops at Denham and goes on to Tynehead.

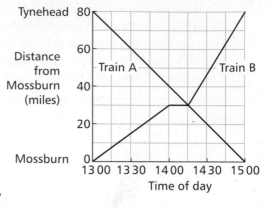

a How far is it from Mossburn to
  i Tynehead
  ii Denham?
b **i** At what time do the trains meet?
  ii Where are they when they meet?
c **i** When does Train B get to Denham?
  ii For how long does Train B stop there?
d Calculate the average speed of Train A.

3 Two buses go from Ancrum to Dundee.
The express bus goes directly, while the ordinary bus stops on the way.

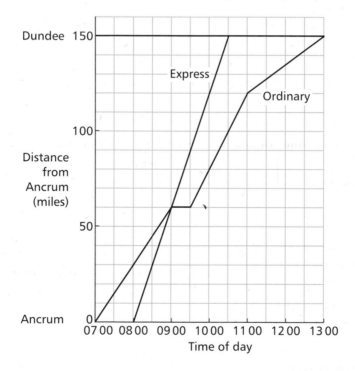

a When does:
  i the ordinary bus
  ii the express bus leave Ancrum?
b When do they arrive in Dundee?
c At what time does the express pass the ordinary bus?
d How far have they gone when they pass?
e Calculate the average speed of:
  i the express bus
  ii the ordinary bus on the first part of its journey.

7 Making sure – which formula?

Remember:

 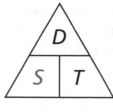 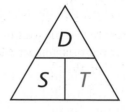

$$D = S \times T \qquad\qquad S = \frac{D}{T} \qquad\qquad T = \frac{D}{S}$$

Exercise 7.1

1 Calculate the missing quantity in each of these situations.
  (Remember: consistent units!)
  a Distance = 50 metres;   Time = 5 seconds;   Speed = ?
  b Distance = 100 km;   Speed = 25 km/h;   Time = ?
  c Speed = 43 mph;   Time = 4 hours;   Distance = ?
  d Distance = 90 miles;   Speed = 60 m/h;   Time = ?
  e Speed = 48 km/h;   Time = $3\frac{1}{2}$ hours; Distance = ?
  f Distance = 259 km;   Time = $3\frac{1}{2}$ hours; Speed = ?

2 **a** Speed, distance or time? Decide which quantity is missing and calculate it.

  b What is the distance round the island?
  c How long does it take to go right round the island?

3 On school sports day, Jen ran 60 metres in 10 seconds.
  Calculate her average speed in m/s.

4 Sheena skied for 25 km at an average speed of 10 km/h.
  a How long did it take her?
  b If she started skiing at 14 35, when did she finish?

5 Rae rode her horse over a cross-country course at an average speed of 15 km/h.
  The course was 22·5 km long.
  How long did it take her?

6 Zak jogged for two and a half hours at an average speed of 8 km/h.
  How far did he travel?

Exercise 7.2

1 Ben drove 189 km at an average speed of 54 km/h.
How long did the journey take him?

2 Lewis drove his quad-bike at an average speed of 5 km/h
for three-quarters of an hour. How far did he travel?

3 Lorna left home at 14 20 and arrived at the cinema at 15 35.
  a How long did the journey take her?
  b If the cinema was 55 km away, what was her average speed?

4 An Olympic runner ran 100 metres in 9·8 seconds.
Calculate his average speed in m/s, rounded to 1 decimal place.

5 The diagram shows how a cross-country race was set out.

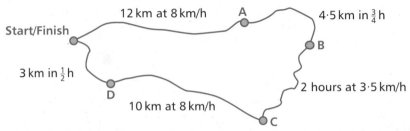

  a Use the information to calculate the quantity missing, either speed, distance or time.
  b i What was the total distance round the cross-country course?
    ii How long did it take to complete the course?

6 a Calculate the average speed in metres per second (m/s) for each of these runners.
    Round your answer to 1 decimal place.
    i Ben: 100 metres in 11·4 seconds
    ii Steve: 110 metres in 13·5 seconds
    iii Seb: 200 metres in 21·8 seconds
  b Which runner had the fastest average speed?
  c How much faster was he than the second fastest person?

7 A travel agent advertises direct flights between various cities.

	Flight number	Route	Flight time
a	BA001	London–Stockholm	4 hours
b	EZ002	Stockholm–Athens	5 hours
c	VA003	London–Athens	4·5 hours
d	BA004	Lisbon–Athens	6 hours

The distance between any two of the cities
can be found from the table.

Calculate the average speed for each flight.

London

1068	Stockholm		
1791	1820	Athens	
1183	1068	2127	Lisbon

Distances in miles

◀◀ RECAP

Speed – Distance – Time

Given any two of these quantities, you can work out the third one using the formulae:

$$D = S \times T \qquad S = \frac{D}{T} \qquad T = \frac{D}{S}$$

This triangle is a useful memory aid.
Cover up the item you want to reveal its formula.

For example, to find speed:

Distance–time graphs

We can chart *Distance moved* against *Time*, although this gives us limited information.
We can't tell how far we are from our starting point with this. The example shows the distance a child travels as he goes round a roundabout twice. The distance round the roundabout is 25 m. The child has travelled 50 m but is back where he started.

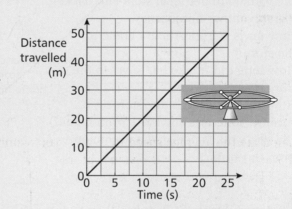

By plotting *Distance from Start* against *Time*, we get a graph from which we can deduce:

- the distance between any two points on a journey
- the distance to the end of the journey
- the average speed between any two points on the journey.

At a glance you can see whether we are moving towards or away from the start, or standing still.

The steeper the line, the faster the speed.

When two lines cross on such a graph, we know that two moving objects are at the same place at the same time.

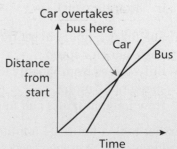

1 **a** Calculate the distance travelled in 3 hours at an average speed of 35 km/h.
   b How long would it take to travel 250 miles at 50 mph?
   c How fast are you travelling if you go 150 km in 2 hours?

2 Calculate the missing quantity in each situation.
   a Distance 150 km; Time 4 hours; Speed?
   b Distance 4500 km; Speed 600 km/h; Time?
   c Speed 8 mph; Time 4 hours; Distance?
   d Distance 440 metres; Time 50 seconds; Speed?

3 **a** Euan leaves home at 7 am and drives 504 miles to London at an average speed of
       48 mph. When does he arrive in London?
   b Emily runs for an hour and a quarter at an average speed of 8 km/h.
       How far does she run?

4 Nishat travels on an overnight bus to Portsmouth. The bus leaves at 22 30 and arrives
   in Portsmouth at 06 50 the next morning. How long is the journey?

5 Abbie walked to her local store and back.
   The graph shows her journey.
   a How far is it from Abbie's home to
       the store?
   b How long did it take her to get to the
       store?
   c How long was she in the store?
   d For how long was she away from home?
   e Did she walk faster on the way to or
       from the store?

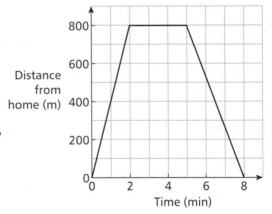

6 Bus A sets out from St Bees to Albany.
   At the same time Bus B sets out from
   Albany to St Bees.
   a How far is it from St Bees to Albany?
   b Calculate the average speed of Bus A.
   c **i**   At what time did the two buses meet?
       ii   How far from St Bees were they?
   d Calculate the average speed of Bus B
       i   before they met
       ii   after they met.

7 **a** Sue takes 2 hours to get from Rowanbank to Hillrise.
       Calculate her speed.
   b Billy drives from Woodly to Rowanbank at an average
       speed of 52 mph.
       How long, in hours and minutes, did it take?

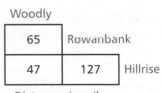

Distances in miles

8 Esther took 4 hours 24 minutes to drive 250 km.
   Calculate her average speed, to the nearest km/h.

REVISE

10 Angles and circles

Engineers use information about angles in many ways.
For example, they know that the amount by which a road is sloped at a corner is important. The bigger the angle, the faster a car can go round the corner.

1 REVIEW

Reminders

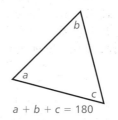

$a + b + c = 180$

◀◀ **Exercise 1.1**

1 Calculate the size of each missing angle.

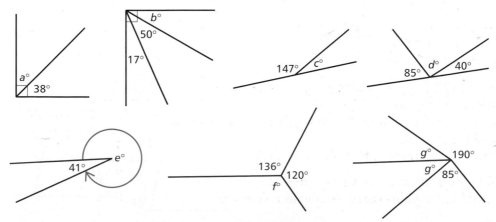

2 Calculate the size of each lettered angle in the triangles.

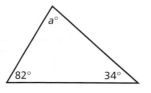

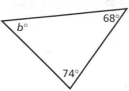

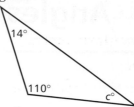

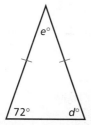

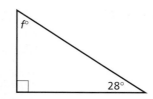

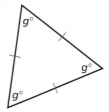

3 The spokes in the big wheel are equally spaced. They are the radii (OA, OB, OC, etc.) of the circle, centre O.

a How many radii are there?

b What size is:

  i ∠AOC

  ii ∠BOC

  iii ∠BOD?

c The radius of the big wheel is 8 metres long. How long is its diameter?

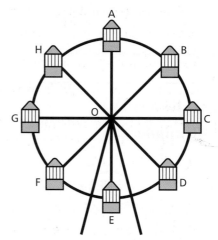

4 Use Pythagoras' theorem to calculate a in each right-angled triangle.

a

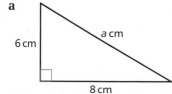

b

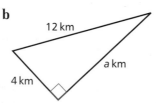

5 The diagram shows how any set of congruent quadrilaterals will tile.

By considering the sum of the angles round a point, find the sum of the angles in a quadrilateral, $a + b + c + d$.

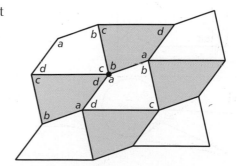

2 Related angles

Complementary angles

$a° + b° = 90°$

We call a and b **complementary** angles.

a is the **complement** of b ... $a = 90 - b$
b is the complement of a ... $b = 90 - a$

For example, 60° is the complement of 30°.

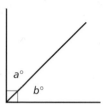

Supplementary angles

$a° + b° = 180°$

We call a and b **supplementary** angles.
a is the **supplement** of b ... $a = 180 - b$
b is the supplement of a ... $b = 180 - a$

For example, 160° is the supplement of 20°.

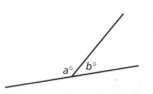

Vertically opposite angles

AB and CD are straight lines which cross at the vertex E.

$\angle AEC + \angle CEB = 180°$ (supplementary angles)
$\angle DEB + \angle CEB = 180°$ (supplementary angles)

$\Rightarrow \angle AEC = \angle DEB$

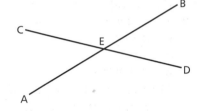

> When two straight lines cross, angles opposite each other are equal.
> We say they are **vertically opposite** angles.

$\angle AEC$ is vertically opposite $\angle DEB$.
$\angle CEB$ is vertically opposite $\angle AED$.

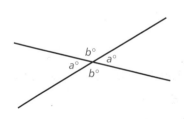

Exercise 2.1

1 In each diagram, the pairs of angles, a and b, are related.
   i State the relationship.　　　　**ii** Work out the value of b when $a° = 40°$.

a　　　　　　**b**　　　　　　**c**

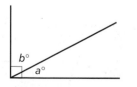　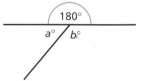　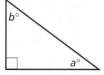

d　　　　　　**e**

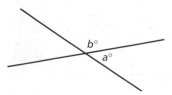　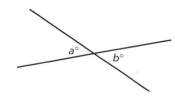

2 Calculate the value of x in each diagram.

a

153°
$x°$

b

87°
$x°$

c

$x°$
122°

3 The diagram represents the side view of a book holder.

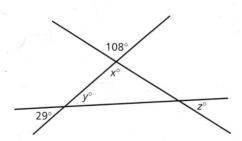

110°
$a°$
125° $b°$
$c°$ $d°$

Calculate, giving reasons, the value of:
a a **b** b
c c **d** d.

4 This diagram shows three straight lines crossing to form a triangle.

108°
$x°$
$y°$
29°
$z°$

Calculate, with reasons, the value of:
a x **b** y **c** z.

5 Two cross-poles for a wigwam form an isosceles triangle with the ground.
They cross at an angle of 26°.
What angle does each make with the ground?

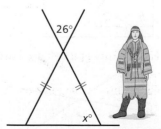

26°

$x°$

Angles and quadrilaterals

Reminder ● Different quadrilaterals have different symmetries.

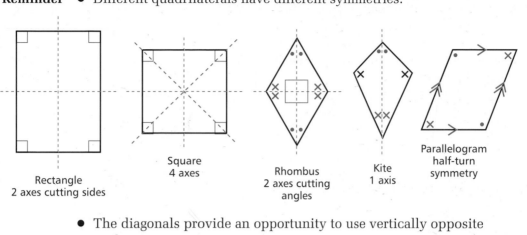

Rectangle
2 axes cutting sides

Square
4 axes

Rhombus
2 axes cutting
angles

Kite
1 axis

Parallelogram
half-turn
symmetry

● The diagonals provide an opportunity to use vertically opposite angles.
● There are complementary and supplementary angles to find.
● The four angles of a quadrilateral add up to 360°.

Exercise 2.2

1 Calculate the size of each labelled angle.

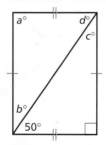
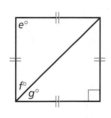

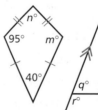
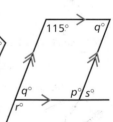

2 Sketch each shape and fill in the sizes of as many angles as you can.

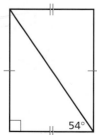
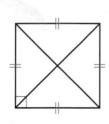

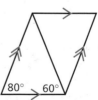

3 a Name four isosceles triangles in the rectangle shown.
b Calculate the size of each angle.

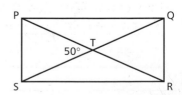

4 In parallelogram ABCD, ∠DAB = 65°.

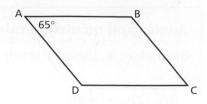

a By thinking of the half-turn symmetry, name another angle which is also 65°.

b i Name another pair of angles that are equal.

   ii What size is each?
   (Remember all four angles add up to 360°.)

c Find the size of all the angles in each parallelogram.

i    **ii** 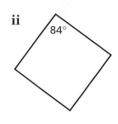   **iii**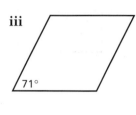

---

3 Angles and parallel lines

Corresponding angles

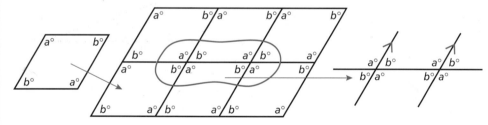

Congruent parallelograms tile. A useful pattern of angles can be found in the tiling.

When a pair of parallel lines is crossed by a third line (a **transversal**) the pattern of angles at each intersection is identical.

In particular, angles in the 'same' position are equal; we call these **corresponding** angles.
There are four pairs of corresponding angles to spot in the diagram above.

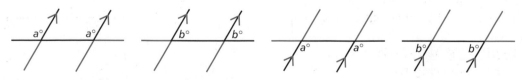

> Corresponding angles are equal.

Exercise 3.1

1 Name all the pairs of corresponding angles in each diagram.

a

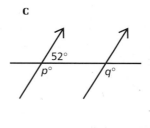

1 pair

b

2 pairs

c

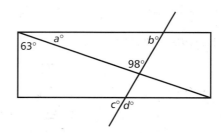

4 pairs

2 Find the size of each lettered angle in the diagrams.

a

63°

$y°$

b

135°
45°

$a°$

c

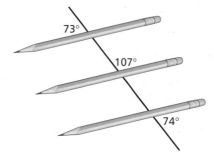

52°

$p°$ $q°$

3 A line cuts a rectangle, as shown.
Calculate the size of each marked angle.

63° $a°$ $b°$

98°

$c° d°$

4 Which two pencils are parallel?
Give a reason.

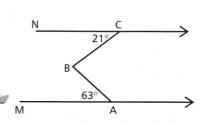

73°

107°

74°

5 A dingy sails from A to B to C.
The banks of the river MA and NC are
parallel.
$\angle MAB = 63°$ and $\angle NCB = 21°$.
a Sketch the diagram.
b i Draw a line through B parallel to MA.
  ii Extend BC upwards.
  iii Extend BA downwards.
c By considering corresponding angles calculate
the size of $\angle CBA$.

N   C

21°

B

63°

M   A

Alternate angles

When a pair of parallel lines is crossed by a transversal the pattern of angles at each intersection is identical.

Another useful pattern produces what are called **alternate** angles.

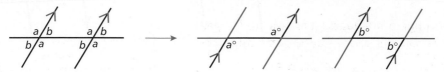

Note that the angle pairs form a zig-zag arrangement.

Alternate angles are equal.

Exercise 3.2

1 Name all the pairs of alternate angles in each diagram.

a

A ← B

1 pair

b

P

Q S
U

2 pairs

R

T

c

J
K
F G H I

L
M
3 pairs N

2 Find the size of each lettered angle in the diagrams.

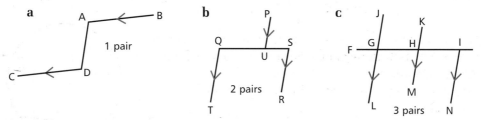

69°

a°

55°

b°

c° 143°

d°

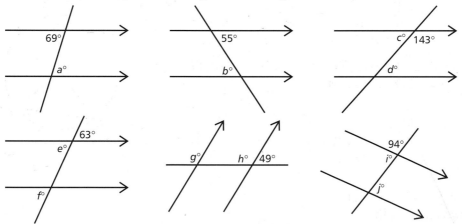

63°
e°

f°

g° h° 49°

94°
i°
j°

3 Find x in each case.

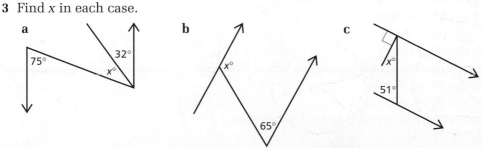

a

75°

32°
x°

b

x°

65°

c

x°

51°

4 Use alternate angles to find the size of ∠ABC.
(Hint: add an extra parallel through B.)

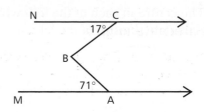

5 Find the size of the lettered angles in this gate
and give reasons. Lines that look parallel are
parallel.

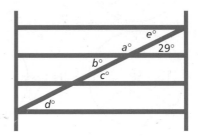

4 Angles in circles

A line that joins two points on the circumference of a circle
without passing through its centre is called a **chord** of the
circle. AB is a chord.
If radii are drawn to the ends of a chord an isosceles
triangle is formed.

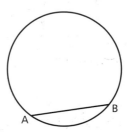

Example   Name the isosceles triangle in the circle
with centre O and name the equal angles.

△AOB is isosceles since AO = OB (radii of circle)
⇒ ∠OAB = ∠OBA

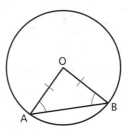

Exercise 4.1

1 In each circle, O is the centre. Name:
  i   the two equal radii
  ii the isosceles triangle
  iii the two equal angles.

a 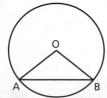   **b**

2 The centre in each of the following circles has been labelled O.
   Calculate the size of the labelled angles.

a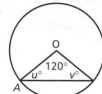

b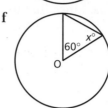

c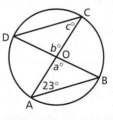

d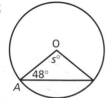

e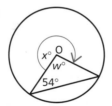

f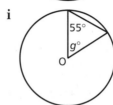

g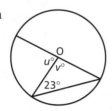

h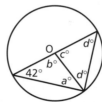

i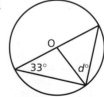

3 Calculate the marked angle in each case.
   The centre of each circle has been marked as O.

a

b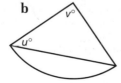

c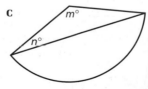

d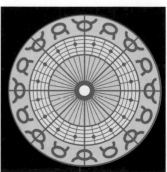

4 AC and BD are diameters. ∠CAB = 23°.
   a Calculate the size of   **i** *a*   **ii** *b*   **iii** *c*.
   b By looking at ∠BAC and ∠ACD comment on the
      chords AB and DC.

5 The circular stained glass window has eight sectors.
   Parts of the window are shown below.
   Calculate the size of the labelled angles.

a
x°
y°

One sector
of window

b
v°
u°

Two sectors
of window

c
m°
n°

Three sectors
of window

Exercise 4.2

1 In each diagram below, AB is a diameter of the circle, centre O.
For each diagram calculate the value of   **i** a **ii** c **iii** d **iv** b **v** $a + b$.

a 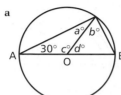   **b** 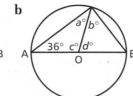   **c** 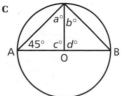   **d**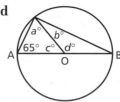

2 a Draw a circle with diameter AB about 8 cm long.
   b Mark any point P on the circumference.
   c Join PA and PB.
   d Measure ∠APB.
   e Pick a different point on the circumference and repeat steps **c** and **d**.
   f Try different sizes of circles.
   g What seems to be true about the size of ∠APB every time?

3 Examine the diagram. AB is a diameter. O is the centre of the circle.
   a Explain why the two angles marked a are equal.
   b Explain why the angle marked c is equal to $180 - 2a$.
   c Explain why the angle marked d is equal to $2a$.
   d Explain why   **i** $2b + d = 180$ **ii** $2b + 2a = 180$ **iii** $b + a = 90$

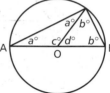

5 The angle in a semicircle

Exercise 4.2 leads us to the following conclusion.

> The angle made by drawing two chords from a point on the circumference to the ends of a diameter is 90°.

We refer to such an angle as the **angle in a semicircle**.

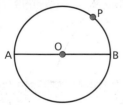   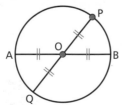   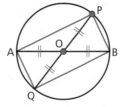 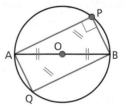

Draw a circle, centre O and diameter AB. Pick any point, P, on the circle (not A or B).

You can always find a diameter from P through O to Q.

The two diameters form the diagonals of a quadrilateral APBQ. Now APBQ must be a rectangle since its diagonals are equal and bisect each other.

So ∠APB is a right angle, being the angle of a rectangle.

> The angle in a semicircle is a right angle.

Exercise 5.1

1 In each diagram, AB is a diameter of a circle, centre O, and P lies on the circle. Calculate the size of each lettered angle.

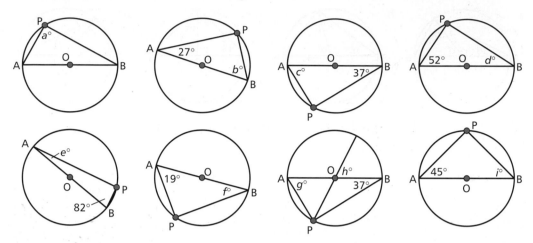

2 Each diagram shows a diameter and points on the circumference. Calculate the size of each lettered angle.

a **b** **c** **d**

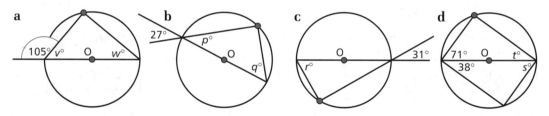

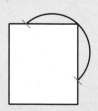

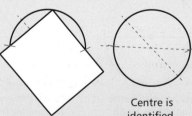

Challenge

Can you explain how the following steps will help you find the centre of a circle?

Take a circle.

Place a rectangle of paper on top so one corner is on the circumference. Mark where the circle disappears under the paper.

Join the marks.

Turn the rectangle through, say, 40° and repeat.

Centre is identified.

Exercise 5.2

1 Each diagram shows a diameter and a point on the circumference.
Calculate the size of each lettered angle.

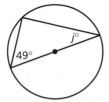 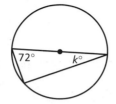 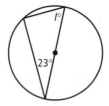 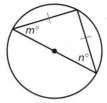

2 Each diagram shows a circle, centre O, a diameter and points on the circumference.
Name each right angle you can find.

a 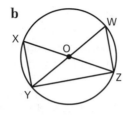   **b** 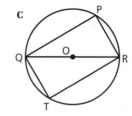   **c** 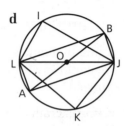   **d**

Diameters AB
and CD

Diameters XZ
and WY

Diameter QR

Diameters AB
and LJ

3 i Sketch each diagram. Each circle has a centre marked O and diameter AC.
B and D are points on the circumference of the circle.

ii Fill in as many angle sizes as you can.

iii Name the quadrilateral inside the circle.

a 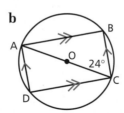   **b** 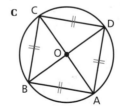   **c**

4 a Three copies of a regular hexagon tile.
What is the size of each angle in a regular hexagon?

b The diagram shows the regular hexagon ABCDEF
with a circle passing through its vertices.
AD is a diameter of the circle and a diagonal of
the hexagon.
Sketch the diagram and mark on it the sizes of as
many angles as you can.

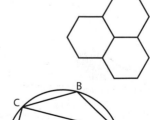

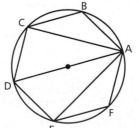

5 The Aberdon Voluntary Organisation has a new logo.
The logo is **symmetrical**.
The letter A stands on a diameter of the circle
representing the letter O.
Sketch the logo and fill in all the missing angles.

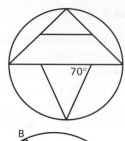
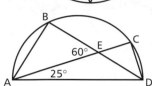

6 The entrance to a tunnel is **semicircular**.
It has become dangerous so struts have been put
in to support it.
Name each angle and give its size.

6 Tangents to a circle

A line that cuts a circle at only one point is called a **tangent** to the circle.
We could say it touches the circle at one point. (In Latin the word for 'I touch' is 'tango'.)

A line is considered to go on forever in both directions. So AB is not a tangent.
It cuts the circle twice even though we have only drawn one of the cuts.

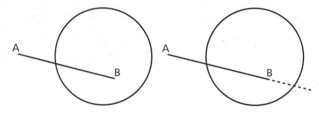

DC touches the circle at T. We say DC is a **tangent to the circle at T.**

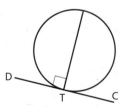

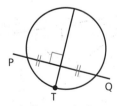

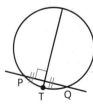

A diameter is drawn at T. A chord cuts the circle at P and Q and the diameter at right angles. Both P and Q will be the same distance from the diameter.

Move the chord towards T, keeping the right angle. P and Q get closer together but stay the same distance from the diameter.

P and Q are now closer still...

... until they become one with T. At this point we have a tangent. Note that it is at right angles to the diameter at T.

> This illustrates a useful fact: A tangent is perpendicular to the radius drawn to the point of contact

Exercise 6.1

1 VW is a tangent to the circle, centre O, at Y.
   a Name three radii.
   b How do you know that OY is shorter than OV?
   c How do you know that OY is the shortest distance
      from the centre of the circle to the tangent?
   d Name two right angles in the diagram.

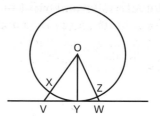

2 Each diagram shows a tangent and its point of contact with a circle, centre O.
   For each name
   i   the tangent
   ii   the point of contact
   iii a radius
   iv   two right angles.

   a 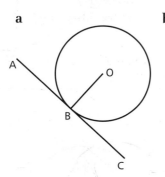   b 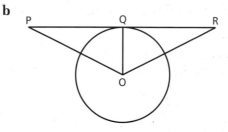   c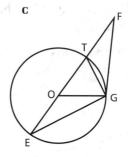

3 Each diagram contains a tangent and a radius drawn to the point of contact.
   Calculate the size of each marked angle.

   a 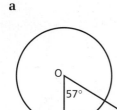   b 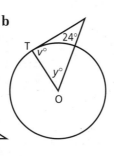   c 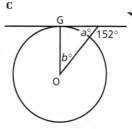   d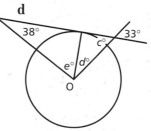

   e 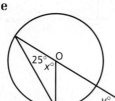   f 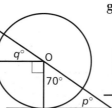   g 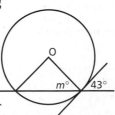   h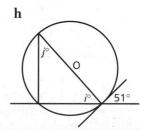

4 Each diagram shows a circle,
centre O, a tangent and a radius
drawn to the point of contact.

Find the value of each letter in
alphabetical order.

a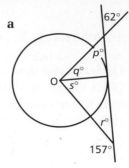

b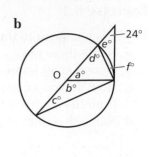

5 The diagram shows a circle, centre O, a diameter BE
and the tangent drawn at B.
D lies on the circumference of the circle.
a Name three right angles in the diagram.
b ∠DEO = 62° and ∠OEC = 37°.
Sketch the diagram and fill in the sizes of all the
angles.

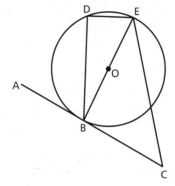

7 Pythagoras in the circle

Example 1   XZ is the diameter of a circle. XY is a chord
of length 7 cm.
ZY is a chord of length 4 cm.
What is the diameter of the circle?

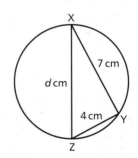

∠XYZ = 90° (angle in a semicircle)
By Pythagoras' theorem
$$d^2 = 7^2 + 4^2$$
$$\Rightarrow d^2 = 49 + 16 = 65$$
$$\Rightarrow d = \sqrt{65} = 8\cdot1 \text{ (to 1 d.p.)}$$
$$\Rightarrow \text{diameter} = 8\cdot1 \text{ cm}$$

Example 2   PQ is a tangent to the circle, centre O.
OP is a radius drawn to the point of contact.
The radius is 3 cm long.
Q is 7 cm from the centre of the circle.
How long is the tangent from P to Q?

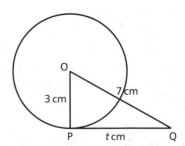

∠OPQ = 90° (angle between a tangent
and radius)
By Pythagoras' theorem
$$7^2 = t^2 + 3^2$$
$$\Rightarrow t^2 = 49 - 9 = 40$$
$$\Rightarrow t = \sqrt{40} = 6\cdot3 \text{ (to 1 d.p.)}$$
$$\Rightarrow \text{tangent PQ} = 6\cdot3 \text{ cm}$$

Exercise 7.1

1 In each diagram O is the centre of the circle, BC is a diameter and A is a point on the circumference. Calculate the labelled lengths.
All measurements are in centimetres.

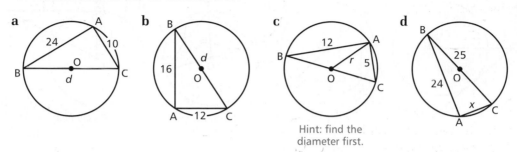

Hint: find the diameter first.

2 In each diagram O is the centre of the circle, SR is a tangent to the circle with S the point of contact. Calculate the labelled lengths.
All measurements are in centimetres.

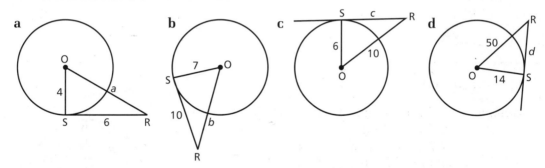

3 A circle with centre O has a diameter AB. A point C lies on the circumference such that the chord AC is 4·5 cm long and the chord BC is 5 cm long.
   a Make a sketch of the situation.
   b Find the diameter of the circle (to 1 d.p.).
   c State the radius of the circle (to 1 d.p.).

4 The diagram shows a circle with centre O and a tangent MN. N is the point of contact. OM cuts the circle at K. Measurements are in centimetres.
   a Calculate the length of OM.
   b What is the length KM?

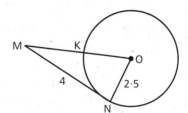

5 An arch under a railway bridge is semicircular.
   Its diameter is BC. A point A on the arch is studied.
   AB = 8·4 m, AC = 6·3 m.
   a What is the diameter of the arch?
   b B is 2 m from the ground.
      How high is the top of the arch above the ground?

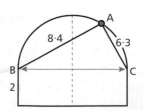

Exercise 7.2

1 In the diagrams AB is a diameter, T is a point on the circumference and ST is a tangent. All measurements are in centimetres. Calculate the labelled lengths to 1 d.p.

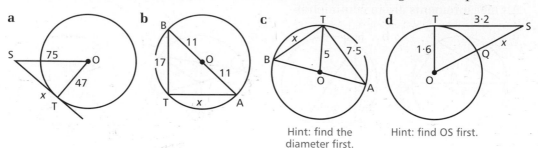

Hint: find the diameter first.

Hint: find OS first.

2 In the diagrams O is the centre of the circle, AB is a diameter, AP is a tangent and T is a point on the circumference. All measurements are in centimetres. Calculate the length of the diameter in each case to 1 d.p.

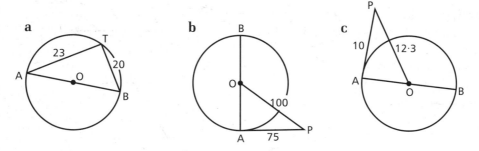

3 In each diagram O is the centre, PQ is a diameter and PS is a tangent to the circle.
R is a point on the circumference of the circle. All measurements are in metres. For each diagram calculate the length of
i x **ii** y.

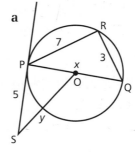

4 The diagram shows the rear view of a tanker.
The cross-section of the tank is circular.
The cross-section of the platform it sits on is rectangular.
GE is a tangent to the circle at G.
HE = 4·9 m. GE = 2·9 m.
a Calculate the height of the tank GH.
b Calculate how far the point E is from the centre of the circle.
c OE cuts the circle at F. What is the length of FE?

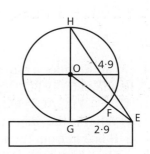

◄◄ **RECAP**

Related angles
Complementary angles add up to 90°.
If $a + b = 90$ then a is the **complement** of b
and b is the complement of a.

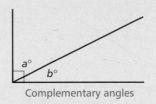

Complementary angles

Supplementary angles add up to 180°.
If $a + b = 180$ then a is the **supplement** of b
and b is the supplement of a.

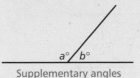

Supplementary angles

When two straight lines intersect, **vertically opposite**
angles are equal.

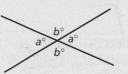

Vertically opposite angles

When parallel lines are cut by a **transversal** the
angle pattern at each intersection is identical.
In particular
● **corresponding** angles are equal
● **alternate** angles are equal.

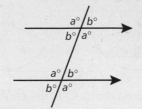

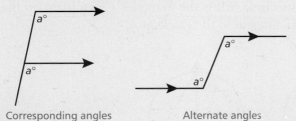

Corresponding angles   Alternate angles

Angles in circles
When radii are drawn to the end of a chord, an
isosceles triangle is formed.

The angle in a semicircle is a right angle.

The angle between a tangent and the radius
drawn to the point of contact is a right angle.

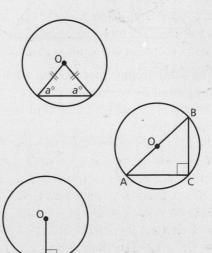

REVISE

1 Find the value of the letter in each diagram. Give a reason for your answer.

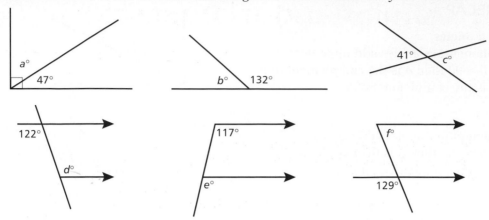

2 Find the size of each lettered angle. O is the centre of the circle in each case.

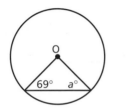 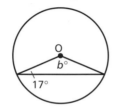 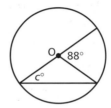

3 In these diagrams O is the centre of the circle, AB is the diameter, C is a point on the circumference of the circle and AT is a tangent to the circle at A.
Calculate the size of each marked angle.

a   **b**   **c**

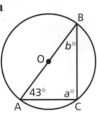 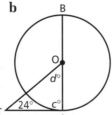 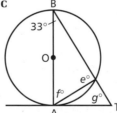

4 The semicircular roof of a pig shelter is supported by wooden struts.
Calculate the width (at ground level) of the shelter.

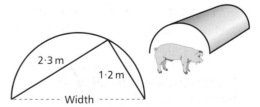

11 Angles and triangles

The Bounty sails 87 km due west from the harbour at H to a port at P, then travels due north to the fishing village at V. ∠VHP is 39°.

We could find the distance from the port to the village by making a scale drawing of triangle HPV.

In this chapter we shall discover another way to find distances and angles in right-angled triangles.

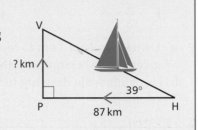

1 REVIEW

◀◀ **Exercise 1.1**

1 a Copy the compass rose and name the four missing directions.
 b What direction is opposite:
   i north-west
   ii south-west?
 c What is the angle between:
   i west and south
   ii east and north-east
   iii north-west and south-west
   iv west and south-east?

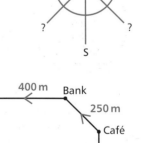

2 Mel left his house and visited several places before arriving back home.
He noted the distances to the nearest 10 m and directions using the points of the compass.
Describe his journey by giving both the direction and the distance travelled for each part.

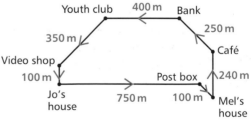

3 Calculate the size of the third angle in each triangle.

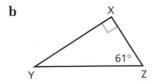

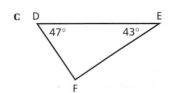

4 Name the hypotenuse of each triangle in question **3**.

5 Use a calculator to find *x* correct to 1 decimal place.

   a $x = \dfrac{7}{13}$ **b** $x = \dfrac{2\cdot3}{4\cdot5}$ **c** $x = \dfrac{6\cdot4}{5\cdot1}$ **d** $x = 0\cdot45 \times 16$

6 a Solve $\dfrac{x}{7} = 5$ by multiplying each side by 7.

   b Use this method to solve:

     i $\dfrac{x}{3} = 8$ **ii** $\dfrac{x}{10} = 2\cdot6$ **iii** $\dfrac{x}{9} = 0\cdot5.$

7 a Using a scale of 1 cm to represent 10 km, make a scale drawing of triangle HPV given at the beginning of the chapter.

   b Use your scale drawing to find the length of PV correct to the nearest kilometre.

2 Three-figure bearings

The captain of the Mimch Lifeboat would like to describe the direction to go in to reach the *Betty B*.

The *Betty B*, however, is not sitting conveniently in one of the named compass directions.

The captain imagines himself facing north, then **turning clockwise** until he faces the desired direction.

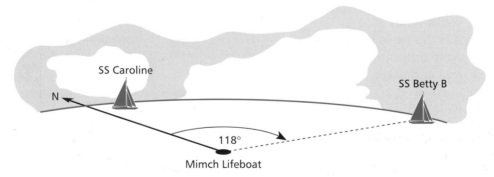

In this case, he turns through 118° before facing the *Betty B*.
He gives instructions for the lifeboat to steer **on a bearing of 118°**.
We say that the *Betty B* is on a bearing of 118° from the lifeboat.
Such bearings are called **3-figure bearings**.
If the desired angle has less than 3 digits, leading zeros are added.

Examples   The direction NE is the 3-figure bearing 045°.
               The *SS Caroline*, which is 7° clockwise round from north, has a bearing of 007°.
               North is the 3-figure bearing 000°.

Exercise 2.1

1 Write down the 3-figure bearing matching each of these compass directions.
   Reminder: the angle is measured **clockwise from the north**.

   a east   **b** south   **c** west   **d** south-west   **e** north-west

2 Estimate the 3-figure bearing of:
   a the castle from the bridge
   b the castle from the cabin
   c the cabin from the bridge
   d the bridge from the tree
   e the bridge from the castle
   f the tree from the cabin.

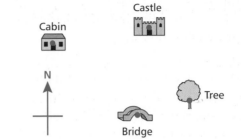

3 The diagram shows the positions
   of five ships A, B, C, D and E,
   and a lighthouse at P.
   a Estimate the bearing of
   each ship from P.
   b Use a protractor to measure
   the bearing of each ship
   from P.

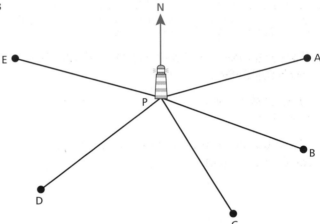

4 The map shows the positions
   of four towns in Ayrshire.
   Estimate, then measure the
   bearing of:
   a Stewarton from Kilwinning
   b Troon from Stewarton
   c Kilwinning from Kilmarnock
   d Kilwinning from Troon.

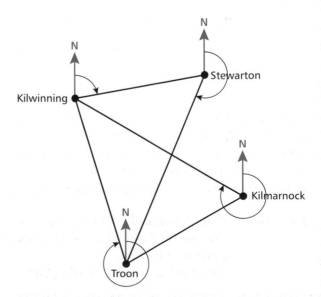

5 Follow these instructions to draw a line that represents a bearing of 120° from a point P.

   a Mark a point to represent P.

   b Draw a north line from P.

   c Draw a line at an angle of 120° to the north line (measured clockwise).

   d All points on this line are on a bearing of 120° from point P.

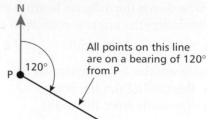

6 On separate diagrams draw lines to represent bearings of:

   a 050°   **b** 130°   **c** 200° (Hint: 200° = 180° + 20°)

   d 250°   **e** 280° (Hint: 280° = 360° − 80°)   **f** 320°

7 A boat at B is 6 kilometres from a boat at A.
The bearing of B from A is 085°.
Using a scale of 1 cm to 1 km, make a scale drawing showing the positions of boats A and B.

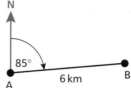

8 A cabin, C, is 8 kilometres from a car park, P.
The bearing of the cabin from the car park is 135°.
Make a scale drawing showing the relative positions of the cabin and the car park.

9 A search party, X, is looking for an injured climber.

   a Mark a point X near the centre of a page of your jotter.
      X represents the search party.

   b Show the positions of the following using a scale of 1 cm to 1 km:

      i   injured climber, C, 7 km from X on a bearing of 165°

      ii campsite, S, 9 km from X on a bearing of 310°

      iii bridge, B, 4·8 km from X on a bearing of 245°

      iv ambulance, A, 6·3 km from X on a bearing of 100°

      v helicopter, H, 5·7 km from X on a bearing of 015°.

3 Using bearings

Example

A boat sails 4·5 kilometres from P on a bearing of 130° to Q.
It then changes course and sails 6·5 kilometres on a bearing of 042° until it reaches R.

   a Using a scale of 1 cm to 1 km, make a scale drawing showing the relative positions of P, Q and R.

   b Find:

      i the bearing of R from P

      ii the distance from P to R.

A sketch will help you plan your steps.

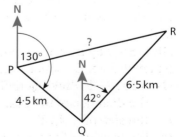

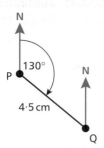
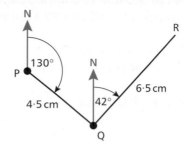
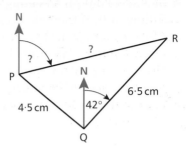

Step 1
Make a point P and draw its north line. Draw an angle of 130° clockwise from P. The length of its arm PQ is 4·5 cm.

Step 2
Draw the north line at Q. Draw an angle of 42° clockwise from Q. The length of its arm QR is 6·5 cm.

Step 3
Join PR.
Measure ∠NPR. It is 76°.
Measure PR. It is 8·0 cm.

i   The bearing of R from P is 076°.
ii The distance PR is 8·0 km.

Try this example for yourself and see if you agree with the answers given.

Exercise 3.1

1 A helicopter flies 50 kilometres from A to B on a bearing of 075°.
It then flies 60 kilometres from B to C on a bearing of 148°.
a Using a scale of 1 cm to represent 10 km, make a scale drawing to show the positions of A, B and C. (Start by marking a point A and its north line.)
b Find the bearing and distance of C from A.

2 A farmhouse (F) is 6 kilometres from a cottage (C) and is on a bearing of 310° from the cottage. From the farmhouse the post office (P) is 8 kilometres on a bearing of 220°.
a *Calculate* the size of:
   i   acute ∠N₁CF
   ii obtuse ∠N₂FP.
b Using a scale of 1 cm to represent 1 km, make a scale drawing to show the positions of C, F and P.
   Hint: Start by marking a point C and drawing its north line. Draw acute ∠N₁CF.
c Use your scale drawing to find:
   i   the distance of the post office from the cottage
   ii   the size of ∠N₁CP
   iii the bearing of the post office from the cottage.

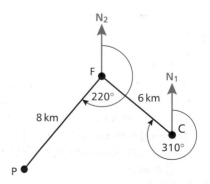

3 A yacht sets out on a bearing of 110° from a harbour at H and sails for 65 kilometres to a buoy at B. It then changes course and sails for 72 kilometres on a bearing of 036° until it hits a rock at R.
   a Make a rough sketch. Include the north lines.
   b Using a scale of 1 cm to represent 10 kilometres, make a scale drawing.
   c Use your scale drawing to find:
      i the distance of the rock from the harbour
      ii the bearing of the rock from the harbour.

4 Mungo the explorer sets out from camp (C) on a bearing of 068° and walks for 16 kilometres until he meets a bear at B. He then walks for 14 kilometres on a bearing of 162° when he realises he is lost (L).
   a Make a sketch of Mungo's journey. Include the north lines.
   b Using a scale of 1 cm to represent 2 km, make a scale drawing of Mungo's journey.
   c Help Mungo by finding how far he is from camp and the bearing he needs to take to arrive back at camp.

4 The bearing of a point from two positions

Example
Two ships positioned at A and B, as shown in the map, pick up a distress signal from a boat at C.
The bearing of the boat from A is 095° and from B is 225°.
Find the position of the boat at C on the map.

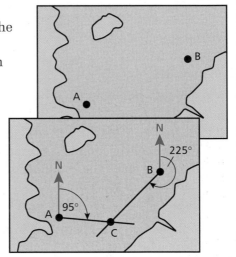

Draw north lines as shown.
Draw a line from A on a bearing of 095°.
Draw a line from B on a bearing of 225°.
C is the point at which these two lines cross.

Exercise 4.1

1 The map shows the positions of two harbours, P and Q.

a Trace the positions of harbours P and Q and their north lines.
b A ship is on a bearing of 136° from the harbour at P.
Its bearing from the harbour at Q is 260°.
Use your tracing to find the position of the ship.
c From your tracing decide if the ship is nearer P or Q.

2 A mountain rescue team at A is 7·5 km due east
of a rescue team at B.
An injured climber is on a bearing of 038° from
B and on a bearing of 305° from A.
a Using 1 cm to represent 1 km, make a scale
drawing to show the positions of the climber
and the two rescue teams.
b How far is the climber from
   i rescue team A   **ii** rescue team B?

3 *The Bounty* (B) is 800 metres due north of *The Star* (S).
There are rocks (R) on a bearing of 085° from *The Bounty*
and on a bearing of 035° from *The Star.*
a Using 1 cm to represent 100 m, make a scale drawing
to show the positions of the boats and the rocks.
b Find the distance of the rocks from:
   i *The Bounty*   **ii** *The Star.*

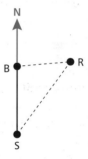

4 The town of Crosbie is 18 kilometres west of the town of Darley.
Barr is a village on a bearing of 155° from Crosbie and on a bearing of 215° from
Darley.
a Make a sketch showing the relative positions of Crosbie, Darley and Barr.
b Using 1 cm to represent 2 km, make a suitable scale drawing.
c From your scale drawing find the distance of:
   i Barr from Crosbie   **ii** Barr from Darley.

5 A cave (C) is 8 kilometres south-east of a tree (T).
From the cave the bearing of a waterfall (W) is 024°.
From the tree the waterfall is on a bearing of 086°.
a Using a scale of 1 cm to 1 km, make a drawing to show the positions of the
waterfall, the cave and the tree.
b How far is the waterfall from   **i** the tree   **ii** the cave?

6 A straight wall XY is 500 metres long.
It runs from north-west to south-east with Y north-west
of X.
A cottage (C) bears 280° from X and bears 160° from Y.
a Make a sketch showing the positions of the wall and
the cottage.
b Choose a suitable scale and make a scale drawing.
c Use the scale drawing to find the distance of the cottage
from the wall.

Challenge

The bearing of B from A is 070°.
How can we find the bearing of A from B?
Extend the north line at B down towards the south.
A property of parallel lines tells us the acute angle at B is 70°.
The bearing of A from B is therefore 180° + 70° = 250°.

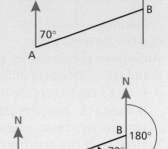

a Find the bearing of A from B if the bearing of B from A is:

   i   35°   **ii** 63°.

b Find the bearing of A from B if the bearing of B from A is:

   i   125°   **ii** 148°

   iii 210°   **iv** 245°

   v 280°   **vi** 300°.

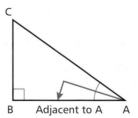

c Without drawing a diagram, try to write down the bearing of A from B if the bearing of B from A is:

   i   52°   **ii** 100°

   iii 190°   **iv** 320°.

5 Trigonometry

Trigonometry is the name given to the study of measurement in triangles.

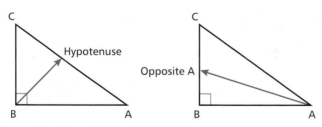

In the right-angled triangle ABC, AC is opposite the right angle. It is called the **hypotenuse**.
CB is the side **opposite** ∠A. AB is the side next to, or **adjacent** to, ∠A.
We can also say AB is **opposite** ∠C and CB is **adjacent to** ∠C.

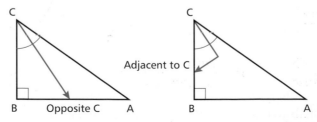

Exercise 5.1

1 a **b** 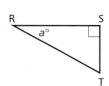 **c** 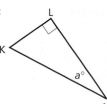 **d**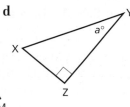

In each right-angled triangle name:
i the hypotenuse
ii the side opposite the marked angle
iii the side adjacent to the marked angle.

2 a 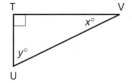 **b** 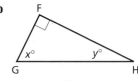 **c**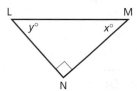

In each right-angled triangle name:
i the hypotenuse
ii the side opposite the angle marked x
iii the side adjacent to the angle marked x
iv the side opposite the angle marked y
v the side adjacent to the angle marked y.

3 In triangle ABC, the ratio $\dfrac{\text{opposite A}}{\text{hypotenuse}} = \dfrac{5}{13} = 0 \cdot 385$ (to 3 d.p.)

In a similar way, calculate the ratio:

a $\dfrac{\text{adjacent to A}}{\text{hypotenuse}}$

b $\dfrac{\text{opposite A}}{\text{adjacent to A}}$

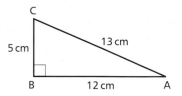

4 In triangle PQR calculate (to 3 d.p.) the ratio:

a i $\dfrac{\text{opposite P}}{\text{hypotenuse}}$ **ii** $\dfrac{\text{adjacent to P}}{\text{hypotenuse}}$

iii $\dfrac{\text{opposite P}}{\text{adjacent to P}}$

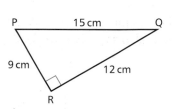

b i $\dfrac{\text{opposite Q}}{\text{hypotenuse}}$ **ii** $\dfrac{\text{adjacent to Q}}{\text{hypotenuse}}$

iii $\dfrac{\text{opposite Q}}{\text{adjacent to Q}}$

6 The tangent

Exercise 6.1 A class activity

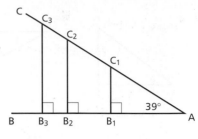

1 a Draw an angle of 39° with arms of reasonable length.
  b Draw three lines at right angles to AB,
    namely B_1C_1, B_2C_2, B_3C_3.
  c Copy and complete the table, measuring
    the lengths as accurately as you can.
    Give Opp ÷ Adj to 3 d.p.

Triangle	Opposite A (Opp)	Adjacent to A (Adj)	Opp ÷ Adj
AB_1C_1	$B_1C_1 =$	$AB_1 =$	
AB_2C_2	$B_2C_2 =$	$AB_2 =$	
AB_3C_3	$B_3C_3 =$	$AB_3 =$	

  d You should find that each time you divided the opposite side by the adjacent side
    you got approximately the same answer.
    Check your answers with others in the class.
    You should all have approximately the same answer.

2 On your calculator, key in   (tan) (3) (9) (=)

  You should get 0·809 784, correct to 6 decimal places.
  Compare this with the answers to question **1** above.

3 Repeat questions **1** and **2** for different acute angles.

  In each case you should find that, for equal angles, the ratios $\dfrac{\text{opposite}}{\text{adjacent}}$ will be equal,

  and for different angles the ratios will be different.

For a particular angle P, the ratio $\dfrac{\text{opposite P}}{\text{adjacent P}}$ is a fixed value known as **the tangent of P**

It is usually written as **tan P**. For example, tan 39° = 0·810 (to 3 decimal places)

Example 1

$$\tan F = \frac{\text{Opp F}}{\text{Adj F}}$$

$$= \frac{6}{8} = 0·75$$

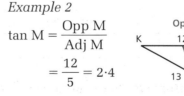

Example 2

$$\tan M = \frac{\text{Opp M}}{\text{Adj M}}$$

$$= \frac{12}{5} = 2·4$$

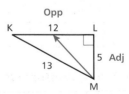

Example 3

$$\tan S = \frac{\text{Opp S}}{\text{Adj S}} = \frac{7}{24}$$

$$= 0·292 \text{ (to 3 d.p.)}$$

Exercise 6.2

1 In part **a**, $\tan A = \dfrac{BC}{AB}$.

In a similar way, write down the ratio for tan A in each of the other triangles.

a 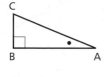   **b**   **c** 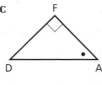   **d**

2 In triangle ABC, $\tan A = \dfrac{\text{Opp A}}{\text{Adj A}} = \dfrac{10}{24} = 0\cdot42$ (to 2 d.p.).

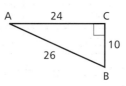

In a similar way, calculate the value of tan A, correct to 2 decimal places, in each triangle.

a 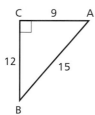   **b**   **c**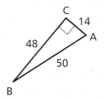

3 For each triangle in question **2**, write down the ratio for tan B, then calculate tan B, to 2 d.p.

Your calculator contains a list of tangent values for all acute angles.

For example, check that $\tan 50° = 1\cdot191\,753\,6$, by keying in

4 Copy the table below.

Use the (tan) key on your calculator to help you find the tangent of each angle, to 2 d.p.

Angle	10°	20°	30°	40°	50°	60°	70°	80°
Tangent								

5 Use your calculator to obtain the values of these tangents, to 2 d.p.
   a tan 0°   **b** tan 15°   **c** tan 24°   **d** tan 35°
   e tan 42°   **f** tan 45°   **g** tan 62°   **h** tan 78°
   i tan 88°   **j** tan 89°   **k** tan 89·5°   **l** tan 89·9°

6 a On squared paper, draw a square and one of its diagonals.
   b Mark all the 45° angles.
   c Explain why the value of tan 45° is 1.

7 Calculating the length of the opposite side

Example 1 Calculate the length of ST in triangle RST.

The triangle is right-angled so we can use the tangent.

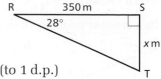

$$\tan 28° = \frac{x}{350} \Rightarrow x = 350 \times \tan 28° = 186\cdot1 \text{ m (to 1 d.p.)}$$

Example 2 At a point, A, 20 m from the foot of the building, the angle to the top of the building, C, is measured as 48°. What is the height of the building BC?

△ABC is right-angled, so we can use trigonometry.

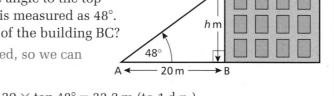

$$\tan 48° = \frac{h}{20} \Rightarrow h = 20 \times \tan 48° = 22\cdot2 \text{ m (to 1 d.p.)}$$

Exercise 7.1

Give lengths correct to 1 decimal place.

1 Copy and complete:

a
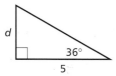

$$\tan 36° = \frac{d}{\dots}$$

$$\Rightarrow d = \dots \times \tan 36°$$

$$\Rightarrow d = \dots$$

b
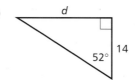

$$\tan \dots° = \frac{d}{\dots}$$

$$\Rightarrow d = \dots \times \tan \dots$$

$$\Rightarrow d = \dots$$

2 Calculate *d* in each triangle below.

a

b

c
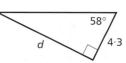

d
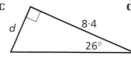

e

f
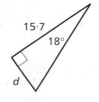

g
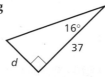

h
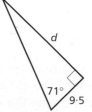

3 Calculate the height, *h* metres, of each tree.

a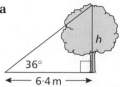

36°
6·4 m

b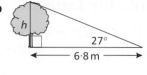

27°
6·8 m

c

34°
8·2 m
h

4 Calculate the width, *w* metres, of each river.

a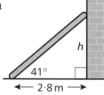

w
35°
18 m

b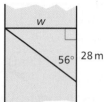

w
56° 28 m

c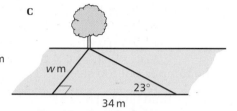

w m
23°
34 m

5 How high up the wall, *h* metres, does each ladder reach?

a

h
41°
2·8 m

b

h
63°
1·9 m

6 Calculate the breadth of rectangle DEFG.

D   E

37°

G   12 cm   F

7 PQRS is a kite.
Diagonal QS = 100 cm.

Calculate the length of the other diagonal, PR.

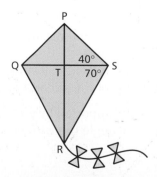

P
40°
Q   T   70°   S
R

8 Calculating angles using the tangent

If we know the lengths of both the opposite side and the adjacent side to an angle in a right-angled triangle, we can find the tangent and hence the size of the angle.

Example

The ramp is too steep if the angle it makes with the ground is greater than 16°. Is the ramp too steep?

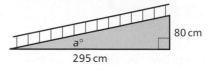

$\tan a° = \dfrac{80}{295} = 0.271$ (to 3 d.p.)

$\Rightarrow a° = 15.2°$ (to 1 d.p.)

or

So the ramp is not too steep.

$$\boxed{2nd}\ \boxed{\tan}\ \boxed{0.271}\ \boxed{=}$$

Note that $\boxed{2nd}\ \boxed{\tan}\ \boxed{0.271}\ \boxed{=}$ gives the angle whose tangent is 0·271.

Exercise 8.1

Give angles to the nearest degree.

1 For each triangle:

   i   write down the ratio for tan x°

   ii use the $\boxed{2nd}$ and $\boxed{\tan}$ keys on your calculator to find x.

   a   b   c   d   e   f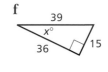

2 a A ladder leans against a wall. It touches the wall 3 m above the ground.
      The foot of the ladder is 3·5 m from the base of the wall.
      What angle does the ladder make with the ground?
   b i Calculate this angle for a ladder which touches the wall 2·8 m up and whose foot is 2·5 m from the base.
      ii What angle does this ladder make with the wall?
   c Repeat part **b** when the lengths are 3·2 m and 4·2 m respectively.

3 A glider reaches a height of 75 metres, having travelled a horizontal distance of 460 metres after leaving the ground.
   Assuming it travelled in a straight line, what is the angle of climb of the glider?

4 A flagpole is supported by a wire as shown.
   Calculate the angle the wire makes with the ground.

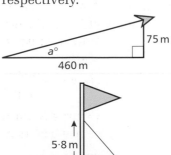

5 The bottom of a gold mine, Q, is 115 metres below the surface.
The entrance to the mine, P, is 760 metres away from the top of the ventilation shaft VQ .
Calculate the angle of slope, $s°$, of the passage PQ.

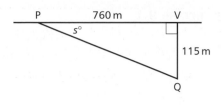

6 a Use the tangent ratio to calculate $\angle A$ and $\angle C$ in $\triangle ABC$.
  b Check that $\angle A + \angle B + \angle C = 180°$.

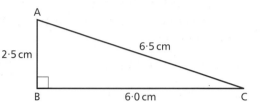

7 Calculate the sizes of the unmarked angles in rectangle JKLM.

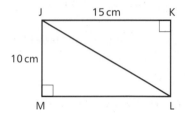

8 Triangle ABC is isosceles. BC = 12 cm and AD = 10 cm.
Calculate the sizes of the three angles of $\triangle ABC$.

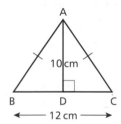

9 The sine of an angle

Another useful ratio in trigonometry is called the **sine** of the angle.
It is defined by

$$\sin A = \frac{\text{opposite A}}{\text{hypotenuse}}$$

Values are obtained from tables or a calculator.

Example   A 4 metre ladder leans against a wall at an angle of 70° to the ground.
How high up the wall, h metres, will the ladder reach?

$$\sin 70° = \frac{\text{opposite 70°}}{\text{hypotenuse}} = \frac{h}{4}$$

$$\Rightarrow h = 4 \times \sin 70°$$
$$\Rightarrow h = 3\cdot76 \text{ m (to 2 d.p.)}$$

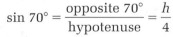

The ladder reaches 3·76 m up the wall.

Exercise 9.1

1 In triangle ABC, $\sin A = \dfrac{\text{Opp A}}{\text{Hyp}} = \dfrac{\text{BC}}{\text{AC}}$.

In a similar way, write down the ratio for sin A
in each triangle below.

a 　　**b** 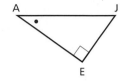　　**c**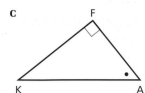

2 In part **a**, $\sin A = \dfrac{\text{Opp A}}{\text{Hyp}} = \dfrac{5}{13} = 0{\cdot}38$ to 2 d.p.

In a similar way, calculate the value of sin A, correct to 2 decimal places, in each of
the other triangles.

a 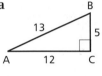　　**b** 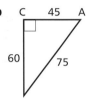　　**c** 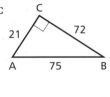　　**d**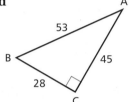

3 For each triangle in question **2**, write down the ratio for sin B, then calculate sin B,
correct to 2 decimal places.

4 Copy the table below.

Use the ⬚ (sin) key on your calculator to help you list the sines of these angles,
correct to 2 decimal places.

A	10°	20°	30°	40°	50°	60°	70°	80°	90°
sin A									

5 Find the values of the following sines, correct to 2 decimal places:
a sin 0°　**b** sin 15°　**c** sin 45°　**d** sin 75°　**e** sin 86°

6 a On squared paper, draw an equilateral triangle PQR with base QR.
b Draw the line of symmetry PS.
c Mark in the sizes of the angles of ΔPSR.
d Explain why the value of sin 30° must be 0·5.

7 Copy and complete:

$\sin 34° = \dfrac{d}{?}$

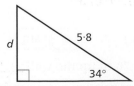

so $d = \ldots \times \sin 34°$

$\quad\; = \ldots$ (to 1 d.p.)

Give your answers to questions **8–12** correct to 1 d.p.

8 Calculate the value of *d* in each of these triangles.

a

b

c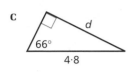

d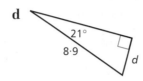

9 Buttresses have been built along a wall to support it.
Calculate the height, *h* m, of each buttress.

a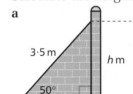

b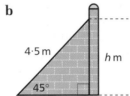

c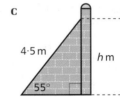

10 Find the height of each kite.
Which kite is flying highest?

a

b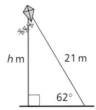

c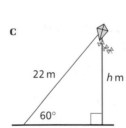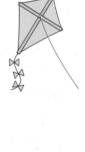

11 A straight stretch of road 180 metres long climbs at 19° to the horizontal.
Calculate the difference in height, *h* metres, between the two ends of the stretch of road.

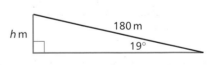

12 Two wires, AC and CD, support a flagpole.
AC is 14 m long and is fixed at A, the top of the pole.
AC makes an angle of 62° with the ground.
CD is 9·5 m long and makes an angle of 50° with the ground.
Calculate:
a the height of the flagpole, AB
b the length AD.

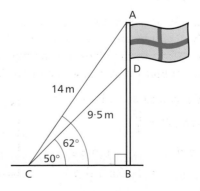

10 Angles and the sine

Example   Calculate the size of ∠PRQ in ΔPQR.
Note that we know the length of the side
opposite the required angle and the
hypotenuse, which suggests we use the
sine rather than the tangent.

$$\sin \angle PRQ = \frac{14}{19} = 0{\cdot}737 \text{ (to 3 d.p.)}$$

What angle has a sine of 0·737?

∠PRQ = 47° (to the nearest degree)

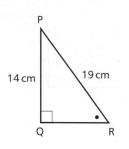

Exercise 10.1

1 Use the (2nd) and (sin) keys on your calculator to find the size of angle P to the
nearest degree, given:

a sin P = 0·5   b sin P = 0·34   c sin P = 0·81   d sin P = 1

e sin P = $\frac{4}{5}$ f sin P = $\frac{2}{7}$ g sin P = $\frac{8}{13}$ h sin P = $\frac{25}{32}$

2 For each triangle: i write down the ratio for sin $a°$ ii calculate $a°$.

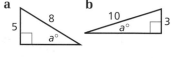

a   b   c   d   e   f

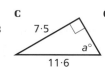

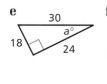

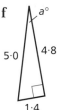

3 Calculate the angle of slope of each roof (marked by a letter in each case).

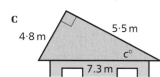

a   b   c

4 Calculate the angle of the slope of each stretch of road.

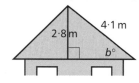

a   b

5 The *Beauty* (B) is 28 km due west of
the *Fearless* (F) and 21 km due north
of *Sparky* (S).
Sparky is 35 km away from the *Fearless*.

Calculate the bearing of the *Fearless*
from *Sparky*.

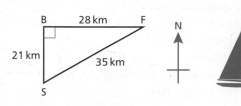

11 The cosine of an angle

An aeroplane takes off at an angle of
18° to the horizontal.
How can we find how far it has
travelled horizontally when it has
flown 1000 metres?

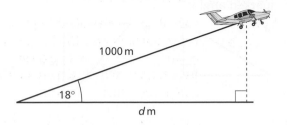

In the right-angled triangle formed we
want to find the side adjacent to the
angle of 18° when we are given the length of the hypotenuse.
Neither the sine nor the tangent can be found.

We define a new ratio, called the **cosine** of the angle.

$$\cos A = \frac{\text{Adjacent to A}}{\text{Hypotenuse}}$$ Values are obtained from tables or a calculator.

For the aeroplane: $\cos 18° = \dfrac{d}{1000}$

$\Rightarrow d = 1000 \times \cos 18°$

$\Rightarrow d = 951$ m to the nearest metre.

Exercise 11.1

1 Write down the ratio for cos A in each triangle below.

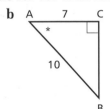

2 Calculate the value of
  i $\cos x°$ **ii** $\cos y°$ in each triangle, correct to 2 decimal places.

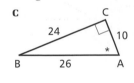
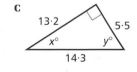
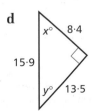
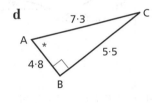

3 Calculate the length of each marked side, correct to 1 d.p. (All sizes are in centimetres.)

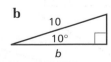
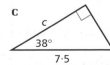

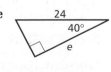

4 Use the (2nd) and (cos) keys on your calculator to help you find the size of each marked angle.

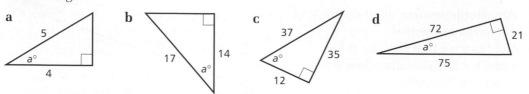

a
5
$a°$
4

b
17
14
$a°$

c
37
$a°$
35
12

d
72
$a°$
75
21

5 Some trees are supported by ropes pegged into the ground as shown. Calculate, in each case, how far from the base of the tree the rope is pegged to the ground. Give your answers correct to 1 decimal place.

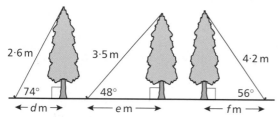

2·6 m
74°
← d m →

3·5 m
48°
← e m →

4·2 m
56°
← f m →

6 A stair and ramp lead up to a doorway.
Calculate the distance d.
(Hint: consider two triangles.)

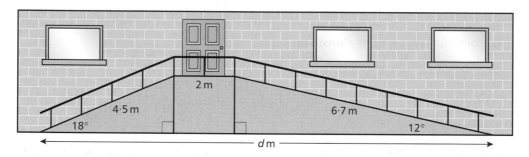

2 m
4·5 m
18°
6·7 m
12°
← d m →

7 Calculate the angle of take-off, $a°$.

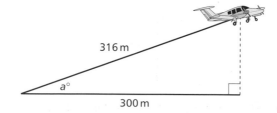

316 m
$a°$
300 m

8 a One bank of a river is higher than the other.
The bridge spanning the river is 18·5 m long and slopes at 15° to the horizontal.
Calculate the width of the river, w m.

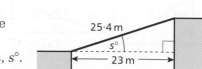

18·5 m
15°
← w m →

b At another spot, the river is 23 m wide and the bridge is 25·4 m long.
Calculate the angle at which the bridge slopes, $s°$.

25·4 m
$s°$
← 23 m →

Investigation

a Copy and complete the table, giving your answers correct to 2 decimal places.

A	0°	10°	20°	30°	40°	50°	60°	70°	80°	90°
sin A										
cos A										

b Look at the table for a connection between the cosines and the sines.

> The cosine means **the complement sine**. The sine of an angle and the cosine of its complement are equal.
> Remember: two angles are complementary if they add up to 90°.
> sin 0° = cos 90°, sin 10° = cos 80°, sin 20° = cos 70°, etc.

c What angle has the same value for its sine and its cosine?
d Copy and complete: **i**   cos 25° = sin …°   **ii**   sin 41° = cos …°
                               iii   cos 1° = sin …°   **iv**   sin …° = cos 63°

12 Which ratio – sine, cosine or tangent?

The following memory aid will help you decide which ratio to use in a problem:

> SOH – CAH – TOA

It represents the initial letters of

$$\sin A = \frac{\text{Opposite A}}{\text{Hypotenuse}} \qquad \cos A = \frac{\text{Adjacent to A}}{\text{Hypotenuse}} \qquad \tan A = \frac{\text{Opposite A}}{\text{Adjacent to A}}$$

Example
Find the size of x in the triangle shown.   Label the sides in relation to the angle:

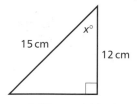 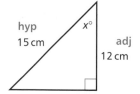

Tick off the sides you have in the memory aid:

$$\sin A = \frac{\text{Opposite A}}{\text{Hypotenuse}} \checkmark \qquad \cos A = \frac{\text{Adjacent to A} \checkmark}{\text{Hypotenuse} \checkmark} \qquad \tan A = \frac{\text{Opposite A}}{\text{Adjacent to A} \checkmark}$$

$$\checkmark \qquad \checkmark\checkmark \qquad \checkmark$$
SOH – CAH – TOA

The ratio that gets two ticks is the one to use.

$$\cos x° = \frac{12}{15} = 0{\cdot}8 \qquad \Rightarrow x° = 37° \text{ (to nearest degree)}$$

Exercise 12.1

In your answers, give angles to the nearest degree and lengths to 1 decimal place.

1 i For each triangle, decide which ratio will help you calculate x.
 ii Calculate x.

 a
 b
 c
 d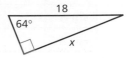

2 The picture shows some measurements
 taken on one bank of a river using a tree
 on the other bank as a point of reference.
 Calculate w, the width of the river.

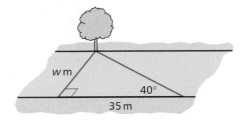

3 An 8·5 m plank of wood just reaches the top of a wall.
 It makes an angle of 42° with the ground.
 a Calculate the height of the wall.
 b How far is the low end of the plank from the foot
 of the wall?

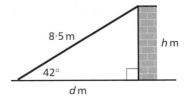

4 Jo stands 240 metres away from the foot of
 the Niagara Falls and needs to look up through 13°
 to see the top.
 How high are the Falls?

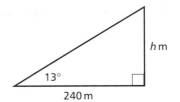

5 The Leaning Tower of Pisa – how far is it
 leaning over?
 Calculate the value of w.

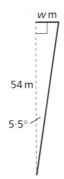

6 Calculate the submarine's angle of dive.

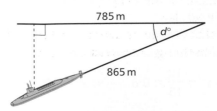

7 Calculate:
   a the width of the road, *w* metres
   b the length of the front of the supermarket,
     d metres.

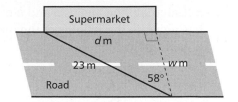

8 Calculate the angle, *a*°, the support of the swing makes with the ground.

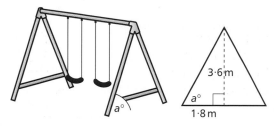

9 a Calculate the size of angle *x* in rectangle PQRS.

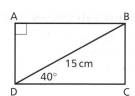

  b Calculate the length and breadth of rectangle ABCD.

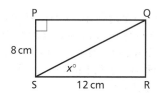

10 The *Sea Spirit* (S) is 4 km due south of the lighthouse (L)
and 7·5 km from the harbour (H).
The harbour is due east of the lighthouse.
Calculate the bearing of the harbour from the *Sea Spirit*.

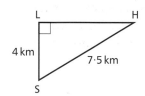

Exercise 12.2

In your answers, give lengths to 1 decimal place and angles to the nearest degree.

1 a Calculate the height, *h* metres, of the
    paraglider.
  b Calculate the horizontal distance, *d* metres,
    of the paraglider from the boat.

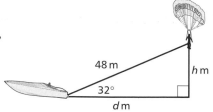

2 a Calculate the angles *a* and *b* of kite DEFG.
  b Calculate the lengths of the diagonals of kite RSTU. Give answers to the nearest centimetre.

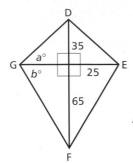

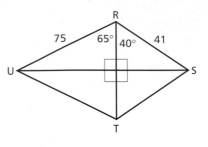

All lengths are in centimetres.

3 A yacht sails 18 km from A to B on a bearing of 042°. Calculate how far it is then:
  a north of A
  b east of A.

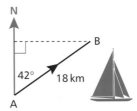

4 Calculate:
  a the width, *w* m, of the house
  b its height, *h* m.

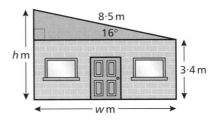

5 The cable car climbs at 18° to the horizontal.
AB = 50 m and BC = 35 m.
Calculate the height the car has risen from:
  a A to B
  b A to C.

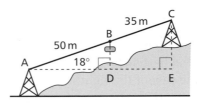

6 a i Calculate the length of RS.
   ii Use Pythagoras' theorem to calculate ST.

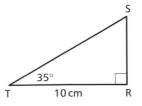

  b i Calculate all the angles in this rectangle.
   ii Use Pythagoras' theorem to calculate the length of the diagonals.

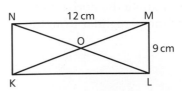

◀◀ RECAP

A **3-figure bearing** is a method of describing the direction from one spot to another.
It is the angle, measured clockwise, from the north line to the desired direction.
It is always expressed using three digits.
If an angle has less than three digits then leading zeros are added.

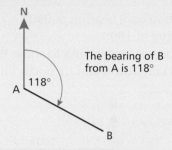

The bearing of B
from A is 118°

Trigonometry can be used to calculate sides and angles of right-angled triangles.

$$\sin A = \frac{\text{Opposite A}}{\text{Hypotenuse}} \qquad \cos A = \frac{\text{Adjacent to A}}{\text{Hypotenuse}} \qquad \tan A = \frac{\text{Opposite A}}{\text{Adjacent to A}}$$

Example 1
Find h, the height of the building.

$$\tan 40° = \frac{h}{28}$$

$$\Rightarrow h = 28 \times \tan 40$$

$$\Rightarrow h = 23 \cdot 5$$

The height is $23 \cdot 5$ m (to 1 d.p.)

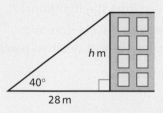

Example 2
Calculate the value of a.

$$\sin a° = \frac{11}{16}$$

$$\Rightarrow \sin a = 0 \cdot 6875$$

$$\Rightarrow a = 43 \cdot 4$$

(using ⎡2nd⎤ and ⎡sin⎤ buttons)

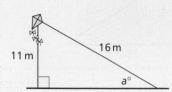

1 Use a protractor to find the 3-figure
bearings of the boats A, B, C and D
from the harbour, H.

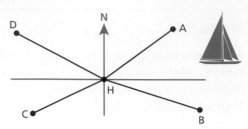

2 The village of Barr is 6 km from Afton on a bearing of 080°.
Croy is 8·5 km from Barr on a bearing of 150°.
Using a scale of 1 cm to 1 km, make a scale drawing to show the positions of
Afton, Barr and Croy. (Start by marking Afton and its north line.)

3 A lighthouse, L, is 700 m due
east of a harbour, H.
The bearing of a cave, C, from
the lighthouse is 200°.
The bearing of the cave from
the harbour is 130°.
  a Using a scale of 1 cm to 100 m,
    make a scale drawing to show the
    positions of the lighthouse, the harbour and the cave.
  b How far is the cave from the lighthouse?

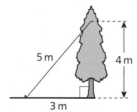

In questions **4–7** do not use a scale drawing.
In your answers, give lengths to 1 decimal place and angles to the nearest degree.

4 Calculate the height of the
chimney.

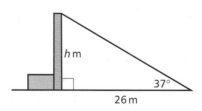

5 What angle does the supporting
rope make with the ground?

6 **a** How far up the wall does the ladder reach?
  b How far is the foot of the ladder from the
    base of the wall?

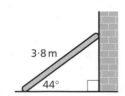

7 **a** Calculate the height of the cliff.

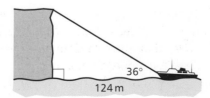

12 More statistics

In the first part of the season Rovers, as the table shows, had a better goal average than Burgh. (Goal average = goals ÷ games played)

The same happened in the second part.

Why was the Rovers' manager surprised when he added the two sets of results together to get a summary of the whole season?

Be very careful with statistics and averages!

Team	Played	Goals	Average
First part			
Rovers	5	4	0·80
Burgh	20	15	0·75
Second part			
Rovers	55	30	0·55
Burgh	40	20	0·50
Summary			
Rovers	60	34	
Burgh	60	35	

1 REVIEW

◀◀ **Exercise 1.1**

1 **a** Calculate   **i** 34 ÷ 60   **ii** 35 ÷ 60
   b Which of the above teams finished with the better goal average?

2 Josie counted the number of cars forming a queue
   at the traffic lights each time they turned green.
   The table shows her findings.
   a Make a frequency table of the data.
   b i   What was the longest queue that formed?
     ii   How often did it happen while she was
             gathering data?
   c What was the most common length of queue?

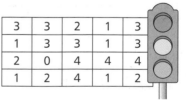

3	3	2	1	3
1	3	3	1	3
2	0	4	4	4
1	2	4	1	2

3 Peter's mobile phone keeps a note of the length of the last ten calls:
   2 min, 3 min, 3 min, 2 min, 1 min, 2 min, 3 min, 10 min, 1 min, 2 min.
   a What is the total amount of time of the last ten calls?
   b What is the average length of a call?
   c What would you say is the typical length of one of Peter's calls?

4 Sharma sat six exams. Her average mark turned out to be 60.
   What was her total for the six exams?

5 The stem-and-leaf diagram records the lengths of a sample of fibres caught in the filter of a vacuum cleaner.

a What was
  i the longest fibre
  ii the shortest fibre measured?
b How many fibres of length 23 mm were measured?
c If you had to guess the average length, what would you say?

Length of fibre						
0	2	3	3	4		
1	0	2	2	4	6	7
2	1	1	3	3	5	8 9
3	0	0	4	5	7	7
4	3	7				

$n = 25$ 2 | 1 represents 21 mm

2 Typical – the mean!

When there is a lot of data, it is often helpful to have an idea of what is typical for the data.

If, for example, you have an exam mark of 62 you may not know whether that is good or bad unless you are given further information such as:

- What is the exam out of?
- What was the highest score?
- What was the lowest score?
- What was the average person's score?

One *average* that you should have come across is the **mean**

> The mean score = the total score ÷ the number of scores

Example   Some cakes were weighed: 50 g, 47 g, 52 g, 49 g, 48 g.
What is the mean weight of the cakes?

There were five weights. The total weight = 50 + 47 + 52 + 49 + 48 = 246 g
The mean weight = 246 ÷ 5 = 49·2 g

Exercise 2.1

1 Calculate the mean of each set of scores.
  a 2, 2, 3, 4, 9, 16
  b 12, 14, 25, 28, 29, 32, 35
  c 17, 25, 37, 49, 123
  d 541, 567, 581, 511, 598, 614, 622, 639, 753, 810

2 A 'Best Buys' magazine priced a certain laptop computer at eight different shops.
The prices quoted are given below.

£899   £845   £866   £950   £850   £874   £830   £848

  a What is the mean cost of the laptop?
  b How many of the shops were selling the computer at a price below the mean?

3 A similar survey was carried out on a personal stereo.
Prices were found to be:

£129   £116   £167   £142   £119   £345   £199   £125

  a What is the mean cost of the personal stereo?
  b How many of the shops were selling the personal stereo
    at a price above the mean?
  c i Which price in the list would seem to be 'out of place'?
    ii If you ignored this price, what would the mean price
      be then?

4 Two different High Street shopping centres are surveyed for the price of a particular
pair of shoes.

Ambledon	£50	£53	£57	£53	£51	£48	
Burby	£62	£59	£68	£70	£71	£59	£66

  a Calculate the mean price of the shoes in   **i** Ambledon   **ii** Burby.
  b What is the difference in the mean prices for these two centres?
  c i What is the mean price for all 13 shoe shops?
    ii How many of the Burby prices are above this mean?

5 Sam and Laura were both training for the same big cycling event.
They each logged how far they cycled in training sessions.

Sam	29 km	36 km	33 km	49 km	48 km	25 km	32 km
Laura	36 km	31 km	37 km	39 km	37 km		

  a Calculate the mean distance cycled per session for
    i Sam   **ii** Laura.
  b How many sessions were below the mean for
    i Sam   **ii** Laura?
  c Make a comment about
    i the cyclists' means   **ii** the cyclists' sessions.

The mean using a frequency table

Data is often presented in a frequency table.

Example   Eleanor's bus is supposed to leave the
terminus each morning at 9 a.m.
Eleanor records the number of minutes
it is late daily.
Her findings have been organised in a
frequency table.
What is the mean number of minutes
that the bus is late?

Minutes late	Frequency
0	5
1	7
2	9
3	4

The number of minutes late could be written out as:

0 0 0 0 0 1 1 1 1 1 1 1 2 2 2 2 2 2 2 2 2 3 3 3 3.

Adding these 25 numbers gives a total of 37, so the mean = 37 ÷ 25 = 1·48.

However, look at this table:

Minutes late	Frequency	Min × freq.
0	5	0
1	7	7
2	9	18
3	4	12
Totals	25	37

5 zeros +
7 ones +
9 twos +
4 threes …
total 37

Total frequency = 25

A third column has been added. This makes it easier to calculate the mean.

Mean = total minutes late ÷ total frequency = 37 ÷ 25 = 1·48

Exercise 2.2

1 For each frequency table:

  i   complete or add a third column … score times frequency

  ii find the total of this column

  iii find the total frequency

  iv calculate the mean score correct to 1 d.p.

a

Score	Frequency	Score × freq.
6	2	12
7	5	
8	8	
9	1	
Totals		

b

Score	Frequency	Score × freq.
20	1	
25	3	
30	5	
35	1	
Totals		

c

Score	Frequency
1	1
2	5
5	3
7	1
9	2
Totals	

d

Score	Frequency
10	7
20	4
30	2
40	3
50	4
Totals	

e

Score	Frequency
4	0
6	5
8	3
10	6
12	1
Totals	

2 The ages of pupils attending a school disco were noted.
Copy and complete the table to help you work out the mean age correct to 1 decimal place.

Age	Frequency	Age × freq.
11	60	660
12	40	
13	30	
14	20	
15	50	
Totals		

3 To see if it is worthwhile keeping a certain bus stop, inspectors visit the stop at various times and note the number of passengers waiting. The frequency table shows their findings.

  a Copy and complete the frequency table.
  b How many visits were made to the bus stop?
  c How many passengers were spotted in total?
  d i Calculate the mean number of passengers at the bus stop to 2 d.p.
  ii If this is greater than 1·5 the bus stop will be kept. Will the bus stop be kept?

Passengers	Frequency	Pass. × freq.
0	4	
1	6	
2	9	
3	5	
4	1	
Totals		

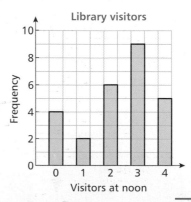

4 People were asked how many cups of coffee they drank each day.
The table shows the results of the survey.
  a How many people were asked?
  b How many cups of coffee were drunk by the people in the sample?
  c Calculate the mean number of cups drunk per person.

Cups	Frequency
0	3
1	5
2	7
3	2
4	3
Totals	

5 The bar graph shows the number of pupils turning up at noon to use the library over 26 days.
  a Use the graph to help you produce a frequency table.
  b Use your frequency table to help you calculate the mean number of visitors to the library at noon.
  c If the mean is more than 3 people, then the library will continue to stay open at lunchtimes. Will it stay open?

Library visitors

6 Fifty packets of a popular brand of breakfast cereal are sampled.
They are labelled as holding 500 g each.

Weight (g)	497	498	499	500	501	502
Frequency	1	5	11	14	17	2

a What is the total weight of the 50 packets?
b What is the mean weight of one packet (to 1 d.p.)?
c Is the 500 g label appropriate?

3 The mode

A football manager noted the number of players in his team at the end of several
games one season. Some players had been sent off and some had been injured.

$$11 \quad 11 \quad 11 \quad 10 \quad 11 \quad 10 \quad 11 \quad 11 \quad 11 \quad 11 \quad 10 \quad 11$$

The mean size of the team $= 129 \div 12 = 10 \cdot 75$ players.
Having 11 players at the end of the game is more than
the mean!

Using such statistics gives a misleading picture of what
is happening.
A more useful figure to use as an average would be the
most commonly occurring number, namely 11.

This is called the **mode**, or **modal score**.

Example 1   A chemist noted the strength (factor) of sun cream
bought by customers:

10 25 15 25 25 15 15 25 30 35
15 20 25 25 30 25 15 10 25

Find the mode (or modal strength) of the sun
cream sold.

From the frequency table we
see that the factor with the
highest frequency is factor
25 with a frequency of 8.
Factor 25 is the mode.

Factor	Tally	Frequency
10	||	2
15	ЖЇ	5
20	|	1
25	ЖЇ |||	8
30	||	2
35	|	1

Example 2 The owner of a hardware store noted the type of light bulb requested over a morning:

60 W 60 W 100 W 60 W   150 W 100 W 150 W 100 W 100 W
40 W 60 W 100 W 150 W   60 W 100 W 60 W   150 W   40 W

Find the modal type of bulb requested.

A frequency table shows that both 60 W and 100 W share the title of having the highest frequency. So both 60 W and 100 W are quoted as modes.

Type	40	60	100	150
Frequency	2	6	6	4

Exercise 3.1

1 Find the mode of each list. State them both where there are two.
a 7 7 7 7 9 9 11 11 11 11 11 12 12 17 17
b 116 116 116 116 116 117 117 118 118 118 118 118 118 118 118 119
c 20 21 22 22 22 23 23 23 24

2 The data need not be numbers. What is the favourite category (the mode) in each case?
a Car colours: red green blue red red green blue green red blue red
b Crisp flavours: tomato bacon bacon cheese tomato tomato cheese cheese cheese
c Best day: Mon Mon Fri Fri Fri Wed Sun Sun Wed Sun Mon Mon Fri Sat Tue

3 What do you think the mode is in each of the following situations?
a The number of days in a month
b The number of wheels on a car
c The number of rugby players in a team at the end of a match
d The number of walls in a room in the school

4 A survey was done on the type of calculator owned by pupils in a class.

Arithmetic   Scientific   Graphic   Arithmetic   Scientific
Scientific   Scientific   Arithmetic   Scientific   Graphic
Scientific   Arithmetic   Scientific   Scientific   Arithmetic

a How many pupils had:
   i   an arithmetic
   ii a scientific
   iii a graphic calculator?
b What is the modal type?
c If the school were to buy batteries for only two of the types, which types would they probably be?

5 In a short test, it was expected that pupils would score 10 out of 12 on average. Here are the results for the class:

7   8   8   10   11   10   12   12   10   11
9   8   9   9   10   11   12   11   10   10
10   11   9   8   11   10   8   8   11   12

  a Make a frequency table of the data.
  b What is the modal score?
  c **i** How many pupils scored the modal score or better?
     ii How many scored worse than the modal score?
  d Do you think the pupils performed to expectations?

Exercise 3.2

1 A video rental shop asked their customers the question 'How many times a week do you rent a video?'
The replies were organised and used to make this bar graph.
  a How many customers said they rented one video per week?
  b Make a frequency table using the graph.
  c What is the modal number of rentals per week?
  d What feature of the graph will allow you to spot the mode without making a frequency table?

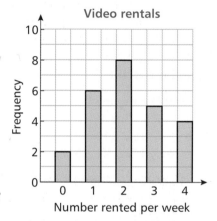

2 On the outside of a packet of sweets there is a claim that 'the average contents are 30 sweets'. A selection of the packets are opened and the contents counted. The table shows the findings.

Contents	27	28	29	30	31	32
Frequency	6	8	14	15	7	4

  a What is the frequency of packets holding 29 sweets?
  b Which size of packet had a frequency of 8?
  c What is the modal number of sweets per packet?

3 A study was made of absentee numbers and day of the week.
Each week, the day with the most absences was given a point.
The graph shows the number of points awarded each day by the end of the study.
  a How often was Wednesday the day with the most absences?
  b For how many weeks was the study done?
  c Which day of the week is the mode?

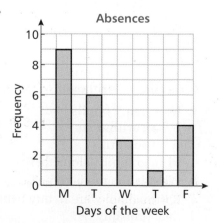

4 Over a period of 24 weeks, the number of times Matt was late for work each week was noted.

The management's policy was that an average of being late once per week was acceptable.

The data shows how many days Matt was late each week.

```
1   3   4   4   1   4
4   0   1   6   4   1
6   1   3   1   4   6
3   6   6   6   1   3
```

a Make a frequency table of the data.

b How many times was Matt late three times a week?

c **i** What is the mode for the number of times late per week?

    ii Does this meet with the management's allowance?

    iii Does it give a picture of what is *typical* for Matt?

d **i** Calculate the mean number of late days per week to 1 d.p.

    ii Does this meet with the management's allowance?

    iii Does it give a picture of what is *typical* for Matt?

4 The median

In the last question, if just one value had been a 6 rather than a 1, then …

Days late	0	1	2	3	4	6
Frequency	1	7	0	4	6	6
Mode	1					

Days late	0	1	2	3	4	6
Frequency	1	6	0	4	6	7
Mode	6					

… the modal score would have jumped from one end of the scale to the other.

An average which is less sensitive to this sort of change is the **median**.

> The value that splits an ordered list of numbers into two smaller lists of equal length is called the median.
> If a list has an odd number of items, the median is the middle item.
> If a list has an even number of items, the median is the mean of the two middle items.

Example   Find the median of each list:

    a 1 1 2 2 2 3 3 3 4 5

    b 6 6 7 7 8 8 9 10 10 10 11 11 12 13

    c 10 10 6 8 4 9 9 4 7 5 10 2 4 3 2

    d p q r s t t

a The list is in order and has an odd number of items: 1 1 2 2 2 **3** 3 3 3 4 5
The median = 3.

b The list is ordered and has an even number of items:

    6 6 7 7 8 8 9 10 10 10 11 11 12 13

The median $= \dfrac{9 + 10}{2} = 9 \cdot 5$

c The list must be put in order first: 2 2 3 4 4 5 5 6 7 8 9 9 10 10 10
The median $= 6$.

d This is not a list of numbers … it has no median.

Exercise 4.1

1 Find the median of each list. Make sure the list is *ordered*.

  a 7 7 8 8 8 8 9 9 10
  b 12 23 36 37 39 41 48
  c 94 96 98 99 99 101
  d 46 46 47 48 49 49 53 56 58 65
  e 3·5 3·6 3·9 4·0 4·6 4·8
  f 6 5 1 8 4 2 9 3 7 4 1
  g 12 35 42 87 12 46 35 75
  h 7·9 1·4 3·1 7·0 8·1 9·2 3·7

2 Terri noted the length of her phone calls in minutes:

    1 3 4 4 7 7 8 10.

  a Calculate:
    i   the median
    ii the mean length of call.
  b She made a mistake. That 10 minute call was actually 100 minutes!
    Recalculate:
    i   the median
    ii the mean length of call.
  c Which of the two averages was unaffected by the error?
  d No. She rechecked. The 10 minute call was a 1 minute call. Phew!
    Recalculate:
    i   the median
    ii the mean length of call.
    Why was the median affected this time?

3 Alan sowed a packet of seeds.
After a few weeks he measured the length of the shoots in centimetres:

    1 1 1 1 2 3 3 4 4 4 4 5 5 5 5 5 6

  a Calculate:
    i   the median   **ii** the modal length of a shoot.
  b Suppose that one of the shoots had been 1 cm rather than 5 cm long.
    How would this affect:
    i   the median   **ii** the modal length?

4 Here is a table of data about some of the planets in our solar system.

Planet	Diameter (miles)	Spins on axis	Goes round sun
Mercury	3000	88 days	88 days
Venus	7600	30 days	225 days
Earth	7900	24 hours	365 days
Mars	4200	24 hours	687 days
Jupiter	87 000	10 hours	12 years
Saturn	72 000	10 hours	29 years
Uranus	29 000	11 hours	84 years
Neptune	28 000	16 hours	165 years
Pluto	2000	?	248 years

a Find
   i   the median diameter   **ii** the mean diameter of a planet.
b i   Which planet has the median diameter?
   ii   Which planet is closest to having the mean diameter?
c We don't know yet how long it takes Pluto to spin on its axis.
    Work out the median time for those we do know.
d i   Work out the median number of days it takes for a planet to go round the sun.
   ii   Difficult! What is the mean number of days (at 365 days a year)?

5 An author's book is examined for sentence length. Twenty sentences are picked at random and the number of words in each is counted.

   6 9 12 13 13 15 9 12 14 23 12 9 21 23 19 13 26 18 24 26

a Put the list in order of size (making a stem-and-leaf diagram will help).
b i   What is the mode in words per sentence?
   ii   Calculate the mean sentence length.
   iii Find the median length.
c Which of the three averages do you think represents the situation best?

Sorting

As the number of pieces of data increases, a stem-and-leaf diagram becomes a good idea for sorting and ordering the data.

Example   Swallows are captured, measured in centimetres and then released in an experiment to find the typical length of the bird. The following data has been collected.

   17·3   18·1   20·0   19·7   19·2   18·5
   18·3   19·0   19·6   19·4   17·6   20·2
   19·1   19·0   17·3   19·5   18·8   20·1
   20·2   18·0   19·1   20·1   19·3   21·0
   21·1   18·6   20·2   18·1   21·1   17·7

What is the median length of a swallow?

A stem-and-leaf diagram will sort the data into numerical order.

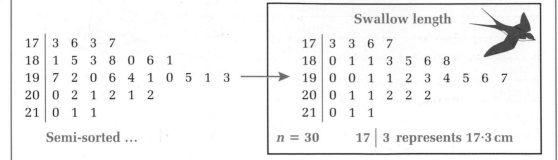

```
17 | 3  6  3  7
18 | 1  5  3  8  0  6  1
19 | 7  2  0  6  4  1  0  5  1  3
20 | 0  2  1  2  1  2
21 | 0  1  1
```

Semi-sorted ...

Swallow length

```
17 | 3  3  6  7
18 | 0  1  1  3  5  6  8
19 | 0  0  1  1  2  3  4  5  6  7
20 | 0  1  1  2  2  2
21 | 0  1  1
```

$n = 30$ 17 | 3 represents 17·3 cm

From the sorted stem-and-leaf diagram we can see that the two middle lengths are the 15th and 16th, i.e. 19·1 and 19·2.

Thus the median size $= \dfrac{19·1 + 19·2}{2} = 19·15$ cm.

Exercise 4.2

1 The heights of some wild poppies are measured to the nearest centimetre.
This is a block of the collected data.

```
45   30   64   37   50
57   51   44   60   48
41   67   31   34   56
53   46   51   65   40
52   41   50   36   54
```

a Organise the data into a sorted stem-and-leaf diagram.

b Use your diagram to help you find the median height.

c How many of the plants have a height that is within 5 cm of this median?

2 The diagram shows the number of visitors to the Miners' Museum over the past 22 open days.

a What's

   i   the least number

   ii the biggest number

   recorded in a day?

b What is the median number of visitors in a day?

c **i**   Calculate the mean number correct to 1 d.p.

   ii On how many days was the number of visitors bigger than the mean?

Visitors

```
1 | 1  2  9
2 | 0  1  1  1  4  7
3 | 2  4  4  6  8  9  9
4 | 4  5  5  8
5 | 6  7
```

$n = 22$ 1 | 1 represents 11 visitors

3 Two types of light bulbs are to be compared. Fifteen of each are tested to destruction and their lifetime in months is noted.

Old model: 15   24   10   16   27   12   32   19   24   7   18   27   34   15   10
New model: 15   29   31   23   42   34   16   23   28   20   21   36   41   20   38

a Calculate the median of   **i** the old model   **ii** the new model.
b Comment on the two medians.

4 The back-to-back stem-and-leaf diagram is the result of comparing two batches of plants.
One of the batches had been given a nutrient and the other hadn't.
The figures are the heights of the plants measured in centimetres.

a Work out the median height for the plants reared
   i with   **ii** without nutrient.
b What is the smallest plant reared
   i with   **ii** without nutrient?
c What is the largest plant reared
   i with   **ii** without nutrient?
d Compare the progress made by the two batches.

		Plant height (cm)		
With nutrient			**Without nutrient**	
	1 1 0	8	0 4 4 4 8	
	5 4 3	9	3 5 6 9	
9 7 7 3 2		10	3 3 8 8	
	5 5 4 0	11	0 2 4	
	6 3 0	12	3 5 6	
	2 1	13	4	

$n = 20$ $n = 20$

8 | 0 **represents 8·0 cm**

5 The range

Lucy and Neil both play darts for their local team.
The table shows how they fared over their last ten visits to the board.
The lists have been sorted.

Neil	1	2	10	24	36	44	53	61	73	100
Lucy	31	32	34	35	39	41	42	43	43	44

Neil's median score $= \dfrac{36 + 44}{2} = 40$; Lucy's median score $= \dfrac{39 + 41}{2} = 40$

Both medians are the same.
However, the difference between Neil's best and worst score is $100 - 1 = 99$ and the difference between Lucy's best and worst score is $44 - 31 = 13$.
Lucy's scoring is less variable than Neil's.
This would be good to know if the team had to nominate someone to go up and score over 30 to win.

The difference between the highest and lowest of a set of scores is known as the **range** of the scores.

> Range = highest score − lowest score

It is used to measure how spread out or how variable the scores are.

Exercise 5.1

1 Calculate the range in each set of data.
  a 1 cm, 3 cm, 5 cm, 12 cm, 17 cm   **b** 3 s, 7 s, 23 s, 79 s, 100 s
  c 20 days, 12 days, 17 days, 49 days   **d** 78 kg, 23 kg, 99 kg, 14 kg, 201 kg
  e 13 °C, 29 °C, 1 °C, −5 °C, −8 °C, 10 °C   **f** −3 °C, −12 °C, −9 °C, − 25 °C

2 **a** Mercury is the nearest planet to the sun and is 36 million miles from it.
     Pluto is furthest away at 3670 million miles.
     What is the range of the distances of the planets to the sun?
  b The largest moon of Jupiter has a diameter of 3100 miles.
     Jupiter's smallest moon has a diameter of 10 miles.
     What is the range in diameters of Jupiter's moons?

3 At six weather stations round the world, the rainfall each month and the average
  temperature each month were recorded over a year.
  The table records the minimum and the maximum figures collected over the year.
  It also gives the total rainfall for the year.

Place	Min. rain	Max. rain	Min. temp	Max. temp	Total annual rain
Greenland	1 mm	30 mm	−20 °C	10 °C (Aug)	90 mm
Canada	10 mm	50 mm	−12 °C	28 °C	380 mm
Burma	2 mm	500 mm	30 °C	32 °C	2600 mm
Greece	6 mm	80 mm	12 °C	37 °C	402 mm
Egypt	0 mm	3 mm	20 °C	38 °C	25 mm
Britain	30 mm	60 mm	−2 °C	20 °C	593 mm

  a Calculate the range in rainfall for
    i Greenland
    ii Burma.
  b Canada or Britain – which has the greater range of temperatures?
  c What is the range of temperatures for
    i Greenland
    ii Burma?
  d For Greece calculate
    i the range in temperatures
    ii the range in rainfall
    iii the mean rainfall per month. (Hint: total ÷ 12)
  e For which country is the range in rainfall figures less than the mean rainfall?

4 In an experiment, ten people were asked to pour what they judged was 1 litre.
  When the amounts were measured they were found to be:

  976 ml, 980 ml, 984 ml, 995 ml, 1002 ml, 1011 ml, 1015 ml, 1019 ml, 1028 ml, 1030 ml.

  a Work out the median guess.
  b What is the range of guesses?
  c Calculate the mean guess.

5 A teacher has to pick a pupil for an inter-school quiz.
She is considering Mel, Les or Don.
She looks at their performance over earlier rounds.

	Number of questions right						
Mel	12	10	14	10	13	11	12
Les	11	19	20	4	12	1	17
Don	8	9	8	7	9	7	8

a Work out the range and median for each player.
b Which player is most consistent (has the lowest range)?
c Which player(s) has the best median score?
d If there is a tie for best median score, which of these are most consistent?
e Who would you pick to be in the team?

6 The median and range from a frequency table

Look at this table.
Writing it out in full will let us see the first, last and
middle terms:

$$0 \quad 0 \quad 0 \quad 1 \quad 1 \quad 1 \quad 1 \quad 1 \quad 2$$
$$2 \quad 2 \quad 2 \quad 2 \quad 2 \quad 2 \quad 3 \quad 3 \quad 4 \quad 4$$

... but this is very clumsy.

Score	Frequency
0	3
1	5
2	7
3	2
4	2

We can add a column to the table to give us a running total of frequencies, which is
very useful.

Score	Frequency	Running total	Notice
0	3	3	the last zero is 3rd in the list
1	5	... + 5 = 8	the last one is 8th in the list
2	7	... + 7 = 15	the last two is 15th in the list
3	2	... + 2 = 17	the last three is 17th in the list
4	2	... + 2 = 19	the last four is 19th in the list

You can tell from the table that the lowest score is 0 and the highest is 4.
The range = 4 − 0 = 4.

There are 19 scores (total of the frequencies), so the middle is the 10th score.
From the table we see that the 9th to the 15th scores are all twos, so the 10th score is 2.
The median is 2

Exercise 6.1

1 Find the median and range of each set of data.

a

Score	Frequency	Running total
3	1	1
8	3	4
9	5	9
11	5	
13	7	

b

Score	Frequency	Running total
5	4	4
10	0	4
15	6	10
20	8	
25	1	

c

Score	Frequency	Running total
1	2	
7	7	
11	3	
21	4	
27	3	

d

Score	Frequency	Running total
87	1	
89	3	
91	5	
94	9	
102	7	

e

Score	Frequency
3·5	10
3·7	8
4·2	5
4·9	3
5·6	1

f

Score	Frequency
324	17
325	25
326	30
327	12
328	4

g

Score	Frequency
1	18
7	6
19	2
97	6
908	3

2 Remember that when there is an even number of items, the median is the mean of the two middle terms. Find the median and range of these sets of data.

a

Score	Frequency
6	3
7	4
8	8
9	2
10	1

b

Score	Frequency
12	7
14	9
16	6
18	7
20	3

c

Score	Frequency
7	2
19	8
28	5
45	7
79	8

Exercise 6.2

1 Inspectors examine the taps in an old housing
scheme to see how many need replaced.
The table shows their findings from one street.
  a What is the range of the data set?
  b How many taps need replaced altogether?
  c What is the median number of taps that
    need replaced?
  d If the median is 3, the inspectors will return
    an *unsatisfactory* report; if 2 an *adequate*
    report; if less than 2, an *excellent* report.
    What kind of report is returned for this street?

Score	Frequency
0	3
1	5
2	4
3	5
4	4
5	2

2 In the tourist season,
the cable cars up the
mountain are busy.
A check is carried out
on the number of
passengers in each car.
  a How many cars
    were checked?
  b What is the range
    of the number of passengers per car?
  c Calculate the median number of passengers per car.
  d Is the median bigger or smaller than the mean number of passengers?

Passengers	Frequency
8	3
9	6
10	7
11	8
12	6

3 Bike enthusiasts were asked to award points out of 10 for two makes of bike,
the Trumps and the Reality. All the scores are shown below.

Trumps

Score	Frequency
6	0
7	0
8	12
9	9
10	3

Reality

Score	Frequency
6	2
7	3
8	5
9	8
10	2

  a i What was the lowest score awarded to the Trumps bike? (Be careful.)
   ii What was the range of scores awarded to the Trumps bike?
  b Calculate the range for the Reality.
  c Calculate the median score for each bike.
  d Compare the scoring by looking at:
   i the medians
   ii how variable the scoring was for each bike.

4 A beekeeper finds that his bees have been infested by a parasite.
He gives one of his hives a new treatment to test its effectiveness.
He takes a sample from the treated hive and one from an untreated hive.
He counts the parasites on each bee.

Without treatment

Parasites	Frequency
0	0
1	1
2	25
3	32
4	46

With treatment

Parasites	Frequency
0	28
1	26
2	18
3	1
4	0

a i What is the lowest number of parasites found in the untreated set?
  ii What is the range for this set?
b i What is the highest number of parasites found in the treated set?
  ii What is the range for this set?
c Calculate   **i** the median   **ii** the mean for both sets.
d Write a few sentences comparing the two sets of bees.

5 The table gives the heights of pupils in Peter's class, measured to the nearest 5 cm.

Height (cm)	135	140	145	150	155	160
Frequency	1	3	7	9	4	2

Peter himself is 155 cm tall.
a Calculate
  i the range of heights
  ii the median height
  iii the mean height.
b Describe Peter's height using these calculated figures.

6 April is traditionally the month for showers.
A local weather station has kept records of April's rain over several years.

Rainfall (mm)	36	37	38	39	40	41	42	43
Frequency	0	4	6	8	9	4	4	0

a For how many years has the rainfall been recorded?
b Calculate
  i the range
  ii the median
  iii the mean amount of rainfall.
c This year 41 mm of rain fell in April.
  Compare this with the average rain for this time of year.

7 Probability

We often want to know how likely an event is to happen, for example 'What are the chances it will rain today?', 'Am I likely to get a phone call today?', 'I've just bought a lottery ticket. What are the chances of winning?' … and so on.

In mathematics we work with a scale from 0 to 1.

> When something is impossible it has a probability of 0.
> When something is certain it has a probability of 1.

Everything else is in-between impossible and certain.

> When something is unlikely it might have a probability of 0·1 … 1 chance in 10.
> When something is very likely it might have a probability of 0·9 … 9 chances in 10.

In a situation where all outcomes are equally likely, the probability of an event happening can be calculated using the formula:

$$P(E) = \frac{\text{number of ways the event can occur}}{\text{number of possible outcomes}}$$

Example 1 I throw a dice. What are the chances of throwing a 3?

Number of threes on the dice = 1
Number of possible outcomes = 6
$P(3) = \frac{1}{6}$

Example 2 I take a card from a pack of playing cards.
What is the probability that it is an ace?

Number of aces in the pack = 4
Number of possible outcomes = 52
$P(\text{Ace}) = \frac{4}{52} = \frac{1}{13}$

Exercise 7.1

1 John has a two-headed coin.
  a What is the probability of a head, P(Head)?
  b What is the probability of a tail, P(Tail)?
  c On a normal coin, what is
    i P(Head)   **ii** P(Tail)?

2 When a normal dice is rolled calculate:
  a P(4)   **b** P(even number)
  c P(number bigger than 4)   **d** P(not 4)
  e P(not an even number)   **f** P(not a number bigger than 4)

3 Calculate for the spinner shown:

  a i   P(6)   **ii** P(not 6)

  b i   P(less than 4)   **ii** P(not less than 4)

  c i   P(divisible by 4)   **ii** P(not divisible by 4)

  d i   P(less than 10)   **ii** P(not less than 10)

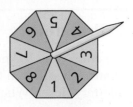

4 **a** What do you notice about the probability of something happening plus the probability of it not happening?

  b If the probability of it raining is $\frac{2}{5}$, what is the probability of it not raining?

  c The probability of getting a total of 6 when you throw two dice is $\frac{5}{36}$.
    What is the probability of not getting a total of 6?

5 Probabilities can be expressed as decimal fractions, for example $\frac{2}{5} = 2 \div 5 = 0\cdot4$.
  In a similar way, express the following probabilities as decimal fractions.
  If you pick a card from a normal pack, find:

  a the probability of picking a red card

  b the probability of picking a spade

  c the probability that it is not a heart.

6 Calculate, correct to 1 significant figure, the following:

  a P(2 of diamonds)

  b P(a heart less than 4)

  c P(anything but the king of spades)
    Assume the ace is 1.

7 Bashir dropped his pen and it struck one of the keys on his calculator at random. Calculate:

  a P(contains a digit)   **b** P(contains a letter)

  c P(contains a symbol)   **d** P(doesn't contain a number)

Exercise 7.2

1 A survey was done to find the favourite film among the pupils in a class.
  The table shows how the voting went.

Film	Frequency
Below the Sea	3
Astronuts	8
Coral Cowboy	6
The Frozen Sky	2
Double Data	1

  a How many voted altogether?

  b How many voted for *The Frozen Sky*?

  c What is the probability if one of the pupils is picked at random he or she will have voted for *The Frozen Sky*?

  d State the probability that the pupil will have voted:
     i   for *Below the Sea*
     ii for a film with two words in its title
     iii not for *Astronuts*.

2 The pupils in a class were asked how often they had visited the hairdresser last term.
The table gives the replies.

Visits	Frequency
1	5
2	6
3	15
4	3
5	1

  a **i**   How many were asked?
     ii How many said '2 times'?
     iii What is the probability that if one of the pupils is chosen at random they will have said '2 times'?
  b What is the probability that if someone from the class is chosen at random they will have said:
     i   4 times
     ii less than 3 times
     iii more than twice?

3 The table shows the responses to the question 'Do you still count on your fingers?'

Reply	Frequency
never	3
hardly ever	5
sometimes	8
often	2
always	2

  a How many people responded?
  b If one of these people is chosen at random what is the probability that they replied
     i   never
     ii not 'always'
     iii more than 'sometimes'?

4 In a word game, letters are mixed up in a bag and then pulled out to try and make words. The 'frequency' row tells us how many of each letter are in the bag.

Letter	A	B	C	D	E	F	G	H	I	J	K	L	M	N	O	P	Q	R	S	T	U	V	W	X	Y	Z
Frequency	9	2	2	4	12	2	3	2	9	1	1	4	2	6	8	2	1	6	4	6	4	2	2	1	2	1
Score	1	3	3	2	1	4	2	4	1	8	5	1	3	1	1	3	10	1	1	1	1	4	4	8	4	10

  a What is the probability that a letter chosen at random is
     i   A
     ii a vowel
     iii after T in the alphabet?
  b The 'score' row tells us what each letter is worth if you use it.
  What is the probability that a letter chosen at random is worth
     i   8 points
     ii 1 point
     iii 10 points?

◀◀ RECAP

When considering a list of values or scores it is useful to have an idea of the *average* score. There are three common averages:

- **the mean**   mean = sum of scores ÷ number of scores
- **the mode**   the most commonly occurring value or score
- **the median**   the score that splits the list into two smaller lists of equal length when the list is put in order.

If the list has an odd number of values, the median is the middle value
If the list has an even number of values, then it's the mean of the two middle values

To get an idea of how variable the values in a list are, or how spread out the list is, we can look at the **range**

The range = the highest mark minus the lowest mark

A frequency table can be used to find the mean and the mode.

Mean = total of scores ÷ number of scores
= 37 ÷ 25 = 1·48
Mode = 2 (by inspection … the score with the highest frequency)

Score	Frequency	Score × frequency
0	5	0
1	7	7
2	9	18
3	4	12
Totals	25	37

A frequency table can be used to find the median and the range.

Score	Frequency	Running total	Notice
0	3	3	the last zero is 3rd in the list
1	5	… + 5 = 8	the last one is 8th in the list
2	7	… + 7 = 15	the last two is 15th in the list
3	2	… + 2 = 17	the last three is 17th in the list
4	2	… + 2 = 19	the last four is 19th in the list

You can tell from the table that the lowest score is 0 and the highest is 4. The range = 4 − 0 = 4.
There are 19 scores so the 10th is the middle one.
The 9th to the 15th scores are all twos, so the 10th score is 2. The median is 2.

Where all outcomes are equally likely, the probability of an event happening can be calculated using the formula:

$$P(E) = \frac{\text{number of ways the event can occur}}{\text{number of possible outcomes}}$$

1 A dice is thrown ten times with these results: 1 2 1 3 5 3 4 6 3 4.
   a State the modal score.
   b Calculate the mean score.

2 The ages, in years, of the pupils on the school committee are:
       12   14   13   15   15   16   13   17   18   13   16.
   a Calculate **i** the range in ages   **ii** the median age.
   b A new member aged 11 years joins the committee.
       Calculate the new **i** range in ages   **ii** median age.

3 Sarah produced this table after counting the wheels on vehicles.
   (She saw 8 vehicles with 2 wheels.)
   a What is the mode?
   b State the range in the number of wheels.
   c Calculate the mean number of wheels to 1 d.p.

Wheels	Frequency
2	8
3	3
4	12
6	2
10	1

4 The temperature was recorded at noon over a few weeks.
   a Calculate the range in temperatures measured.
   b State the modal temperature.
   c Complete the third column to get a running total of the frequencies.
   d Work out the median temperature for the period.
   e On the 24th day the noon temperature was −1 °C.
       Compare that with the rest of the period.

Temp. °C	No. of days	Running total
−3	3	3
−2	2	5
−1	4	
0	5	
1	6	
2	2	
3	1	

5 Tess recorded the number of hours of sunshine daily for the first fortnight and the second fortnight in June.

1st fortnight

Hours of sunshine	5	6	7	8	9
Frequency	1	2	6	4	1

2nd fortnight

Hours of sunshine	5	6	7	8	9
Frequency	0	7	0	5	2

   a For each table calculate
      i   the mean
      ii   the median
      iii the range in temperatures.
   b Use these calculations to help you compare the two periods of time.

REVISE

6 a What is the probability that a month selected at random will start with a J?
   b What is the probability that a day selected at random in 2007 will be in February?
      Give your answer to 1 significant figure.

7 The table shows the distance pupils live from school.

Distance (miles)	0	1	2	3	4	5
Frequency	7	11	23	34	65	6

What is the probability that a pupil selected at random will be:
a 3 miles from school?
b more than 3 miles from school?

13 Chapter revision

Revising Chapter 1　Calculations and the calculator

1 Calculate these without the use of a calculator:
   a $5 + 4 \times 2$　　**b** $6 \times (3 + 1)$　　**c** $10 - 8 \div 4$　　　　**d** $\frac{1}{2}$ of $6 + 5$

2 Calculate these without using your calculator:
   a 5^2　　　　**b** 12^2　　　　**c** 2^3　　　　**d** 1^5　　　　**e** 3^4
   f $\sqrt{16}$　　　**g** $\sqrt{49}$　　　**h** $\sqrt{1}$　　　**i** $\sqrt{121}$　　**j** $\sqrt{196}$

3 Use the appropriate key on your calculator to help you calculate:
   a 17^2　　　　　　　　**b** $2 \cdot 6^2$　　　　　　　**c** $\sqrt{361}$
   d $\sqrt{7 \cdot 29}$　　　　　　**e** 16^3　　　　　　　　**f** 2^7

4 Use your fraction key to calculate:
   a $\frac{7}{8}$ of $144\,kg$　　**b** $\frac{3}{4} + \frac{1}{3}$　　　　**c** $4\frac{1}{2} - 2\frac{5}{8}$　　　　　**d** $\frac{2}{7} \times \frac{5}{8}$

5 Calculate the following, giving your answer to 1 decimal place where necessary:
   a $56 \div (25 - 18)$　　　　**b** $3 \cdot 2 \times (1 \cdot 4 + 0 \cdot 8)$　　　**c** $(13 + 26)^2$
   d $\dfrac{60}{18 \cdot 2 + 11 \cdot 8}$　　　　　**e** $\dfrac{19 - 6}{2 \times 4}$　　　　　　**f** $\sqrt{(19 \cdot 4 - 5 \cdot 3)}$

6 Write the numbers in scientific notation:
   a 3400　　　　　　　**b** $15\,000\,000$　　　　**c** $6\,000\,000\,000$
   d $0 \cdot 000\,23$　　　　　**e** $0 \cdot 009$　　　　　　**f** $0 \cdot 000\,000\,405$

7 Write these numbers in full:
   a 4×10^3　　　**b** $5 \cdot 6 \times 10^7$　　**c** $1 \cdot 4 \times 10^{-3}$　　**d** 3×10^{-5}

8 Anna and Ben were given £50 for the work they did for their neighbour.
They calculated that it should be shared in a ratio of 1 : 3, as this reflected the work each had done.
How much did　**a** Anna　　**b** Ben get?

9 To make light green paint, white and green paint are mixed in the ratio 4 : 1.
How much white paint is needed to make 20 litres of paint?

Remember to estimate, calculate and check!

10 Saida spent £24·99 on a jacket, £35·50 on winter boots and then she bought 2 tops at £11·49 each. How much would she have left out of £100?

11 Mhairi earns £23 448 per annum. How much does she earn in
   a month
   b a week (to the nearest penny)?

REVISE

12 Jars of face cream are sold in two sizes.
Compare the prices by working out the cost
per millilitre.
Which is the better buy?

Revising Chapter 2   Integers

1 Which of these are true and which are false?
a $-2 < -8$ **b** $7 < -3$ **c** $-1 > -2$ **d** $-2 > 0$ **e** $-7 < 0$

2 Write down the number that is:
a 5 bigger than -1 **b** 2 smaller than 0.

3 Arrange these numbers in order, smallest first: $7, 3, -7, -3, 0, -1$.

4 Calculate the following:
a $8 + (-2)$	**b** $-4 + 5$	**c** $-1 - 6$
d $5 + (-9)$	**e** -4×3	**f** $9 - (-2)$
g $-5 - (-3)$	**h** -4×4	**i** $-7 + (-1)$
j $6 \times (-9)$	**k** $5 \times (-8)$	**l** $-1 - (-1)$
m $-8 + (-3)$	**n** -5×7	**o** $3 - 8$

5 The sensors of a spacecraft located on the moon detected
a temperature of $-217\,°C$ at night and a temperature of
$134\,°C$ in the day.
Calculate the difference in temperature between night and
day on the moon.

6 Find the value of:
a $4 \times (-7) \times 5$ **b** $4 + (-8) - 1$ **c** $-3 - (-6) + (-5)$

7 A parallelogram has vertices A(-1, -1), B(-1, 2), C(3, 3) and D(3, 0).
a Plot the points and draw the parallelogram.
b All the coordinates are doubled so that, for example, C becomes (6, 6).
Find what happens to the other points.
c **i** Plot the new points and join them to make a new shape.
    ii What kind of shape is it?

8 A diver climbs down a ladder attached to the leg of an oil rig.
The rungs are 50 cm apart. He starts 10 rungs above sea level. One rung is at sea level.
a How many metres above sea level is he?
b Work out how much above sea level he is after going down
    i 8 rungs
    ii 12 rungs
    iii 15 rungs.
c At one point his depth gauge reads -23 metres.
On which rung is he standing?

9 Evaluate:
a $-2 + 5 \times 3$ **b** $9 - 9 \times (-1)$
c $(6 - (-3)) \times 4$ **d** $-6 \times 1 + 5 \times (-1)$

REVISE

Revising Chapter 3 Brackets and equations

1 Remove the brackets:

  a $3(x - 3)$ **b** $7(y + 5)$

  c $4(b + 4)$ **d** $3(f - 5)$

  e $7(v + 3)$ **f** $6(4 - y)$

  g $4(3 - x)$ **h** $4(e + f)$

  i $9(x - y)$ **j** $10(a - b)$

2 Multiply out the brackets:

  a $3(6m + 5)$ **b** $4(2k - 1)$

  c $3(7x + 2)$ **d** $5(2n + 6)$

  e $4(5y - 2)$ **f** $9(5e + 3)$

  g $9(3m - 4)$ **h** $2(9h + 1)$

  i $5(5x - 2)$ **j** $7(8m - 3)$

3 Multiply out the brackets and simplify the expression:

  a $4(n - 2) - 2n$ **b** $7 + 3(y + 2)$

  c $5(k + 3) - 5k$ **d** $3(q + 2) - 6$

  e $2(y - 1) + 2(y + 2)$ **f** $3(k + 2) + 5(k - 1)$

  g $3(x + y) + 5(x + y)$ **h** $4(2m + n) + 3(m - n)$

4 Solve these equations (remember to check your solutions):

  a $4y - 2 = 6$ **b** $23 = 7m + 2$

  c $8k - 3 = 53$ **d** $3n = n + 8$

  e $4a - 3 = a$ **f** $2x + 16 = 5x - 2$

  g $8y - 3 = 5y + 18$ **h** $12 - m = 5m - 6$

5 Make an equation, with brackets, and solve it to find the IN number:

  a 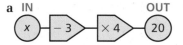   **b** 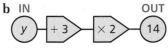   **c**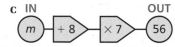

6 Solve these equations, showing each step of your working:

  a $3(x - 2) = 15$ **b** $6(y + 3) = 60$ **c** $7(m - 3) = 14$

  d $2(e - 1) + 2 = 10$ **e** $7 + 3(m + 7) = 34$ **f** $4(2y + 1) + 2 = 22$

7

> I think of a number.
> I add 12 to it then multiply by 3 to get 60.
> What's my number?

Write an equation and solve it to find the number.

8 Each pair of straws is the same length. All measurements are in centimetres.
In each case:

  i make an equation and solve it   **ii** calculate the length of the straws.

  a 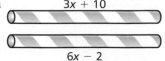   **b** 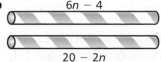   **c**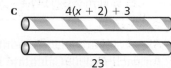

REVISE

Revising Chapter 4   Money

1 Calculate the selling price for each item:

a
> **BINOCULARS**
> *COST PRICE* £158
> *PROFIT* 25%

b
> **TELESCOPE**
> *COST PRICE* £486
> *PROFIT* 18%

c
> **TRIPOD**
> *COST PRICE* £74·80
> *PROFIT* 15%

2 Calculate
  i   the VAT at 17·5%
  ii the cost including VAT of each item, giving your answers correct to the nearest penny:

a
> *POCKET RADIO*
> £9·95 + VAT

b
> *SPEAKERS*
> £58·59 + VAT

c
> *SCANNER*
> £147·25 + VAT

d
> *CD REWRITER*
> £79·45 + VAT

3 Calculate entries A, B and C for this phone bill:

STATEMENT FOR 0011 888 9999	6 Apr – 5 Jul
Total cost of calls	£63·48
Line rental	£34·65
Total	A
VAT @ 17·5%	B
Total this period	C

4 Mr Spark's gas bill shows the following charges:
first 1250 units at 1·860p per unit; remaining 3720 units at 1·415p per unit.
Calculate, in pounds and pence, to the nearest penny:
  a the cost of   **i** the first 1250 units   **ii** the remaining units
  b the total cost.

5 Using £1 = 1·98 Swiss francs, convert:
  a i £5   **ii** £200 into Swiss francs
  b i 30 Swiss francs   **ii** 650 Swiss francs into pounds.

6 Keith's car insurance premium for the next year is
£954 before any no-claims discount.
He is due a 40% no-claims discount.
Calculate the amount he has to pay.

7 For the following items, calculate:
  i   the hire purchase price   **ii** the difference between the HP and the cash price.

a
> **PIANO**
> CASH PRICE *£560*
> or £80 deposit &
> 12 payments of £49·45

b
> **CAR**
> CASH PRICE *£7999*
> or 10% deposit &
> 36 instalments of £249·99

8 Simon insurances the contents of his flat for £12 000. The cost for one year is £2·85 for each £1000. Calculate his premium.

REVISE

Revising Chapter 5   Factors

1 List all the factors of:

   a 48   **b** 72   **c** 360.

2 List the common factors of 90 and 126.

3 List all the prime numbers between 20 and 50.

4 Find the prime factors of 4620.

5 Copy and complete to find the missing factor:

   a $45 = 5 \times \ldots$ **b** $56 = \ldots \times 7$

   c $ab = a \times \ldots$ **d** $3pq = 3q \times \ldots$

   e $4mn = 2n \times \ldots$ **f** $k^2 = k \times \ldots$

   g $3y^2 = 3y \times \ldots$ **h** $12ab = 4b \times \ldots$

6 Write each number or expression as a product of two factors in as many different ways as you can:

   a 16   **b** ef

   c n^2 **d** $9ab$

7 Factorise fully:

   a $7k - 14$ **b** $8n + 24$ **c** $50 - 10n$

   d $8 + 20xy$ **e** $18 - 24b$ **f** $12l - 18$

   g $24e + 16$ **h** $4ab + 6$ **i** $4 + 10x^2$

   j $2y^2 - 22$ **k** $16k - 24lm$ **l** $32xy + 18z$

8 Copy and complete the table.

Each pair of factors multiply to give the expression at the top.

	a	b	c
	$12pq$	$6x^2$	$12mn$
i	$3 \times \ldots$	$1 \times \ldots$	$2 \times \ldots$
ii	$4q \times \ldots$	$3 \times \ldots$	$3n \times \ldots$
iii	$12pq \times \ldots$	$x \times \ldots$	$12 \times \ldots$
iv	$2q \times \ldots$	$2x \times \ldots$	$mn \times \ldots$

Revising Chapter 6   Statistics – charts and tables

1 A cafeteria keeps a note of the different flavours of chocolate biscuits it sells.

   mint   mint   mint   mint   mint

   coffee   orange   orange   mint   orange

   mint   mint   mint   mint   mint

   toffee   coffee   orange   mint   mint

   mint   orange   orange   mint   coffee

   a Use a frequency table to help you sort out the data.

   b Which flavour was requested **i** most often   **ii** least often?

REVISE

2 Pupils on a nature trail had the opportunity to see a variety of things.
  After the walk each was asked to say what impressed them most.
  The frequency table records the responses.
  a How many pupils in total went on the trail?
  b What fraction voted for
    i magpies ii the badger's set?
  c Draw a pie chart to illustrate the findings.

Sight	Frequency
Ant's nest	14
Badger's set	36
Heron	25
Magpies	15

3 The shelves in a supermarket were inspected.
  Twelve batches of cans were examined.
  The number of days past the 'best before' date were noted.
  The table shows the number of cans in each category.
  For example, batch 1 was made up of five cans
  4 days past their 'best before' date.

Batch No.	1	2	3	4	5	6	7	8	9	10	11	12
Days past	4	4	3	2	8	7	2	9	5	1	10	5
No. of cans	5	4	5	7	2	1	5	1	3	6	1	4

  a Make a scatter diagram from the data to show the relation between 'Days past' (use *x* axis) and 'No. of cans' (use *y* axis).
  b Describe the relation in words.
  c Draw a line of best fit.
  d Estimate how many cans are 6 days past their 'best before' date.

4 Twenty people were asked to count the number of coins they had in their pockets.
  The table gives the responses.
  a Make a stem-and-leaf diagram to help you sort the list.
  b 10s, 20s, 30s, 40s, 50s … which of these was the most common response?

30	20	24	38
41	35	19	46
23	17	41	30
42	27	38	52
34	40	31	23

Revising Chapter 7   Proportion and variation

1 Gerry buys six disposable barbeques for £10·50.
  How much would eight cost?

2 Janice arranges 20 pots each with three hyacinth bulbs.
  She rearranges them so that there are four bulbs in each pot.
  How many pots of bulbs are there now?

3 There are 32 g of fat in each 100 g of Peter's sausages.
  He eats 180 g of sausages for lunch.
  Calculate the weight of fat in his sausages.

REVISE

4 This is Jane's recipe to make six jam tarts:

> 100 g plain flour
> 50 g margarine
> 20 ml water
> 80 g jam

How much of each ingredient is needed to make 15 jam tarts?

5 Chris cleans carpets. A 20 m² carpet takes him 30 minutes.
  a How long would it take him to clean a 42 m² carpet?
  b Calculate the size of a carpet which takes him 72 minutes to clean.

6 $H \propto t$. When $H = 7 \cdot 2$, $t = 6$.
  a Find a formula for H in terms of t.   **b** Calculate H when $t = 9$.

7 The total time (T min) taken to serve pupils in a school canteen varies directly with the number of pupils (n).
200 pupils are served in 40 minutes.
  a Find a formula for T in terms of n.   **b** Calculate T when $n = 280$.

8 The table shows the annual interest earned at Western Bank.

Money deposited (£D)	100	200	300	400	500
Interest (£I)	4	8	12	16	20

  a Draw a graph to illustrate the table.
  b Explain how the graph shows that the interest varies directly as the money deposited.
  c Find a formula for I in terms of D.
  d Dawn invests £320 for a year. How much interest does she receive?

Revising Chapter 8   Pythagoras

1 Without actually doing the calculation, are these statements true or false?
  a The hypotenuse is close to 11 cm.
  b The hypotenuse is close to 15 cm.
  c The hypotenuse is close to 23 cm.
  d The hypotenuse is close to 7 cm.

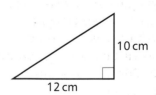

Work to 1 d.p. in questions **2**–**4**.

2 Calculate the missing lengths in these right-angled triangles.
All measurements are in centimetres.

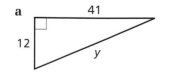
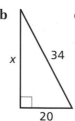
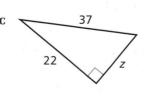
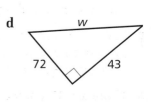

3 Calculate the height of the frame
  for these swings.

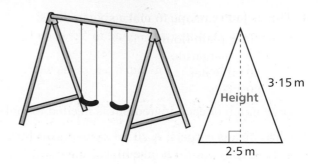

Height   3·15 m

2·5 m

4 Calculate the length of the sloping
  edge of this grit box.

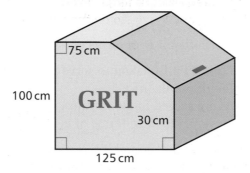

75 cm

100 cm   GRIT

30 cm

125 cm

REVISE

Revising Chapter 9   Time, distance and speed

1 a Calculate the average speed of a journey of 108 miles which takes 4 hours.
   b How long does it take to travel 360 km at an average speed of 60 km/h?
   c How far does a plane fly in 7 hours at 430 km/h?
   d A runner averages a speed of 8 m/s. How far would he run in 20 seconds?

2 The timetable shows the times a bus arrives at each destination and the distances
   between the towns.
   a Calculate the average speeds for
      each of the three parts of the journey.
   b i   How long did the whole journey
          from Fleetwood to Newcroft take?
      ii How far is it from Fleetwood to
          Newcroft?
      iii Calculate the average speed for the whole journey.
          Give your answer to the nearest whole number.

Town	Time	Distance
Fleetwood	23:30	72 km
Harrow	01:00	104 km
Drymen	03:00	95 km
Newcroft	05:30	

3 Sarah ran a half-marathon, 13 miles, at an average speed of 5·2 miles per hour.
   How long, in hours and minutes, did it take her?

4 Tessa set out from home at 10 45 to drive to her boyfriend's house 90 kilometres
   away.
   She arrived at his house at 12 15.
   a How long did her journey take?
   b Calculate her average speed for the journey.
   c On the way home she averaged 72 km/h.
      If she left at 16 50, when would she arrive home?

5 a How far is it from Teviot to Newmills?

b Calculate the average speed of the direct bus.

c i At what time did the buses pass each other?

   ii How far from Teviot were they then?

d i For how long did the tourer bus stop?

   ii How far had it gone when it stopped?

e Calculate the average speed of the tourer bus on the last part of its journey.

f Which bus took longer to do the journey and by how much?

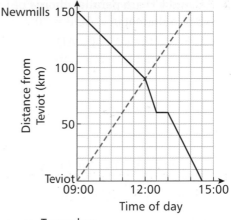

— Tourer bus
---- Direct bus

6 Selina walked from home to the library and back. On the way there she met a friend and stopped for a chat.

a How far is it between Selina's house and the library?

b When did Selina

   i leave home

   ii arrive at the library

   iii arrive back home?

c How long did she stay at the library?

d i When did she meet her friend?

   ii For how long did they stop and talk?

e Calculate her average speed on the way home.

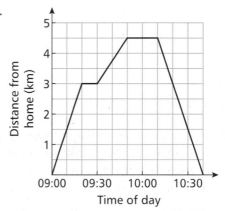

Revising Chapter 10   Angles and circles

1 Calculate the size of each lettered angle.
Give reasons for your steps.

a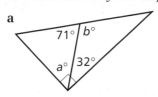

b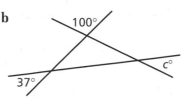

c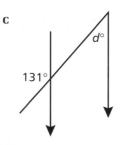

d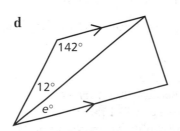

e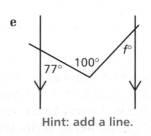

Hint: add a line.

REVISE

2 AB and CD are parallel chords of the circle, centre O.
AD is a diameter. ∠AOB = 70°.

Calculate the size of ∠ADC.
Give reasons for your steps.

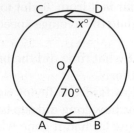

3 AB is a diameter to the circle, centre O.
SAT is a tangent.
∠SAD = 21°. ∠ATO = 40°.
Calculate:
  a ∠DBA
  b ∠DBC.

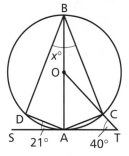

4 A watch is represented by a circle set in a rhombus.
The circle, centre O, has a radius OT of 10 mm.
The sides of the rhombus form tangents to the circle.
PO = 12 mm and TS = 17 mm.
Calculate (to 1 d.p.):
  a the length of OS
  b the length of PT
  c the perimeter of the rhombus.

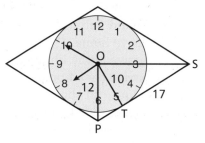

Revising Chapter 11   Angles and triangles

1 Use a protractor to find the 3-figure bearing of each plane from the airport.

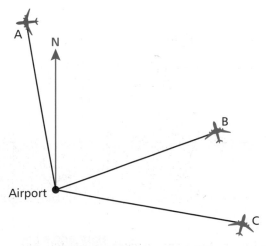

REVISE

2 An aircraft at a point P picks up a radio signal coming from an airport on a bearing of 050°.
It then flies due east for 10 km to a point Q.
It picks the signal up again on a bearing of 300°.
   a Make a scale drawing, letting 1 cm represent 1 km.
   b Use a protractor to help you pinpoint the airport on your drawing.
   c Use your diagram to help you measure how close the plane got to the airport.

3 A piano is 2·3 m wide.
The lid is being held up by a support CB which is 1·15 m long.
The support meets the lid at right angles.

Calculate the angle through which the lid has been lifted (∠BAC).

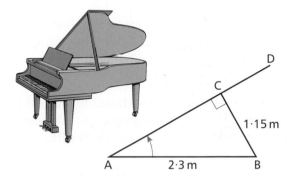

4 A submarine starts to dive at P.
After a kilometre it reaches a depth of 140 m.
Calculate the angle, $a°$, of the dive.
(Be careful with units.)

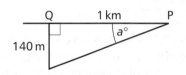

5 Triangle ABC is right-angled at C.
The hypotenuse is 24 cm long.
∠CAB = 37°.
Calculate the perimeter of the triangle, correct to 1 d.p.

Revising Chapter 12   More statistics

1 Over two working weeks Harry was late every day.
The number of minutes late was recorded:

   2, 5, 3, 2, 2, 4, 2, 3, 5, 5.

   a State the mode number of minutes late.
   b Calculate the mean number of minutes late, correct to 1 d.p.

2 Along the banks of Loch Ness, watchers keep a look-out for Nessie.
A group were asked their age.
The following are the replies:

   18, 18, 19, 20, 21, 21, 23, 25, 26, 26, 27, 28, 28.

   a What is the range in ages?
   b State the median age.
   c It was found that these were a group of students and their teacher joined them.
   He was 54 years old.
   Calculate the range in ages and the median of the group including the teacher.

REVISE

3 Pupils were asked: 'How many days last week did you have a school lunch?'
The table shows the responses.

No. of days	Frequency	Running total
0	3	3
1	5	8
2	5	13
3	7	
4	3	
5	1	

  a What is the range of possible responses?
  b What was the modal response?
  c Complete the running total of frequencies column and use it to find the median response.
  d In another school six people had school lunches on 3 days that week. How does that compare with the figures for this school?

4 The results of an experiment to study the effects of fertiliser are shown.
The tables show the lengths (in centimetres) of flowers not fed the fertiliser and a sample that had been fed the fertiliser.

Without fertiliser

Length	3	4	5	6	7
Frequency	1	2	3	3	4

With fertiliser

Length	3	4	5	6	7
Frequency	0	3	4	6	2

  a Find the mean and range of both samples.
  b Use your answers to help you write a few sentences comparing the samples.
  c If a flower from the sample fed fertiliser is picked at random, what is the probability that it is 4 cm long?

5 a What is the probability that a number picked at random
   i   from 1 to 10 is prime
   ii from 1 to 20 is prime
   iii from 1 to 50 is prime?
  b Would you say that it is more likely or less likely to get a prime when you pick from a bigger range of numbers?

REVISE

Answers

1 Calculations and the calculator

Page 1 Exercise 1.1

1 a 857   **b** 1081   **c** 145   **d** 1238
 e 2430   **f** 2367   **g** 122   **h** 562
 i 110   **j** 240   **k** 1500   **l** 8000
 m 3   **n** 35 000   **o** 10

2 a 9·9   **b** 24·4   **c** 25·85   **d** 3·2
 e 4·6   **f** 5·9   **g** 13·2   **h** 4·5
 i 277·2   **j** 3·7   **k** 2·06   **l** 1·59
 m £1·25   **n** 115 m

3 a 133·3   **b** 78·2   **c** 997·5   **d** 2278
 e 184   **f** 543

4 a i 80   **ii** 30   **iii** 70
   iv 180   **v** 470
 b i 500   **ii** 800   **iii** 1300
   iv 5600   **v** 10 900
 c i 5   **ii** 8   **iii** 14
   iv 3   **v** 1

5

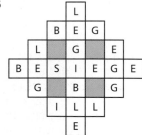

Page 3 Exercise 2.1

1 a 8·3   **b** 12·3   **c** 8·0

2 a 4·3   **b** 7·8   **c** 11·5
 d 0·9   **e** 9·0   **f** 4·0
 g 6·8 s   **h** 24·5 cm   **i** 52·7 litres
 j 0·4 kg   **k** 43·1 m

3 a 8·149   **b** 14·55

4 a i 5·4   **ii** 5·37
 b i 3·1   **ii** 3·14
 c i 28·1   **ii** 28·08

5 a 1·57   **b** 6·05   **c** 21·29
 d 403·20   **e** 0·75   **f** 13·99

6 a £4·72   **b** £16·55   **c** £29·97
 d £344·52   **e** £100·07   **f** £0·05
 g £33·33

7 a £50·71   **b** pupil's check

8 a 0·33   **b** 46·03   **c** 7·44
 d 5·36   **e** 7·69

9 a To round to three decimal places: look at the
   digit in the fourth decimal place; if it is 4 or
   less then round down otherwise round up
 b i 3·715   **ii** 78·190   **iii** 0·050
   iv 0·092   **v** 0·250

Page 4 Exercise 2.2

1 a 40   **b** 80   **c** 100   **d** 400
 e 2000   **f** 5   **g** 0·8   **h** 0·006

2 a 370   **b** 520   **c** 450   **d** 4400
 e 9·8   **f** 57   **g** 0·13   **h** 0·60
 i 0·042   **j** 0·071   **k** 0·0084   **l** 0·060
 m 50   **n** 0·000 46   **o** 1·0   **p** 0·70
 q 0·010   **r** 150   **s** 9·7

3 a 40 kg   **b** 9 cm   **c** 300 min
 d 0·7 litre   **e** £2000   **f** 0·08 g
 g 0·009 mm   **h** 0·01 s   **i** 0·7 m²
 j 500 kg

4 a 80 000   **b** 84 000   **c** 84 300   **d** 84 290

5 a 1·1   **b** 0·079   **c** 23   **d** 0·20
 e 0·16   **f** £0·42   **g** 2·6   **h** 0·091

Page 5 Exercise 3.1

1 a iii   **b** ii   **c** iii   **d** i

2 a i estimate   **ii** 1   **iii** 81
 b i estimate   **ii** 9   **iii** 149
 c i estimate   **ii** 0   **iii** 420
 d i estimate   **ii** 6   **iii** 26
 e i estimate   **ii** 6   **iii** 526
 f i estimate   **ii** 6   **iii** 81·6
 g i estimate   **ii** 8   **iii** 53·8
 h i estimate   **ii** 2   **iii** 98·2
 i i estimate   **ii** 7   **iii** 3·27

3 a £48·18   **b** 89·9 cm   **c** £481·68

4 £17 131·50

5 a 1350   **b** 12

6 a 30·9 cm²   **b** 16·3 cm²   **c** 46·0 cm²

7 £394· 72

8 a $381·60   **b** £53·46

9 a £135·50   **b** £84·54

10 a 22·4   **b** 32·4   **c** 1·7

Page 7 Exercise 3.2

1 a yes   **b** no   **c** yes

2 15·2p per km

3 135p

4 a estimates

   b i 47p   **ii** £1·88   **iii** £5·64

   c 851

5 a £0·012 32

   b £0·011 31

   c larger tube is cheaper per ml so is a better buy

6 a small   **b** large   **c** medium

Page 8 Exercise 4·1

1 a 20	**b** 14	**c** 41	**d** 18
e 8	**f** 52	**g** 21	**h** 11
i 21	**j** 16	**k** 32	**l** 8
m 16	**n** 20	**o** 54	**p** 49
q 55	**r** 7	**s** 13	**t** 5
u 15	**v** 80	**w** 60	**x** 10

2 calculator exploration

Page 9 Exercise 5.1

1 a 9	**b** 49	**c** 1	**d** 64
e 100	**f** 169	**g** 289	**h** 625
i 70·56	**j** 11449	**k** 0·16	**l** 15·21
2 a 25	**b** 314	**c** 15·65	**d** 49
e 105	**f** 30·45	**g** 175	**h** 2
i 36	**j** 143		
3 a 5	**b** 6	**c** 2	**d** 9
e 1	**f** 12	**g** 37	**h** 16
i 66	**j** 105	**k** 3·4	**l** 0·4
m 5·63			
4 a 6·16	**b** 7·68	**c** 8·89	**d** 23·54
e 0·92	**f** 0·26		

5 a 2209 cm^2 **b** 2970·25 cm^2 **c** 10 816 cm^2

6 a 6 cm   **b** 17 cm   **c** 1·4 m   **d** 0·8 m

7 a 27	**b** 16	**c** 1
d 3125	**e** 49	**f** 81
g 343	**h** 128	**i** 14 641
j 1 000 000	**k** 1 860 867	**l** 0·000 064
8 a 3^5	**b** 3^2	**c** 3^4
d 2^4	**e** $\sqrt{2\cdot25}$	**f** 21^2

9 a 1728 cm^3 **b** 12 167 cm^3

   c 19 683 mm^3 **d** 1·728 m^3

Page 11 Exercise 6.1

1 a 4	**b** 25·01	**c** 47·6	**d** 529
e 3249	**f** 2000·376	**g** 25	**h** 0·22
i 2	**j** 5·184		
2 a 10	**b** 15	**c** 13	**d** 2·5

3 a i 15·7   **ii** 7·32

   iii 22·42   **iv** 41·28

   b i 15·8   **ii** 21·84

   iii −11·5   **iv** 4·32

4 1, 3, 5, 7

5 a i €32·46   **ii** €105·50

   iii €740·09   **iv** €1175·05

   b i £18·48   **ii** £3080·71

   iii £240·91   **iv** £545·29

c i £4·49   **ii** £12·82   **iii** £48·08

   iv £96·15   **v** £4346·15

Page 12 Exercise 7·1

1 a £7·30	**b** £34·20	**c** 56 m	**d** £49·50
e 29 t	**f** £74·25	**g** £3·23	**h** £665
2 a $\frac{14}{3}$	**b** $\frac{5}{4}$	**c** $\frac{13}{5}$	
d $\frac{7}{2}$	**e** $\frac{61}{8}$	**f** $\frac{29}{6}$	
3 a $5\frac{2}{3}$	**b** $3\frac{1}{9}$	**c** $5\frac{1}{6}$	
d $10\frac{3}{5}$	**e** $1\frac{3}{8}$	**f** $1\frac{5}{12}$	
4 a $\frac{3}{4}$	**b** $\frac{1}{4}$	**c** $\frac{5}{6}$	**d** $\frac{1}{2}$
e $\frac{1}{9}$	**f** $\frac{3}{8}$	**g** $1\frac{5}{8}$	**h** $1\frac{7}{8}$
i $\frac{9}{20}$	**j** $7\frac{7}{24}$	**k** $6\frac{19}{35}$	**l** $2\frac{7}{30}$
m $\frac{3}{20}$	**n** $\frac{1}{14}$	**o** $\frac{4}{33}$	**p** $3\frac{1}{2}$

5 a $12\frac{11}{12}$ m   **b** $2\frac{1}{4}$ m

Page 13 Exercise 7.2

1 Tom £100, Sarah £400

2 a 120 g, 20 g   **b** 7 m, 49 m

   c 360 t, 90 t   **d** 900 s, 7200 s

   e 70 ml, 14 ml   **f** 250 g, 750 g

   g 120 mm, 1200 mm   **h** 300 days, 25 days

3 sand 270 kg, cement 90 kg

4 6 hours sleep, 18 hours work

5 a 550 ml   **b** 90 ml

6 a i £120, £240   **ii** £90, £270   **iii** £72, £288

   iv £60, £300   **v** £180, £180

   b i 1:1   **ii** 1:5

Page 15 Exercise 8.1

1 a 6×10^2	**b** 6×10^3	**c** 6×10^4
d 6×10^5	**e** 6×10^8	**f** 2×10^2
g 9×10^1	**h** 4×10^3	**i** 5×10^5
j 1×10^8	**k** $3\cdot2 \times 10^2$	**l** $5\cdot8 \times 10^3$
m $9\cdot13 \times 10^3$	**n** $6\cdot45 \times 10^5$	**o** $8\cdot7 \times 10^4$
p $2\cdot43 \times 10^3$	**q** $4\cdot6 \times 10^1$	**r** $4\cdot55 \times 10^5$
s $3\cdot01 \times 10^5$	**t** $1\cdot764 \times 10^{11}$	**u** $7\cdot92 \times 10^1$
v $8\cdot14 \times 10^1$	**w** $6\cdot15 \times 10^0$	**x** $9\cdot04 \times 10^0$
y $1\cdot0445 \times 10^2$		
2 a 2×10^3	**b** $3\cdot65 \times 10^2$	**c** $1\cdot75 \times 10^4$
d $1\cdot27 \times 10^4$	**e** $4\cdot42 \times 10^8$	
3 a $1\cdot69 \times 10^8$	**b** 3×10^{10}	**c** $5\cdot98 \times 10^{24}$
d $1\cdot49 \times 10^8$	**e** $8\cdot22 \times 10^8$	
4 a 4000	**b** 5 000 000	**c** 200 000
d 40 000	**e** 4200	**f** 67 000
g 580	**h** 8 900 000	**i** 1250
j 904 000	**k** 655	
l 235 700 000	**m** 2·18	**n** 61
o 4·11	**p** 71·7	

5 a $6\cdot5 \times 10^{14}$ **b** pupil's own answer

6 a $3\cdot33 \times 10^{12}$; 3 330 000 000 000

   b $5\cdot265 \times 10^{11}$; 526 500 000 000

   c $4\cdot201868 \times 10^{10}$; 42 018 680 000

   d $2\cdot0 \times 10^8$; 199 999 998

7 a $£1\cdot53 \times 10^{10}$ **b** £15 300 000 000

8 a $3 \cdot 1536 \times 10^{10}$

   b $4 \cdot 415 \times 10^8$ for age 14; $4 \cdot 0997 \times 10^8$ for age 13

9 a $132\,000\,000\,\text{ft}$ **b** $2 \cdot 64 \times 10^{10}$

   c $26\,400\,000\,000$

Page 16 Investigation 1

1 a i $1\,999\,998$ **ii** $2\,999\,997$ **iii** $3\,999\,996$

   b i $4\,999\,995$ **ii** $8\,999\,991$

2 a i 121 **ii** $12\,321$ **iii** $1\,234\,321$

   b i $123\,454\,321$ **ii** $12\,345\,654\,321$

3 a i 81 **ii** 9801

   iii $998\,001$ **iv** $99\,980\,001$

   b i $9\,999\,800\,001$ **ii** $999\,998\,000\,001$

Page 16 Investigation 2

1 a $7\,000\,000$ **b** 5000 **c** $80\,000$ **d** 300

   e $8 \cdot 1$ **f** 63 **g** $7\,010\,000$

   h $13\,100\,000$

2 $0 \cdot 561$ is not between 1 and 10. Yes, it is $56\,100$.

Page 17 Exercise 8.2

1 a 5×10^{-2} **b** 7×10^{-3} **c** 2×10^{-5}

   d 1×10^{-2} **e** 9×10^{-1} **f** $5 \cdot 3 \times 10^{-2}$

   g $4 \cdot 3 \times 10^{-2}$ **h** $2 \cdot 5 \times 10^{-2}$ **i** $3 \cdot 1 \times 10^{-5}$

   j $6 \cdot 9 \times 10^{-3}$ **k** $3 \cdot 56 \times 10^{-2}$ **l** $1 \cdot 74 \times 10^{-3}$

   m $8 \cdot 62 \times 10^{-5}$ **n** $3 \cdot 333 \times 10^{-1}$ **o** $5 \cdot 5 \times 10^{-12}$

2 a $1 \cdot 13 \times 10^{-1}$ **b** 8×10^{-7}

   c $9 \cdot 11 \times 10^{-31}\,\text{kg}$

3 a $2 \cdot 8 \times 10^{-4}$ **b** $1 \cdot 9 \times 10^{-6}$

   c 1×10^{-6} **d** $1 \cdot 64 \times 10^{-24}$

4 a $0 \cdot 002$ **b** $0 \cdot 0005$ **c** $0 \cdot 06$

   d $0 \cdot 3$ **e** $0 \cdot 000\,86$ **f** $0 \cdot 002\,32$

   g $0 \cdot 000\,047$ **h** $0 \cdot 000\,000\,006\,67$

5 a $7 \cdot 5 \times 10^{-9}$, $0 \cdot 000\,000\,007\,5$

   b $2 \cdot 5 \times 10^{-11}$, $0 \cdot 000\,000\,000\,025$

   c $1 \cdot 296 \times 10^{-11}$, $0 \cdot 000\,000\,000\,012\,96$

   d $2 \cdot 46 \times 10^{-9}$, $0 \cdot 000\,000\,002\,46$

   e $1 \cdot 28 \times 10^{-8}$, $0 \cdot 000\,000\,012\,8$

   f 1×10^{-9}, $0 \cdot 000\,000\,001$

6 14 days

Page 19 Revise

1 a 17 **b** 8 **c** 4 **d** 2

2 a 9 **b** $67 \cdot 24$ **c** 16

   d $29 \cdot 791$ **e** $0 \cdot 7$ **f** $1 \cdot 1$

3 a i $3 \cdot 9$ **ii** $8 \cdot 6$ **iii** $1 \cdot 3$

   iv $345 \cdot 6$ **v** $2 \cdot 5$ **vi** $4 \cdot 3$

   b i $7 \cdot 35$ **ii** $35 \cdot 05$ **iii** $0 \cdot 88$

   iv $0 \cdot 05$ **v** $0 \cdot 01$

   c i 100 **ii** 5000

   iii 5 **iv** $0 \cdot 02$

   d i 370 **ii** 4100

   iii $4 \cdot 0$ **iv** $0 \cdot 0071$

   e i £$3 \cdot 50$ **ii** $5 \cdot 0\,\text{g}$ **iii** $1 \cdot 9$

4 a ii 0 **iii** 690

   b ii 1 **iii** 471

   c ii 2 **iii** 1222

   d ii difficult to tell   **iii** 49

5 a $13 \cdot 56$ **b** $33 \cdot 64$ **c** 16 **d** $20\,736$

   e $5 \cdot 2052$ **f** $2 \cdot 8224$ **g** 41 **h** $22 \cdot 04$

   i $60 \cdot 041$

6 a £357 **b** £$24 \cdot 58$

7 a $\$15 \cdot 30$ **b** $\$82 \cdot 62$ **c** $\$1836$ **d** $\$19 \cdot 28$

8 a i $2\frac{5}{7}$ **ii** $12\frac{1}{2}$ **iii** $3\frac{9}{10}$

   b i $\frac{16}{5}$ **ii** $\frac{9}{7}$ **iii** $\frac{47}{11}$

   c i 12 **ii** 10 **iii** 21

   iv $\frac{31}{40}$ **v** $2\frac{1}{8}$ **vi** $\frac{1}{4}$

9 a £192 , £24

   b mint extract 7 ml, mashed potato 140 ml

10 a i $1 \cdot 2 \times 10^3$ **ii** 4×10^1 **iii** $3 \cdot 05 \times 10^8$

   iv $3 \cdot 4 \times 10^{-3}$ **v** 8×10^{-3}

   b i $1\,500\,000$ **ii** $0 \cdot 0056$

   iii $0 \cdot 000\,09$ **iv** $3 \cdot 7$

2 Integers

Page 21 Exercise 1.1

1 a Dundee $-7\,^\circ\text{C}$, Edinburgh $-6\,^\circ\text{C}$,

   Aberdeen $-5\,^\circ\text{C}$, Glasgow $-4\,^\circ\text{C}$,

   Lerwick $-2\,^\circ\text{C}$, Ayr $-1\,^\circ\text{C}$, Belfast $0\,^\circ\text{C}$,

   London $1\,^\circ\text{C}$, Dover $2\,^\circ\text{C}$, Liverpool $3\,^\circ\text{C}$,

   Cardiff $4\,^\circ\text{C}$, Plymouth $5\,^\circ\text{C}$

   b 6° **c** 3° **d** 12°

2 a Bruce $(0, 0)$, Vine $(1, 2)$, Kirn $(6, 3)$,

   Don $(-2, 4)$, Col $(-6, 2)$, Ruby $(-3, -3)$,

   Grace $(-9, -2)$, Fern $(4, -3)$, Holly $(5, -2)$

   b Bruce $(-1, -2)$, Vine $(0, 0)$, Kirn $(5, 1)$,

   Don $(-3, 2)$, Col $(-7, 0)$, Ruby $(-4, -5)$,

   Grace $(-10, -4)$, Fern $(3 , -5)$, Holly $(4, -4)$

3 a $8000\,\text{m}$ **b** $3500\,\text{m}$ **c** $8000\,\text{m}$

   d $5500\,\text{m}$ **e** $1500\,\text{m}$

   f i $20\,000\,\text{m}$ **ii** $8500\,\text{m}$

   iii $6500\,\text{m}$ **iv** $1500\,\text{m}$

4 a 7 months   **b** 5 months

   c an overall profit of £$26\,000$

Page 23 Exercise 2.1

1 a $5 > 3$ **b** $0 < 4$ **c** $3 > -4$

   d $6 > -2$ **e** $-3 > -6$ **f** $-2 > -5$

   g $-6 < -5$ **h** $-4 < 0$ **i** $0 > -1$

   j $-1 > -9$

2 a $-2, -1, 0, 3$ **b** $-3, -2, -1, 1$

   c $-6, -2, 1, 3$ **d** $-4, -1, 2, 5$

   e $-4, -3, -1, 3$ **f** $-6, -2, 4, 7$

3 a 8 **b** -5 **c** -2 **d** -7 **e** 0

4 a 4 **b** -2 **c** -8 **d** -1 **e** -4

5 a 5 **b** 8 **c** -1 **d** -2

   e -2 **f** 2 **g** -7 **h** -3

6 Moscow $-1\,^\circ\text{C}$, Anchorage $-3\,^\circ\text{C}$, Ontario $2\,^\circ\text{C}$,

   Godthab $1\,^\circ\text{C}$, Helsinki $5\,^\circ\text{C}$

7 $A(-5, -1)$, $B(-1, -1)$, $C(-1, 3)$, $D(-5, 3)$

Page 24 Challenge

$=\text{INT}(-4 \cdot 3)$ gives -5

Page 25 Exercise 3.1

1 a 2 **b** 3 **c** 4 **d** -3
e 0 **f** -1 **g** -3 **h** 4
i -3 **j** 1 **k** -1 **l** -4
m -3 **n** -6 **o** 0

2 a 2 **b** 2 **c** 5 **d** -3
e 1 **f** -5 **g** -6 **h** -6
i -9 **j** -7 **k** -9 **l** -2
m -9 **n** -6 **o** -9

3 a i 18, 22, 26 **ii** 4
b i 9, 6, 3 **ii** -3
c i 30, 25, 20 **ii** -5
d i $-1, 0, 1$ **ii** 1
e i $-1, -3, -5$ **ii** -2
f i $-3, -6, -9$ **ii** -3
g i 0, 5, 10 **ii** 5
h i 2, 5, 8 **ii** 3
i i 0, 2, 4 **ii** 2
j i $-3, -8, -13$ **ii** 5

4 a -2 **b** -4

5 a i 2 **ii** 2
b i 4 **ii** 4
c i 2 **ii** 2
d i 4 **ii** 4
e i 0 **ii** 0
f i 2 **ii** 2

Each pair of answers is the same.

Page 26 Exercise 4.1

1 a/b

−	−5	−4	−3	−2	−1	0	1	2	3	4	5
5	10	9	8	7	6	5	4	3	2	1	0
4	9	8	7	6	5	4	3	2	1	0	−1
3	8	7	6	5	4	3	2	1	0	−1	−2
2	7	6	5	4	3	2	1	0	−1	−2	−3
1	6	5	4	3	2	1	0	−1	−2	−3	−4
0	5	4	3	2	1	0	−1	−2	−3	−4	−5
−1	4	3	2	1	0	−1	−2	−3	−4	−5	−6
−2	3	2	1	0	−1	−2	−3	−4	−5	−6	−7
−3	2	1	0	−1	−2	−3	−4	−5	−6	−7	−8
−4	1	0	−1	−2	−3	−4	−5	−6	−7	−8	−9
−5	0	−1	−2	−3	−4	−5	−6	−7	−8	−9	−10

2 a 6 **b** 7 **c** 7
d 5 **e** 4 **f** -2
g -2 **h** 4 **i** -3
j -5 **k** -7 **l** 2
m 1 **n** -1 **o** 0

3 a i 3 **ii** 3
b i -1 **ii** -1
c i -2 **ii** -2
d i -4 **ii** -4
e i -4 **ii** -4
f i -7 **ii** -7
g i 1 **ii** 1
h i -3 **ii** -3

Page 27 Exercise 4.2

1 a -1 **b** -2 **c** -4 **d** -2
e -4 **f** -8 **g** -5 **h** -4
i -10 **j** -3 **k** 4 **l** 7
m 5 **n** 4 **o** 3 **p** 1
q 2 **r** 3 **s** -1 **t** -4

2 a -2 **b** 5 **c** -6 **d** -5
e 0 **f** 8 **g** -5 **h** -7
i 6 **j** 0 **k** -7 **l** 1
m -5 **n** 15 **o** -10

3 a $(6, 2)$ **b** $(-3, 0)$ **c** $(-1, -2)$
d $(1, -3)$ **e** $(3, -6)$

4 Moscow 10 °C, Oslo -5 °C, Calgary 2 °C,
Bergen -2 °C, Anchorage -8 °C, Stanley -3 °C,
Hobart -1 °C, Dunedin -1 °C

5 a profit of £1000

6 a 4 **b** -7

7 a i 274 °C **ii** 606 °C
b i 32 °C **ii** 240 °C
c Neptune (by 11°)
d i 519 °C **ii** -13 °C

8 a 19 883 m **b** 4600 m

Page 28 Challenge

a i 3 **ii**

4	−1	0
−3	1	5
2	3	−2

b i -3 **ii**

−2	−3	2
3	−1	−5
−4	1	0

c i -2 **ii**

7	−6	−7	4
−4	1	2	−1
0	−3	−2	3
−5	6	5	−8

Page 29 Exercise 5.1

1 a–c

×	−5	−4	−3	−2	−1	0	1	2	3	4	5
5	−25	−20	−15	−10	−5	0	5	10	15	20	25
4	−20	−16	−12	−8	−4	0	4	8	12	16	20
3	−15	−12	−9	−6	−3	0	3	6	9	12	15
2	−10	−8	−6	−4	−2	0	2	4	6	8	10
1	−5	−4	−3	−2	−1	0	1	2	3	4	5
0	0	0	0	0	0	0	0	0	0	0	0
−1						0	−1	−2	−3	−4	−5
−2						0	−2	−4	−6	−8	−10
−3						0	−3	−6	−9	−12	−15
−4						0	−4	−8	−12	−16	−20
−5						0	−5	−10	−15	−20	−25

2 a -4 **b** -15 **c** -6 **d** -15
e -16 **f** -8 **g** -10 **h** -15
i 0 **j** 12
3 a 42 **b** -18 **c** -36 **d** -40
e -24 **f** -45 **g** -28 **h** -30
i -8 **j** -42 **k** -56 **l** -54
m -64 **n** -48 **o** -49
4 a -24 **b** -42
5 a -30 **b** -8 **c** -48
d -28 **e** -72 **f** -8
g -54 **h** -30 **i** -28

Page 30 Exercise 6.1

1 a -13 **b** -13 **c** 8 **d** -5
e 11 **f** 9 **g** -32 **h** -27
i -30 **j** -36 **k** -35 **l** -36
m 7 **n** -3 **o** 17 **p** -2
q -8 **r** 2 **s** -6 **t** -28
u -32
2 a 13 **b** 18 **c** 28 **d** -23
e -7 **f** 5 **g** 9 **h** -7
3 a -55 **b** It is 55 m below sea level
4 a $3\cdot4 \times 10^4$ **b** $2\cdot55 \times 10^8$
c $2\cdot75 \times 10^{11}$ **d** $1\cdot85 \times 10^{-4}$
e $4\cdot56 \times 10^{-3}$ **f** $1\cdot2 \times 10^{-10}$

Page 31 Challenge

1

Page 32 Revise

1 a true **b** true **c** true
d false **e** false **f** true
2 a -4 **b** -4
3 $-5, -3, -2, 1, 4$
4 a -1 **b** 2 **c** -6 **d** 5 **e** -3
f 8 **g** -4 **h** -45 **i** -10 **j** -49
k 0 **l** 0 **m** -2 **n** -36 **o** -5
5 a -403 m **b** 1746 m
6 a -48 **b** -6 **c** -4
7 P$(1, -1)$, Q$(4, -6)$, R$(-2, -3)$
8 a -3 **b** 19 **c** 20 **d** -13

3 Brackets and equations

Page 33 Exercise 1.1

1 a $3b$ **b** $2x$ **c** $7y$ **d** $3e$
e a^2 **f** $4xy$ **g** $3a + 2b$ **h** $5y$
2 a £$3m$ **b** £$(2n + 1)$ **c** £$(8w + 3)$
3 a $3x - 4$ **b** $5x + 7$
4 a $6x$ cm **b** $4y$ cm **c** $8a$ cm **d** $10y$ cm
5 a m^2 cm^2 **b** ab cm^2 **c** $2xy$ cm^2

Page 34 Exercise 2.1

1 a i 12 **ii** 12
b i 35 **ii** 35
c i 2 **ii** 2
d i 49 **ii** 49; they are equal

2 a i 6 **ii** 6
b i 39 **ii** 39
c i 70 **ii** 70
d i 24 **ii** 24; they are equal
3 a i 24 **ii** 24
b i 52 **ii** 52
c i 12 **ii** 12
d i 16 **ii** 16
e i 21 **ii** 21
f i 21 **ii** 21
g i 60 **ii** 60
h i 110 **ii** 110; they are equal
4 a i 12 **ii** 12
b i 3 **ii** 3
c i 6 **ii** 6
d i 27 **ii** 27; they are equal

Page 35 Exercise 3.1

1 a $3x + 6$ **b** $2y - 6$ **c** $4a + 8$
d $3t - 3$ **e** $2m + 12$ **f** $4c - 20$
g $5x + 15$ **h** $2h - 12$ **i** $5y + 35$
j $4n - 8$ **k** $5y + 5$ **l** $7w - 7$
m $4a + 28$ **n** $3e - 27$ **o** $8x + 32$
p $3k + 15$ **q** $5a - 30$ **r** $4x + 32$
s $9h - 72$ **t** $3u + 24$ **u** $11x - 33$
v $8y + 8$ **w** $5r - 30$ **x** $7n + 14$
y $9x + 81$
2 a i $3(y + 2)$ **ii** $3y + 6$ **b i** $4(x - 3)$ **ii** $4x - 12$
c i $5(t - 1)$ **ii** $5t - 5$ **d i** $2(m + 3)$ **ii** $2m + 6$
e i $3(n + 5)$ **ii** $3n + 15$ **f i** $7(y - 6)$ **ii** $7y - 42$
3 a $40 - 8x$ **b** $44 - 4m$ **c** $33 + 11n$
d $2k + 6$ **e** $5m - 5$ **f** $21 + 3y$
g $10 + 5b$ **h** $6h + 60$ **i** $7y - 56$
j $12 + 6k$ **k** $15 - 3n$ **l** $48 - 12c$
m $72 - 8a$ **n** $2z + 10$ **o** $42 - 7x$
p $24 + 4e$ **q** $72 - 9f$ **r** $10r - 90$
s $36 - 9u$ **t** $10w + 70$

Page 36 Exercise 3.2

1 a $6x - 6$ **b** $20y + 8$ **c** $12c - 6$
d $20a - 25$ **e** $42z + 7$ **f** $40 - 5x$
g $12e + 8$ **h** $4y - 6$ **i** $24w + 32$
j $54x - 18$ **k** $32y + 24$ **l** $6a + 3$
m $15k - 3$ **n** $24c - 18$ **o** $9y + 6$
p $11a + 11b$ **q** $2u - 2v$ **r** $9w - 9y$
s $14a + 21$ **t** $30b - 40$ **u** $8a + 12b$
v $20b - 15c$ **w** $60x - 12y$
2 a $2(y + 4)$ cm; $2y + 8$ cm
b $2(2m + 3)$ cm; $4m + 6$ cm
c $2(3y + 7)$ cm; $6y + 14$ cm
3 a $3y + 1$ **b** $3m - 6$ **c** $4x + 6$ **d** $1 + 3a$
e $k - 12$ **f** $3 + 2y$ **g** $9n - 7$ **h** $1 + 3h$
i $5c + 10$ **j** $r + 3$ **k** $5y$ **l** $6x + 6$
m $5n + 1$ **n** $9a + b$ **o** $8x + 2y$ **p** $9m + 5n$
4 a $3(x + 2)$ m^2; $3x + 6$ m^2
b $25(y + 20)$ mm^2; $25y + 500$ mm^2
c $250(m + 80)$ cm^2; $250m + 20000$ cm^2

Page 37 Challenge

$2(x - 3) + 2(x + 4) = 4x + 2$ or $2x - 6 + 2(x + 4)$ or $2(x - 3) + 2x + 8$, etc. (all cm)

Page 37 Exercise 4.1

1 a $y = 5$ **b** $t = 12$ **c** $m = 4$ **d** $n = 0$
  e $x = 6$ **f** $y = 9$ **g** $y = 3$ **h** $k = 5$
  i $z = 13$ **j** $x = 0$
2 a $x = 2$ **b** $m = 3$ **c** $k = 7$ **d** $n = 10$
  e $y = \frac{3}{2}$ **f** $y = \frac{4}{3}$ **g** $a = \frac{3}{4}$ **h** $n = \frac{7}{2}$
  i $t = 2$ **j** $x = 2$ **k** $e = \frac{11}{2}$ **l** $k = \frac{5}{2}$
  m $x = 1$ **n** $y = \frac{1}{2}$
3 a $y = 3$ **b** $x = 5$ **c** $a = 2$ **d** $e = 3$
  e $k = 3$ **f** $r = 3$ **g** $h = 4$ **h** $c = 8$
  i $x = 5$ **j** $y = 9$ **k** $m = 4$ **l** $k = 6$

Page 38 Exercise 4.2

1 a $y = 7$ **b** $x = 2$ **c** $m = 2$ **d** $x = 5$
  e $k = 3$ **f** $h = 1$ **g** $y = 1$ **h** $w = \frac{5}{2}$
  i $x = \frac{3}{2}$ **j** $x = \frac{1}{2}$ **k** $k = 1$ **l** $y = 3$
  m $a = 2$ **n** $c = 3$ **o** $n = 3$ **p** $r = 7$
  q $e = 1$ **r** $x = \frac{17}{2}$

2 a $5x = 3x + 6$; $x = 3$; length 15 cm
  b $4y = y + 12$; $y = 4$; length 16 cm
  c $2x - 7 = x$; $x = 7$; length 7 cm
3 a $x = 2$ **b** $y = 1$ **c** $m = 3$ **d** $k = 2$
  e $x = 3$ **f** $y = 3$ **g** $e = 7$ **h** $k = 3$
  i $w = 7$ **j** $n = 4$ **k** $x = 3$ **l** $y = \frac{1}{2}$

Page 39 Exercise 5.1

1 a $n = 4$ **b** $m = 7$ **c** $e = 7$ **d** $d = 1$
  e $h = 0$ **f** $a = 3$ **g** $c = 6$ **h** $z = 13$
  i $x = 14$ **j** $m = 0$ **k** $w = 3$ **l** $b = 12$
  m $n = 11$ **n** $y = 1$
2 a i $5(x + 2) = 35$ **ii** $x = 5$ **iii** 7 m
  b i $3(y - 3) = 27$ **ii** $y = 12$ **iii** £9
  c i $5(x + 3) = 40$ **ii** $x = 5$ **iii** 5 m
  d i $3(y + 4) = 15$ **ii** $y = 1$ **iii** 1 m
3 a $y = 12$ **b** $x = 2$ **c** $m = 1$ **d** $n = 1$
  e $x = 0$ **f** $k = 3$ **g** $y = 8$ **h** $m = 9$
  i $t = 3$ **j** $n = 11$ **k** $x = 16$ **l** $y = 0$
4 a ii $x = 10$; £10
  b ii $y = 9$; 9p
  c ii $x = 5$; 5 kg
5 a $x + 4$ **b** $10(x + 4)$
  c $10(x + 4) = 190$ **d** $x = 15$; 15 sweets
6 a $x - 2$
  b $100(x - 2)$
  c $100(x - 2) = 1000$; $x = 12$; 12 screws
7 $6(x - 15) = 384$; $x = 79$; 79 pence

Page 40 Exercise 5.2

1 a $x = 3$ **b** $y = 2$ **c** $n = 2$ **d** $m = 1$
  e $y = 2$ **f** $x = 4$ **g** $x = 5$ **h** $y = 3$
  i $n = 8$ **j** $m = 3$ **k** $x = 0$ **l** $k = 5$
2 a i $5(x + 3) = 50$ **ii** $x = 7$

b i $6(m - 3) = 54$ **ii** $m = 12$
c i $8(t - 6) = 8$ **ii** $t = 7$
d i $9(t + 7) = 81$ **ii** $t = 2$
e i $11(y - 2) = 66$ **ii** $y = 8$
f i $8(w + 7) = 56$ **ii** $w = 0$
3 a $x = 4$; number was 4
  b i $2(x - 6) = 6$; $x = 9$; number was 9
    ii $3(x + 7) = 45$; $x = 8$; number was 8
    iii $2(x + 12) = 38$; $x = 7$; number was 7

Page 41 Challenges

1 a $3(x + 1) = 4(x - 1)$; $x = 7$; IN number is 7
  b $2(3y + 6) = 4(5y - 4)$; $y = 2$; IN number is 2
2 a $3(x + 7) - 10 = 7(x - 3)$; $x = 8$;
    they both thought of 8
  b 35

Page 43 Revise

1 a 10 **b** 6 **c** 16
2 a $5m + 5$ **b** $6n - 18$
  c $6 - 3x$ **d** $12a + 8b$
3 a i $4(w + 3)$
    ii $4w + 12$
  b i $2(k + 5)$ cm
    ii $2k + 10$ cm
4 a $5x$ **b** $n + 8$ **c** $6 + 3h$
5 a $x = 3$ **b** $y = 15$ **c** $y = 7$
  d $x = \frac{3}{2}$ **e** $x = 5$ **f** $m = 2$
  g $n = 4$ **h** $k = 8$ **i** $x = 7$
6 a $x = 12$ **b** $y = 4$ **c** $a = 3$
7 a $7(x - 12) = 21$; $x = 15$; number is 15
  b $4(y + 2) = 28$; $y = 5$; width is 5 m
  c $4x - 2 = 2x + 6$; $x = 4$; 14 cm lengths
8 a $5(x - 15) = 165$
  b $x = 48$; £48

4 Money

Page 44 Exercise 1.1

1 a £4·72 **b** £6·43 **c** £6·59 **d** £3·46
  e £20·64 **f** £25·31 **g** £1·082
2 £2·05
3 a £56·44 **b** £3·56
4 a £11 **b** £848 **c** £1·53
  d £1·99 **e** £6470 **f** 84p
5 a £8·70 **b** 14p
6 a i £26 **ii** £52
  b i £7·80 **ii** £13·10
7 a sixty-four pounds nine pence
  b two hundred and six pounds eighty pence
8 a £4·60 **b** 7p
  c 60p **d** £40
9 a £67 **b** £67·03
10 £153·55
11 a £9·96 **b** 44p **c** £63·58

Page 45 Exercise 2.1
1a £3·49   **b** £1·51   **c** £6·32   **d** £1·73
2 £148
3 £13·16
4 a £80   **b** £79·79
5 a £170   **b** £77·94   **c** £13·96
6 £57·80
7 £4·75
8 a £7   **b** £28
9 £2·51
10 82·9p
11 £11·10; £5·70; £5·95; £2·96; total £25·71

Page 47 Exercise 3.1
1 44p
2 £1·69
3 £205
4 a £40·99   **b** £76·15   **c** £57·15
5 a £22·50   **b** £8·55   **c** £13·95 profit
6 a £1·50   **b** £4·50   **c** £2·40
7 a i £7   **ii** £77
   b i £25   **ii** £275
   c i £135   **ii** £1485
8 a £3·60   **b** £21·60
9 £4·50
10 £208, £168 and £136

Page 49 Exercise 3.2
1 a 5p   **b** 10%
2 a £2   **b** 25%
3 a i £10   **ii** 50%
   b i 12p   **ii** 15%
   c i £25 loss   **ii** 20% loss
4 17%
5 24%
6 a 40% profit   **b** 26% profit   **c** 12·5% loss
7a £14·99   **b** 33·3%
8 28%
9 a 500%   **b** 84%
10 28·8%

Page 50 Exercise 4.1
1 a £5   **b** 90p   **c** £58·30
   d 6p   **e** £640   **f** 75p
2 a £2   **b** £1·50   **c** £35   **d** 25p
   e 4p   **f** £185   **g** 46p
3 £3·60; £1·80; £0·90; £6·30
4 a £10·50   **b** 70p   **c** £875
   d £8·40   **e** 46p
5 a £3·60   **b** £75·60
6 a £35   **b** £3·15   **c** 21p   **d** £245
7 a £4·55   **b** £30·55
8 a £5·26   **b** £110·42
9 a i £4·29   **ii** £28·78
   b i £454·83   **ii** £3053·83
   c i £29·36   **ii** £197·11
   d i £1400·00   **ii** £9399·99

Page 51 Exercise 4.2
1 £101·64
2 £50·53
3 a electricity bill   **b** by £9·75
4 a £98·99   **b** £10·56
   c £276·70   **d** £14 799·13
5 £179; £237·40; £41·55; total £278·95
6 a Spanish Villas   **b** by £123·91

Page 52 Brainstormer
£680

Page 53 Exercise 5.1
1 a weekend   **b** peak
   c off-peak   **d** off-peak
2 a 4p   **b** 2p   **c** 24p   **d** 8p
3 12p
4 £3·15
5 £1·84
6 a Mandy's call   **b** by 5p
7 a 95p   **b** 125p   **c** 175p
8 a 36p   **b** 63p   **c** 117p
9 £8·79

Page 54 Exercise 5.2
1 A = £61·48;   B = £10·76;   C = £72·24
2 A = £95·09;   B = £16·64;   C = £111·73
3 A = £161·88;   B = £28·33;   C = £190·21
4a £88·11   **b** £56·26

Page 56 Exercise 6.1
1 a 866   **b** 1144
2 £25·38
3 a £44·49   **b** £100·24
4 a i £21·12   **ii** £61·22
   b £82·34
5 a £3·14   **b** £65·94
6 A = £1·70;   B = £35·76

Page 57 Exercise 6.2
1 A = 880; B = £49·63; C = £5·11; D = £54·74
2 a £21·26   **b i** 5298   **ii** £64·05   **c** £85·31
3 £106·57
4 720 units cost £40·61; £5·54; £46·15;
   VAT £2·31; total £48·46

Page 57 Investigation
a 49p   **b** 1·4p

Page 58 Exercise 7.1
1a 14·2 euro   **b** 16·2 dollars
   c 1833·3 yen   **d** 100·4 kroner
2 a $1620   **b** $81
3 a 284 euro   **b** 163·20 Swiss francs
4 109 998 yen
5 a i €28   **ii** €70   **iii** €105
   b i £61   **ii** £43   **iii** £79
6 a £7·04   **b** £6·17   **c** £49·02   **d** £99·60
7 a £21·10   **b** £45·80   **c** £12·70   **d** £90·10

Page 59 Exercise 7.2

1 Ken, his cost £5·56; Karl's cost £5·63

2 a €8·09   **b** $101·66

  c 262·14 francs   **d** 52 120·72 yen

  e 7650·23 rupees   **f** 4526·03 kroner

3 a £53·20   **b** £386·30   **c** £6·60

  d £696·20   **e** £9·70   **f** £382·70

4 Germany by £16·22

5 a £518·52   **b** $56·13

6 £53

Page 60 Exercise 8.1

1 £308

2a £1920   **b** £120

3a £5360   **b** £360

4a £98·94   **b** £8·95

5a £229·90   **b** £34·41

6a £329·88   **b** £16·93

7a £959·76   **b** £59·77

8a £18 719·64   **b** £1720·64

Page 61 Exercise 8.2

1 a £77·94   **b** £97·94   **c** £8·94

2 a £239·88   **b** £279·87   **c** £29·92

3 a £79·50   **b** £779·40

  c £858·90   **d** £63·90

4 a £1123·75   **b** £8398·80

  c £9522·55   **d** £532·55

5 a £263·76, £287·64   **b** £34·76, £58·64

6 a £659·88, £677·76   **b** £59·89, £77·77

  c the 24 month plan only costs £17·88 more than the 12 month plan.

Page 63 Exercise 9.1

1 a £380   **b** £1264   **c** £487

2 a £625   **b** £500

3 a £292   **b** £295·80

4 £937·50

5 a £986   **b** £98·60   **c** £887·40

6 £294

7 £335·60

Page 64 Exercise 10.1

1 £14·50

2 £45·37

3 £9·75

4 £49·70

5 £128·60

6 a £38   **b** £14·25   **c** £76   **d** £451·25

Page 65 Exercise 10.2

1 £17·85

2 £42·84

3 £31·80

4 £121·90

5 a i £23·85   **ii** £53·55   **b** £77·40

6 a i £60·95   **ii** £82·11   **b** £143·06

7 a i £413·40   **ii** £428·40   **b** £841·80

Page 67 Revise

1 a £30   **b i** £29·95   **ii** £10·05

2 a £299·50   **b** £524·50   **c** £225

3 a 24p   **b** 45p   **c** 99p

4 a £234   **b** £546

5 a £40·32   **b** 20·7%

6 a i £4·23   **ii** £88·83   **b** £107·61

7 a £61·30

  b A = 781, B = £45·45, C = £5·60, D=£51·05, E = £2·55, F = £53·60

8 a $456·40   **b** £37·70

9 a £177·68   **b** £19·68

10 a £55·80   **b** £87·00

5 Factors

Page 69 Exercise 1.1

1 a 2, 4, 6, 8, 10

  b 9, 18, 27, 36, 45

  c 7, 14, 21, 28, 35

  d 11, 22, 33, 44, 55

  e 100, 200, 300, 400, 500

2 a 15

  b i 21, 42, 63   **ii** 10, 20, 30   **iii** 6, 12, 18

  c i 21   **ii** 10   **iii** 6

3 a $5x$ **b** w^2 **c** $15c$ **d** $6y^2$

  e $10ab$ **f** 25   **g** t^3 **h** $14k^2$

  i $4y^2$ **j** $24a^2$

4 a $7x - 21$ **b** $10 - 5y$ **c** $3a + 3b$

  d $30x - 25$ **e** $x^2 - 2x$ **f** $6y + y^2$

  g $a^2 + ab$ **h** $30x - 25$ **i** $g^2 - g$

  j $8m + m^2$ **k** $3a^2 + a$ **l** $9 - 18x$

Page 70 Exercise 2.1

1 a 1, 2, 5, 10   **b** 1, 13

  c 1, 2, 4, 8   **d** 1, 2, 3, 4, 6, 12

  e 1, 5, 25   **f** 1, 2, 5, 10, 25, 50

2 a i 16: 1, 2, 4, 8, 16; 30: 1, 2, 3, 5, 6, 10, 15, 30

  ii 1, 2

  iii 2

  b i 24: 1, 2, 3, 4, 6, 8, 12, 24; 84: 1, 2, 3, 4, 6, 7, 12, 14, 21, 28, 42, 84

  ii 1, 2, 3, 4, 6, 12

  iii 12

  c i 63: 1, 3, 7, 9, 21, 63; 8: 1, 2, 4, 8

  ii 1

  iii 1

  d i 100: 1, 2, 4, 5, 10, 20, 25, 50, 100; 40: 1, 2, 4, 5, 8, 10, 20, 40

  ii 1, 2, 4, 5, 10, 20

  iii 20

3 a 33   **b** 25   **c** 1

4 a 1: 1; 2: 1, 2; 3: 1, 3; 4: 1, 2, 4; 5: 1, 5; 6: 1, 2, 3, 6; 7: 1, 7; 8: 1, 2, 4, 8; 9: 1, 3, 9; 10: 1, 2, 5, 10

  b 2, 3, 5, 7

  c 2, 3, 5, 7, 11, 13, 17, 19, 23, 29

5 a 2

  b 53

  c 6 (for 23 and 29; 31 and 37)

6 The numbers circled should be: 2, 3, 5, 7, 11, 13, 17, 19, 23, 29, 31, 37, 41, 43, 47, 53, 59, 61, 67, 71, 73, 79, 83, 89, 97

7 a 2, 5   **b** 13   **c** 2   **d** 2, 3

  e 5   **f** 2, 5   **g** 3, 11

Page 72 Exercise 2.2

1 a 2, 3, 7   **b** 2, 3   **c** 2, 5, 7

  d 2, 7   **e** 3, 5   **f** 3, 5, 7

  g 2, 3, 7   **h** 2, 3, 11   **i** 2, 5, 11

  j 2, 3, 19   **k** 3, 11, 23   **l** 5, 7, 19

2 a 1, 2, 3, 4, 6, 12

  b 1, 5, 7, 35

  c 1, 2, 3, 4, 6, 8, 12, 16, 24, 48

  d 1, 71

  e 1, 2, 3, 6, 13, 26, 39, 78

  f 1, 2, 3, 4, 5, 6, 8, 10, 12, 15, 16, 20, 24, 30, 40, 48, 60, 80, 120, 240

  g 1, 2, 3, 4, 5, 6, 10, 12, 15, 20, 25, 30, 50, 60, 75, 100, 150, 300

  h 1, 3, 5, 9, 15, 27, 45, 81, 135, 405

  i 1, 5, 13, 25, 65, 325

  j 1, 3, 5, 11, 15, 33, 55, 165

  k 1, 13, 17, 221

  l 1, 2, 4, 5, 8, 10, 20, 25, 40, 50, 100, 125, 200, 250, 500, 1000

3 a 1, 3, 5,15   **b** 15

  c i 4   **ii** 8   **iii** 6

4 a 1, 2, 3, 5, 6, 10, 15, 30 (all cm lengths)

  b 30 cm

5 a 20   **b i** 81   **ii** 245

Page 73 Challenges

a 28

b 1 two: no; 2 twos: 3 prime; 3 twos: 7 prime; 4 twos: 15 not prime; 5 twos: 31 prime

Page 74 Exercise 3.1

1 a $1 \times 6, 2 \times 3$ **b** $1 \times 9, 3 \times 3$

  c $1 \times 10, 2 \times 5$ **d** $1 \times 15, 3 \times 5$

  e $1 \times 18, 2 \times 9, 3 \times 6$ **f** 1×19

  g $1 \times 20, 2 \times 10, 4 \times 5$ **h** $1 \times 25, 5 \times 5$

  i $1 \times 32, 2 \times 16, 4 \times 8$

  j $1 \times 36, 2 \times 18, 3 \times 12, 4 \times 9, 6 \times 6$

2 a $1 \times 3y, 3 \times y$

  b $1 \times 7a, 7 \times a$

  c $1 \times 5x, 5 \times x$

  d $1 \times 4w, 2 \times 2w, 4 \times w$

  e $1 \times 9k, 3 \times 3k, 9 \times k$

  f $1 \times 6m, 2 \times 3m, 3 \times 2m, 6 \times m$

  g $1 \times 10b, 2 \times 5b, 5 \times 2b, 10 \times b$

  h $1 \times mn, m \times n$

  i $1 \times x^2, x \times x,$

  j $1 \times pq, p \times q$

  k $1 \times c^2, c \times c$

  l $1 \times 2ab, 2 \times ab, a \times 2b, b \times 2a$

  m $1 \times 3y^2, 3 \times y^2, y \times 3y$

3 a 2   **b** n **c** $4r$ **d** $3k$

  e 3   **f** $2y$ **g** $7m$ **h** x

  i 2   **j** a **k** k^2 **l** n

  m e^2 **n** a **o** $3x$

4 a 1, 2, 3, 6, k, $2k$, $3k$, $6k$

  b 1, 2, 7, 14, b, $2b$, $7b$, $14b$

  c 1, 7, a, b, $7a$, $7b$, ab, $7ab$

  d 1, 2, 3, 4, 6, 12, q, $2q$, $3q$, $4q$, $6q$, $12q$

  e 1, 2, 4, k, $2k$, $4k$, t, $2t$, $4t$, kt, $2kt$, $4kt$

  f 1, p, q, r, pq, pr, qr, pqr

  g 1, 13, g, $13g$

  h 1, f, g, fg

  i 1, 3, x, $3x$, x^2, $3x^2$

  j 1, 2, 4, x, $2x$, $4x$, x^2, $2x^2$, $4x^2$

  k 1, x, x^2, y, xy, x^2y

  l 1, 2, x, $2x$, x^2, $2x^2$, y, $2y$, xy, $2xy$, x^2y, $2x^2y$

Page 74 Challenges

1 a i diagram leading to $2a$, 2, a, 1

    ii diagram leading to $7xy$, $7x$, $7y$, 7, xy, x, y, 1

    iii diagram leading to 70, 10, 14, 2, 35, 5, 7, 1

  b i diagram leading to $2a^2$, $2a$, $2a$ (repeat), 2, a^2, a, a (repeat), 1

    ii diagram leading to $4a$, 4, $2a$, 2, $2a$ (repeat), 2 (repeat), a, 1

    iii diagram leading to 12, 4, 6, 2, 6 (repeat), 2 (repeat), 3, 1

2 A–11, B–23, C–13, D–12, E–10, F–22, G–6, H–8, I–19, J–1, K–18, L–3, M–15, N–21, O–9, P–16, Q–4, R–24, S–7, T–2, U–17, V–5, W–20, X–14

Page 75 Exercise 3.2

1 a i 1, 2, 4, a, $2a$, $4a$

    ii 1, 2, 4, 8

  b 1, 2, 4

  c 4

2 a i 1, 3, x, $3x$, y, $3y$, xy, $3xy$

    ii 1, 2, 3, 4, 6, 12, y, $2y$, $3y$, $4y$, $6y$, $12y$

  b 1, 3, y, $3y$

  c $3y$

3 a 3   **b** 4   **c** 7   **d** 6

  e $12t$ **f** $6x$ **g** d **h** $5g$

  i x **j** y **k** $4x$ **l** $7x$

  m a **n** $6b$ **o** b **p** ab

  q ab **r** ab **s** 5   **t** $2ab$

4 a i $3x + 12$ **ii** 3

  b i $14a + 35$ **ii** 7

  c i $5t - 40$ **ii** 5

  d i $8x + 4$ **ii** 4

  e i $2x^2 + 5x$ **ii** x

  f i $4g - g^2$ **ii** g

  g i $x + x^2$ **ii** x

  h i $6x^2 + 2x$ **ii** $2x$

i i $3a^2 + 3ab$ **ii** $3a$
j i $3pq + p^2q$ **ii** pq
k i $12f - 4f^2$ **ii** $4f$
l i $5d^2 + 5d$ **ii** $5d$
   The highest common factor is the same as the term outside the brackets

5 a 2   **b** $6x + 12$
  c 6   **d** $2x$ and 4 have HCF of 2

Page 76 Exercise 4.1

1 a $2x + 3$ **b** $y + 3$ **c** $m - 2$
  d $k + 2$ **e** $2 - n$ **f** $3a - 4b$
  g $2k + 3m$ **h** $a + 1$ **i** $a - 1$
  j $2e - 1$ **k** $2k - m$ **l** $2x + 3y$
  m $6y - 1$

2 a $3(a + 2)$ **b** $5(y - 2)$ **c** $2(3 - k)$
  d $2(m + 2)$ **e** $7(k + 3)$ **f** $3(a - b)$
  g $5(p - 2q)$ **h** $2(2x - 3)$ **i** $2(4 - 3y)$
  j $2(3 - 2k)$ **k** $2(a + 2b)$ **l** $7(x - 2y)$
  m $2(a + 1)$ **n** $3(y - 1)$ **o** $7(r - 1)$
  p $5(1 - x)$ **q** $2(x + 5)$ **r** $2(8 - y)$
  s $3(a + 1)$ **t** $2(6a - 7b)$

3 a $10(x + 2)$ **b** $4(2y - 3)$ **c** $4(4 - a)$
  d $9(2 - b)$ **e** $4(a - 2b)$ **f** $6(m + 3n)$
  g $4(3 - w)$ **h** $6(1 - 2ab)$ **i** $4(5xy - 1)$
  j $10(x^2 + 4)$ **k** $4(2 - y^2)$ **l** $4(7 - 2mn)$
  m $6(6k + 5)$ **n** $6(3x - 2y)$ **o** $10(5ab - 2)$
  p $12(4y^2 + 3)$

4 a $6(a + 4)$ **b** not possible **c** $4(2 - m)$
  d not possible **e** not possible **f** $2(7 - 13g)$
  g not possible **h** not possible **i** not possible
  j not possible **k** $2(a + 2b)$ **l** $7(x - 2y)$
  m $2(a + 1)$ **n** $3(y - 1)$ **o** $7(r - 1)$
  p not possible **q** not possible **r** $9(9 - 5y)$
  s not possible **t** $a(17 - 1) = 16a$

Page 77 Exercise 4.2

1 a $y(y + 3)$ **b** $x(x - 5)$ **c** $a(a + 7)$
  d $t(t - 2)$ **e** $m(m + 6)$ **f** $k(k - 1)$
  g $2a(a + 2)$ **h** $3a(2a - 1)$ **i** $5n(n + 3)$
  j $3w(3 - w)$ **k** $4a(1 + 3a)$ **l** $6p(1 - 3p)$

2 a $a(x + y)$ **b** $c(a - b)$ **c** $k(a + 1)$
  d $a(a + b)$ **e** $q(p - q)$ **f** $2x(x + 3y)$

3 a $x(a - b)$ **b** $m(n - p)$ **c** $a(2 + b)$
  d $n(m - 5)$ **e** $x(2x - 1)$ **f** $x(2x - y)$
  g $a(a - b)$ **h** $y(x + y)$ **i** $2x(1 - y)$
  j $3a(1 + b)$ **k** $m(5n - m)$ **l** $4x(2 - 3x)$
  m $2m(3m - 1)$ **n** $a(2x + y)$ **o** $3k(5k - 2m)$
  p $2pq(5p + 6q)$

4 a i $3a + 12 + 4a + 44$
    ii $7a + 56$
    iii $7(a + 8)$
  b i $5x + 10 + 2x + 18$
    ii $7x + 28$
    iii $7(x + 4)$

c i $2x + 12 + 7x + 105$
  ii $9x + 117$
  iii $9(x + 13)$
d i $8y + 8 + 3y + 36$
  ii $11y + 44$
  iii $11(y + 4)$
e i $2x - 8 + 3x + 18$
  ii $5x + 10$
  iii $5(x + 2)$
f i $5y - 25 + 2y + 4$
  ii $7y - 21$
  iii $7(y - 3)$

Page 78 Challenges

1 a i 700   **ii** 260   **iii** 13
  b i 800   **ii** 140   **iii** 5·1
  c i 5   **ii** 7·2   **iii** 84
  d i £6   **ii** £15
  e 100 seconds; 1 min 40 s

2 a i 4 is a factor of $9 - 1 = 8$
    ii 7 is a factor of $16 - 9 = 7$
    iii 10 is a factor of $49 - 9 = 40$
  b/c pupil's own answers
  d true for given values, not true for others

Page 80 Revise

1 a 1, 2, 4, 8
  b 1, 3, 5, 15
  c 1, 2, 3, 4, 6, 9, 12, 18, 36

2 1, 5, 25

3 a 12
  b 17

4 7, 11, 13, 17, 19

5 $2 \times 3 \times 5 \times 5$

6 a $1 \times 6x, 2 \times 3x, 3 \times 2x, 6 \times x$
  b 1, 2, 3, 6, x, $2x$, $3x$, $6x$

7 1, 2, 4, 8, p, $2p$, $4p$, $8p$, q, $2q$, $4q$, $8q$, pq, $2pq$, $4pq$, $8pq$

8 a 4
  b $3xy$
  c x

9 a 1, 5, x, $5x$
  b 1, 2, 4, x, $2x$, $4x$

10 a 8   **b** $9x$
11 a $3(w - 2)$ **b** $2(p + 2q)$ **c** $2(8ab - 1)$
12 a $6(a + 3b)$ **b** $4(3 - 2x)$ **c** $6(3x^2 - 1)$
  d $a(m - n)$ **e** $x(x + 1)$ **f** $2b(2a - 3b)$

6 Statistics – charts and tables

Page 81 Exercise 1.1

1 a 15   **b** cola   **c** 65
2 a 10   **b** 8   **c** 2
3 a 1950   **c** 30 hundred million
  c 15 hundred million **d** going up with time
4 a vegetables; flowers; shrubs; lawn
  b i $\frac{1}{2}$ **ii** $\frac{1}{4}$ **iii** $\frac{1}{4}$

5 a 15   **b** 23   **c** 26
d

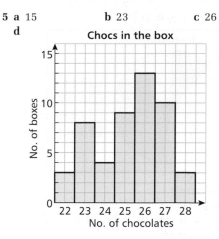

Chocs in the box

Page 83 Exercise 2.1

1 a BBC 1 (7); BBC 2 (7); ITV (5); Ch 4 (7); Ch 5 (4)
   b 2 (8); 3 (5); 4 (15); 5 (0); 6 (2)
   c golf (7); keep-fit (7); tennis (5); football (9);
     volleyball (2)

2 a 7
   b

Distance (m)	100	125	150	175	200	225	250
Frequency	5	7	9	12	7	6	4

   c i 4   **ii** 9   **iii** 17
   d

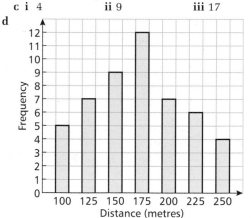

3 a 50
   b i 60 seconds   **ii** 120 seconds
   c

Length (s)	60	70	80	90	100	110	120
Frequency	1	5	8	9	16	7	4

   d i 5
     ii 16
     iii 11
   e 100 seconds

Page 85 Exercise 2.2

1 a

Letter	A	B	C	D	E	F	G	H	I	J	K	L	M	N	O	P	Q	R	S	T	U	V	W	X	Y	Z
Frequency	1	7	0	2	0	18	1	2	12	34	4	0	25	5	0	0	2	7	24	9	6	0	3	10	8	5

   b J
   c A man entered a shop and spent one half of the
     money he had. When he came out he had the
     same number of pennies as he had pounds when
     he went in and half as many pounds as he had
     pennies when he went in. How much did he
     have when he entered?
   d £99·98
2 a left (9); right (7); ahead (14)
   b ahead
   c no

Page 87 Exercise 3.1

1 a $\frac{1}{5}, \frac{2}{5}, \frac{3}{10}, \frac{1}{10}$
   b i 72°   **ii** 36°
   c

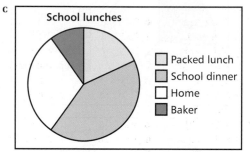

School lunches

2 a i $\frac{1}{5}$ **ii** $\frac{1}{4}$
   b i 120°   **ii** 78°
   c

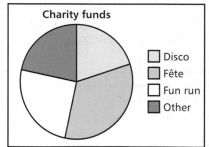

Charity funds

3 a 1
   b

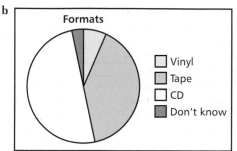

Formats

Page 88 Exercise 3.2

1 a

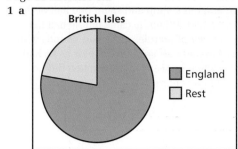

b

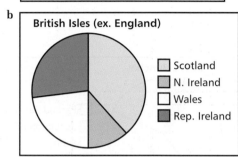

2 a

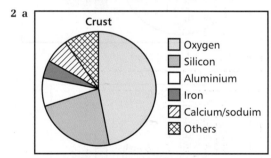

b

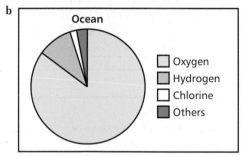

3 a

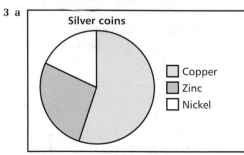

b i 89%   **ii** 11%
c iron

4 a i 17·6%   **ii** 41·2%
b

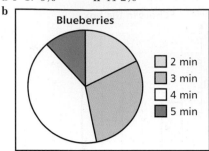

Page 90 Exercise 4.1

1 a dropped   **b** no   **c** positive correlation
2 a with **iv**   **b** with **iii**   **c** with **ii**   **d** with **i**
3 a type **d** of question 2
   b type **b** of question 2
   c type **c** of question 2

Page 91 Exercise 4.2

1 a

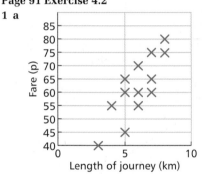

b positive
2 a

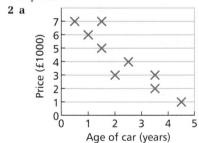

b negative
c i 2·5 years   **ii** £2000
d overpriced
3 a

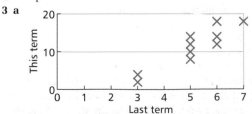

b positive correlation
c 8   **d** 5 or 6
e i 5·1   **ii** 11·2

Page 92 Exercise 5.1

1 a 20 pairs   **b** 15 °C

2 a/b

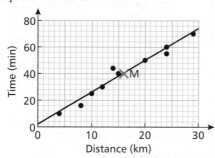

c 45 min

3 a i 34·3 min   **ii** 42·8 papers

b/c

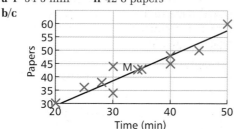

d 48 minutes

4 a 17·5 goals; 13·2 points

b

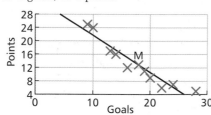

c negative correlation

d 11 goals

Page 94 Exercise 6.1

1 a 21, 25, 26 houses

  b 43 houses

  c 308 houses

2 a 12, 14, 17 visitors

  b 3, 5, 12, 14, 17, 20, 23, 23, 24, 28, 31, 31, 36, 42, 44

  c 15

3 a i 10·1 cm   **ii** 6·2 cm

  b level 8

  c 8·6 cm

  d 8·6 cm

4 a i £10 300   **ii** £14 000

  b level 11   **c** £12 100, £12 600, £12 700

5 a £3·60, £3·80, £4·00, £4·20, £4·20, £4·50, £4·70, £4·90, £4·90, £5·30, £5·40, £5·60, £5·80, £5·80, £5·90, £6·00, £6·20, £6·50, £6·70, £7·10

  b 9

  c 20

Page 96 Exercise 6.2

1

Christmas cards						
1	4	5	6	8	9	
2	0	1	2	2	3	6 7
3	1	3	5			
4	0	1	6			

$n = 18$ 1 | 4 = 14 cards

2

Interest rates						
4	2	2	3	5	8	8 9
5	0	2	2	4	5	6
6	0	2	4	7		
7	1	5	6			

$n = 20$ 4 | 2 = 4·2%

3

Holiday costs						
1	3	3	5	6		
2	0	0	2	2	3	6
3	1	9				
4	2	4				
5	6					

$n = 15$ 1 | 3 = £130

4

Times between programmes					
1	2	3	5	9	
2	0	4	6	8	
3	1	3	3	6	8
4	2	7	8	9	
5	0	1	7		

$n = 20$ 1 | 3 = 1·3 min

Page 97 Exercise 7.1

1 a i 102   **ii** 65

  b no, fewer books borrowed

2 a 3rd year: £6·00, £6·50, £6·60; 4th year: £6·50

  b i £9·80   **ii** 4th year

3 a

Plant height (cm)		
With feed		Without feed
1 1 0	8	0 4 4 4 8
5 4 3	9	3 5 6 9
9 7 7 3 2	10	3 3 8 8
5 5 4 0	11	0 2 4
6 3 0	12	3 5 6
2 1	13	4
$n = 20$		$n = 20$

9 | 3 = 9·3 cm

  b yes, median risen from 10·3 cm to 10·8 cm

4 a

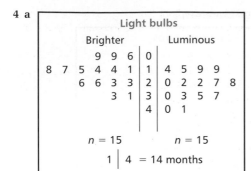

Light bulbs

```
        Brighter        Luminous
        9  9  6 │ 0 │
8 7 5 4 4 4 1 │ 1 │ 4 5 9 9
      6 6 3 3 │ 2 │ 0 2 2 7 8
          3 1 │ 3 │ 0 3 5 7
              4 │ 0 1
```

n = 15   n = 15

1 │ 4 = 14 months

b Luminous

Page 100 Revise

1 a

Colour	Frequency
green	10
amber	6
red	4

b i green   **ii** red
2 a 60   **b i** $\frac{1}{3}$ **ii** $\frac{1}{10}$
c

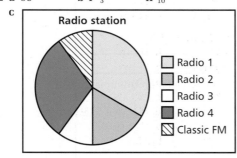

Radio station

Radio 1
Radio 2
Radio 3
Radio 4
Classic FM

3 a/c

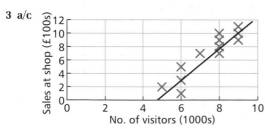

b positive correlation
d £400
e 7500 visitors

4 a

Ages of audience

```
0 │ 3  7  8  8
1 │ 1  3  4  5  6  6  7  8
2 │ 0  4  6  6
3 │ 0
4 │ 4  4  5
```

n = 20   1 │ 3 = 13 years old

b those in their teens (10 to 19)

5 a 9
b

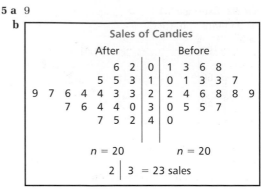

Sales of Candies

```
              After        Before
          6  2 │ 0 │ 1  3  6  8
        5  5  3 │ 1 │ 0  1  3  3  7
9 7 6 4 4  3  3 │ 2 │ 2  4  6  8  8  9
    7 6 4 4  0 │ 3 │ 0  5  5  7
        7  5  2 │ 4 │ 0
```

n = 20   n = 20

2 │ 3 = 23 sales

c yes

7 Proportion and variation

Page 102 Exercise 1.1
1a 120 min   **b** 600 min   **c** 30 min
2 a £6   **b** £360   **c** £59·94
    d 24p   **e** £146   **f** £9·30
3 £5·97
4 17 m²
5 a £52   **b** £104   **c** £208   **d** £416
6 a increase   **b** decrease
7 a 35   **b** 6
8 a 3 : 1   **b** 1 : 4   **c** 1 : 6   **d** 3 : 4
9 2 : 5
10

2·50 ─────────── (5, 2·50)

Cost (£)

0   Time (h)   5

Page 103 Exercise 2.1
1 0·45, 0·90, 1·35, 1·80, 2·25, 2·70, 3·15, 3·60, 4·05
2 a, b and e
3 a Yes   **b** 28 kg
4 a Yes   **b** 240p
5 a, b and c
6 a £5   **b** £15
7 a 3 min   **b** 24 min
8 a £4   **b** £16
9 a 400 g   **b** 3200 g
10 a 30p   **b** £2·70
11 1050 g
12 £16·58

Page 105 Exercise 2.2
1 £15
2 £44
3 £1·50
4 100 min

5 15 m
6 a 36 km **b** 24 km
7 a 270 calories **b** 48 min
8 a 1248 cm² **b** £31·25
9 a 5650 g **b** 450 cm³
10 a 8·1 m² **b** 200 ml
11 a 288 calories **b** 65 g
12 a 4p **b** 4p
13 a €812 **b** £450

Page 106 Brainstormer
a 200 ml and 80 ml
b 150 ml bottle should cost £23·40

Page 106 Exercise 3.1
1 a 1 lemon, 25 g sugar, 250 ml water
  b 6 lemons, 150 g sugar, 1500 ml water
2 a 10 g butter, 5 ml syrup, 20 g oats
  b 100 g butter, 50 ml syrup, 200 g oats
3 120 g rice, 800 ml milk, 68 g sugar, 4 ml vanilla
4 675 g sugar, 345 g treacle, 165 g butter, 3 tbsp water, 1·5 tbsp vinegar

Page 107 Exercise 4.1
1 £60; £60 ÷ 6 = £10
2 60
3 a 12 h **b** 4 h
4 a 72 **b** 12
5 a 90 h **b** 9 h
6 a £4·80 **b** 80p
7 a 2 h **b** 1 h **c** 40 min **d** 30 min
8 36 min
9 6
10 40 min

Page 108 Exercise 4.2
1 12
2 100 m²
3 £600 000
4 £84
5 a 15 **b** 36
6 45 min or 0·75 hour
7 a 0·3 m² **b** 24
8 a 200 **b** 120

Page 110 Exercise 5.1
1 a inverse **b** direct **c** inverse **d** direct
2 halved
3 trebled
4 £3·60
5 6 h
6 408·5 calories
7 £300
8 35 days
9 a 220 calories **b** 5 min
10 a 810 g **b** 2000 cm³
11 a 32 km **b** 76·8 km
  c 30 miles **d** 12·5 miles

Page 111 Exercise 5.2
1 a direct **b** inverse **c** inverse **d** direct
2 £360
3 17·5 km
4 £300
5 a 10 days **b** 15 days
6 a £50·40 **b** £57·60
7 a 7·5 m **b** 5·6 m
8 a 8·4 kg **b** 12·2 kg

Page 113 Exercise 6.1
1 a $T \propto n$ **b** $D \propto n$ **c** doesn't apply
  d $D \propto t$ **e** doesn't apply
2 a 5 **b** $A = 5B$
3 a 0·5 **b** $P = 0·5Q$
4 a 5·08 **b** 25·4
5 a 2·80 **b** 14
6 a $C = kt$; $140 = k \times 4$; $k = 140 \div 4 = 35$; $C = 35t$
  b $C = 35 \times 7 = 245p$
7 a $D \propto n$; $D = kn$; $20 = k \times 10$; $k = 20 \div 10 = 2$;
    $D = 2n$
  b $D = 2 \times 25 = 50$ m
8 a $F = 32w$ **b** 110
9 a $W = 9n$ **b** £72
10 a $D = 30s$ **b** 210 m

Page 115 Exercise 6.2
1 a $D = 7t$ **b** 160 m
2 a $W = 0·25t$ **b** 11 cm
3 a $W = 1·5V$ **b** 450 g
4 a $T = 2·8d$ **b** £18·20
5 a $C = 4·6n$ **b** 1610p or £16·10
6 a $V = 0·625I$ **b** 12·5 volts
7 a $S = 0·1t$ **b** 8·5 g

Page 116 Exercise 7.1
1 a Straight line through (0, 0)
  b 60° **c** 6 **d** $A = 6t$
2 a Straight line through (0, 0) **b** 1·5; $C = 1·5t$
3 a

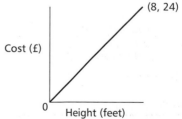

  b Yes, cost varies directly as height
  c $C = 3h$
4 a Straight line through (0, 0)
  b 0, 80, 160, 240, 320, 400
  c $D = 8t$
5 a Distance travelled varies directly as the petrol used
  b 7·5, 15, 22·5, 30, 37·5, 45
  c $D = 7·5P$

Page 119 Exercise 7.2

1 a Amount of data downloaded varies directly as the time

b 0, 9, 18, 27, 36, 45

c $D = 4{\cdot}5t$

d 67·5 kb

2 a

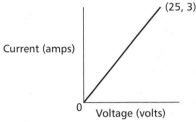

b straight line through (0, 0)

c $I = 0{\cdot}12V$

d 4·2 amps

3 a

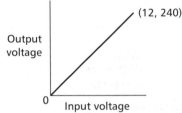

b straight line through (0, 0)

c $V = 20v$

d 170 volts

4 a

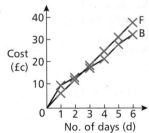

b Freewheelers; $C = 6d$

c Freewheelers £42, Beta Bikes £35 (assuming same increase for 6 to 7 days as from 5 to 6 days)

Page 121 Revise

1 yes

2 a direct   **b** inverse

   c direct   **d** inverse

3 36 kg

4 40

5 5 eggs, 25 g butter, 125 ml milk

6 a 2·4p

   b 8 min

7 a $M = 0{\cdot}6n$

   b 12

8 a $F = 0{\cdot}028w$

   b 12·6 g

9 a

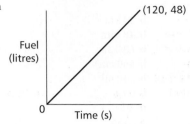

b straight line through (0, 0)

c $F = 0{\cdot}4t$

d 18 litres

8 Pythagoras

Page 122 Exercise 1.1

1 a i 9   **ii** 25   **iii** 64   **iv** 100

   b i 16   **ii** 289   **iii** 625   **iv** 10 000

   c i 7   **ii** 9   **iii** 11   **iv** 15

   d i 4   **ii** 8   **iii** 13   **iv** 25

2 a 81 cm^2 **b** 132·25 cm^2

3 a 17 cm   **b** 37 cm

4 a 5   **b** 49, 49, 7

   c 6   **d** 8, 8, 64

5 a 106   **b** 274   **c** 730

6 a   **b**   **c**

 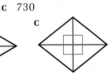

Page 124 Exercise 2.1

1 a LN   **b** FD   **c** PR   **d** FH

   e XZ

2 Check number of squares.

3 a i 25 cm^2 **ii** 5 cm

   b i 169 cm^2 **ii** 13 cm

   c i 100 cm^2 **ii** 10 cm

   d i 289 cm^2 **ii** 17 cm

Page 125 Exercise 3.1

1 $x^2 = 5^2 + 12^2$

   $x^2 = 25 + 144$

   $x^2 = 169$

   $x = \sqrt{169}$

   $x = 13$

2 a 17 cm   **b** 15 cm   **c** 26 cm

   d 7·5 cm   **e** 75 cm

3 a 20 cm   **b** 17·5 cm   **c** 50 cm

   d 42·5 cm   **e** 19·5 cm

4 a 25·1 cm   **b** 20·6 cm   **c** 21·2 cm

   d 11·7 cm   **e** 22·8 cm

5 a 22·0 cm   **b** 39·6 cm   **c** 9·9 cm

   d 9·9 cm   **e** 15·4 cm   **f** 8·1 cm

Page 126 Exercise 3.2

1 4 m   **2** 13 m   **3** 18·5 m

4 25 cm   **5** 4·5 m   **6** 137 m

Page 127 Exercise 4.1

1 $15^2 = 9^2 + x^2$
$x^2 = 15^2 - 9^2$
$x^2 = 225 - 81$
$x^2 = 144$
$x = \sqrt{144} = 12$

2 a 30 cm   **b** 72 cm   **c** 14·4 cm
   d 12·5 cm   **e** 22·5 cm

3 a 26·0 cm   **b** 12·4 cm   **c** 5·7 cm
   d 6·1 cm   **e** 6·2 cm

Page 128 Exercise 4.2

1 20 m

2 40 mm

3 0·8 m

4 a 1 m   **b** 2·4 m

5 a 5 cm   **b** $x = 2·4$ cm, $y = 2·6$ cm
   c 9·4 cm   **d** $p = 3·6$ cm, $q = 3·5$ cm

Page 128 Exercise 5.1

1 a 32·7   **b** 63·6   **c** 12·8
   d 60·0   **e** 20·7

2 a    **b** 1·2 m

3 a   **b** 132 km

4 a
2 m   2·25 m
   b 1·03 m

5 3·79 m

6 9·17 m

Page 130 Exercise 5.2

1 a ABD, DBC
   b EIH, HIG, IGF, EIF
   c KJN, KNL, JNM, NLM
   d SPQ, PQR, SQR, PSR

2 $a = 29·2$ cm, $b = 13·6$ cm, $c = 17·2$ cm,
$d = 21·0$ cm, $e = 6·4$ cm

3 a $x = 21·9$ m, $y = 45·0$ m   **b** $z = 23·1$ m

4 $a = 3·05$ m, $b = 2·42$ m

5 a $x = 10$ mm, $y = 22·6$ mm
   b 28·6 mm
   c 68 mm

6 9·57 cm

7 a 0·9 m
   b 2·22 m

Page 132 Exercise 6.1

1 $a = 11·6$ cm, $b = 20·7$ cm, $c = 50·5$ cm, $d = 7·7$ cm

2 32 m

3 a 7·5 cm   **b** 10·1 cm

4 a 10·0 cm   **b** 14·9 m

5 3·9 m

6 2·5 m

7 a

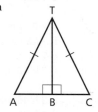

   b TB = 42 m

Page 133 Exercise 6.2

1 20·9 m

2 14 cm

3 a 2·5 cm   **b** 16 cm

4 34 cm

5 a 6 m   **b** 10 m

6 a 30 yards   **b** 70 yards

7 a 8·5 cm   **b** 4·24 cm

Page 134 Exercise 7.1

1 a 7·3   **b** 7·1   **c** 6·4   **d** 8·1

2 a 5   **b** 13   **c** 7·3

3 4·5 m

4 a AC = 5·8   **b** PR = 7·2   **c** YZ = 7·8

5 Oscar = 5·8 km; Oliver = 6·3 km;
Oliver by 0·5 km

6 a pupil's own diagram
   b PQ = 4·1, QR = 4·1
   c isosceles

7 a 8·1 km   **b** 23·5 km   **c** 15·4 km

Page 137 Revise

1 a YZ   **b** AV

2 a 30 cm   **b** 7·1 cm   **c** 19·7 cm

3 4·1 km

4 7·17 m

5 5·7

6 4·3 m

9 Time, distance and speed

Page 138 Exercise 1.1

1 7.50

2 a 70 mph   **b** 110 km/h   **c** 97 432 miles

3 a i 60 min   **ii** 30 min
    iii 15 min   **iv** 150 min
   b i $\frac{1}{2}$ **ii** $\frac{1}{4}$ **iii** $\frac{3}{4}$
     iv $\frac{1}{6}$ **v** $\frac{1}{3}$

4 a 0·5   **b** 0·25   **c** 0·75
   d 6·5   **e** 1·75   **f** 4·25

5 a i 19 miles   **ii** 47 miles
  b Redly and Dunbeg
6 a 45 min   **b** 1 h 45 min   **c** 2 h 30 min
7 a i 20 km   **ii** 20 km
  b i after 3 hours   **ii** 30 km

Page 140 Exercise 2.1

1 a 11 00   **b** 05 00   **c** 14 30
  d 23 50   **e** 00 10
2 a 7.30 am   **b** 2 pm   **c** 7.57 pm
  d 11.15 am   **e** 12.20 pm   **f** 12.35 am
3 a 2 h 30 min   **b** 2 h 15 min   **c** 7 h
  d 3 h 40 min   **e** 4 h 50 min   **f** 7 h 55 min
  g 7 h   **h** 5 h 30 min
4 a 4 h   **b** 5 h 20 min   **c** 2 h 45 min
  d 14 h 40 min   **e** 3 h   **f** 5 h 30 m
  g 12 h 25 min
5 42 min
6 8.25 pm
7 6.15 am
8 6 h 20 min
9 4 h 25 min
10 a 10 55   **b** 35 min   **c** 1 h 15 min
   d 4 h 20 min   **e** 2.18 pm   **f** 40 min

Page 141 Exercise 2.2

1 a 5 h 45 min   **b** 8 h 8 min   **c** 13 h 43 min
  d 4 h 15 min   **e** 7 h 3 min
2 a 4 h 20 min   **b** 11 h 40 min   **c** 7 h 41 min
  d 6 h 40 min   **e** 6 h 22 min   **f** 6 h 8 min
3 a i 09 05   **ii** 11 43   **iii** 23 26
  b Berry and Norseman
  c i 27 min   **ii** 55 min   **iii** 2 h 55 min
  d Hilton 10.35 pm, Berry 11.26 pm,
     Dunmore 11.45 pm, Little Don 12.12 am,
     Norseman 1.07 am, Camptown 1.30 am
  e i 12 35 or 19 35   **ii** 2 h 49 min

Page 142 Exercise 3.1

1 a 32 km   **b** 60 km
  c 150 km   **d** 450 km
2 a 12 miles   **b** 36 miles
  c 14 miles   **d** 230 miles
3 a 180 m   **b** 175 m
4 a 24 km   **b** 7 km
  c 350 miles   **d** 147 miles

Page 142 Exercise 3.2

1 a 300 km   **b** 252 miles   **c** 360 m
  d 220 km   **e** 240 miles   **f** 80 m
2 a 32·5 km   **b** 340 miles
  c 330 metres   **d** 123 km
3 900 miles
4 8050 km
5 a 180 seconds   **b** 1260 m
6 6820 km
7 a Matthew   **b** 0·5 mile
8 a 1 h 30 m   **b** 82·5 miles

9 a/b

Spode	Distances in km	
11	Trimby	
26	9	Beechgrove

Page 144 Exercise 4.1

1 a 50 km/h   **b** 5 km/h
  c 35 km/h   **d** 70 km/h
2 a 6 mph   **b** 11 mph   **c** 90 mph
3 a 10 m/s   **b** 60 m/s   **c** 20 m/s
4 a 9 km/h   **b** 75 mph   **c** 10 m/s
  d 70 mph   **e** 3 m/s
5 a 1840 km/h   **b** 83 km/h
6 10 km/h
7 50 mph
8 a 1·5 hours   **b** 46 km/h

Page 145 Exercise 4·2

1 a 1·25   **b** 3·5   **c** 0·75   **d** 5·5
2 a 1·25   **b** 3·5   **c** 5·75   **d** 2·4
  e 4·1   **f** 1·15   **g** 0·45   **h** 0·7
  i 2·33
3 a 4 km/h   **b** 6 km/h   **c** 12 km/h
  d 52 km/h **e** 14 km/h
4 30 km/h
5 6 km/h
6 a 98 km/h   **b** 96 km/h

Page 146 Exercise 5·1

1 a 2 h   **b** 3 h   **c** 3 h   **d** 1·5 h
2 a 2 h   **b** 6 h   **c** 50 s   **d** 60 s
  e 5 h   **f** 4 s   **g** 1·5 h   **h** 2·5 h
3 a 2 h   **b** 11 00
4 15 45
5 a 2 h   **b** 3 h   **c** 2·5 h

Page 147 Exercise 5·2

1 a 5 h   **b** 5 h   **c** 22 s
  d 3 h   **e** 2·5 h   **f** 5·5 s
2 a 3 h 30 min   **b** 5 h 15 min   **c** 1 h 45 min
  d 4 h 30 min   **e** 3 h 15 min
3 5 h 45 min
4 a 3 h 15 min   **b** 17 55   **c** 3 h
5 a i 2 h   **ii** 0·5 h
     iii 1·5 h   **iv** 0·75 h
  b i 4 h 45 min   **ii** 15 00
6 a 2 h 12 min   **b** 1 h 24 min   **c** 5 h 6 min
7 9.25 pm
8 3·4 s
9 14 56
10 500 s

Page 149 Exercise 6·1

1 a i 400 m   **ii** 600 m   **iii** 900 m
  b 900 m
  c i 1 minute   **ii** 2 minutes
  d approx. 820 m
  e i first part   **ii** yes

2 a 3.00 **b** 5 miles **c** 15 min **d** 30 min
  e 4.15 **f** 1 h 15 m **g** 10 miles
  h 2·5 miles **i** to the supermarket
3 a i 4 km **ii** 6 km
  b 2·4 km
  c 9 km
  d i 12·5min **ii** 2 min
  e last
4 a 3 km **b** 10 min **c** 40 min **d** 6 km
  e 60 min **f** before
5 a 250 miles
  b i 100 miles **ii** 50 mph
  c 1 hour **d** 150 miles **e** 50 mph
6 a i 09 00 **ii** 14 00
  b 30 km
  c i 11 30 **ii** 50 km **iii** 1 hour
  d 35 km **e** last stop to home **(iv)**
  f i 30 km/h **ii** 20 km/h
    iii 30 km/h **iv** 70 km/h

Page 151 Exercise 6.2
1 a 6 hours **b** 50 km/h
  c i 09 30 **ii** 120 km
  d 12 00
  e i 72 km/h **ii** 48 km/h
2 a i 80 miles **ii** 30 miles
  b i 14 15
    ii 30 miles from Mossburn at Denham
  c i 14 00 **ii** 15 min **d** 40 mph
3 a i 07 00 **ii** 08 00
  b ordinary 13 00, express 10 30
  c 09 00 **d** 60 miles
  e i 60 mph **ii** 30 mph

Page 153 Exercise 7.1
1 a 10 m/s **b** 4 h **c** 172 miles
  d 1·5 hours **e** 168 km **f** 74 km/h
2 a i 27 km/h **ii** 105 km
    iii 2·5 hours **iv** 93 km
  b 372 km **c** 9 hours
3 6 m/s
4 a 2·5 hours **b** 17 05
5 1·5 h
6 20 km

Page 154 Exercise 7.2
1 3·5 hours
2 3·75 km
3 a 1 h 15 min **b** 44 km/h
4 10·2 m/s
5 a Start → A 1·5 h; A → B 6 km/h; B → C 7 km;
    C → D 1·25 h; D → Finish 6 km/h
  b i 36·5 km **ii** 6 hours
6 a i 8·8 m/s **ii** 8·1 m/s **iii** 9·2 m/s
  b Seb **c** 0·4 m/s
7 a 267 mph **b** 364 mph
  c 398 mph **d** 354·5 mph

Page 156 Revise
1 a 105 km **b** 5 hours
  c 75 km/h
2 a 37·5 km/h **b** 7·5 hours
  c 32 miles **d** 8·8 m/s
3 a 5.30 pm
  b 10 km
4 8 h 20 min
5 a 800 m **b** 2 min
  c 3 min **d** 8 min
  e to the store
6 a 120 miles
  b 40 mph
  c i 12 00 **ii** 80 miles
  d i 20 mph **ii** 80 mph
7 a 63·5 mph
  b 1 h 15 m
8 57 km/h

10 Angles and circles

Page 157 Exercise 1.1
1 $a = 52, b = 23, c = 33, d = 55, e = 319,$
  $f = 104, g = 42·5$
2 $a = 64, b = 38, c = 56, d = 72, e = 36,$
  $f = 62, g = 60$
3 a 8
  b i 90° **ii** 45° **iii** 90°
  c 16 m
4 a 10 cm
  b 11·3 km to 1 d.p.
5 360°

Page 159 Exercise 2.1
1 a i complementary **ii** 50°
  b i supplementary **ii** 140°
  c i complementary **ii** 50°
  d i supplementary **ii** 140°
  e i vertically opposite **ii** 40°
2 a 153°
  b 87°
  c 122°
3 a 70°, supplementary
  b 55°, supplementary
  c 55°, angles in a triangle
  d 125°, supplementary
4 a 108°, vertically opposite
  b 29°, vertically opposite
  c 43°, angles in a triangle and vertically opposite
5 77°

Page 161 Exercise 2.2
1 $a = 90°, b = 40°, c = 40°, d = 50°, e = 90°, f = 45°,$
  $g = 45°, h = 55°, i = 62·5°, j = 62·5°, k = 62·5°,$
  $m = 95°, n = 130°, p = 115°, q = 65°, r = 115°,$
  $s = 65°$

2

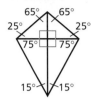 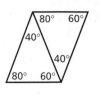

3 a PTQ, PTS, STR, RTQ

b $\angle$SPT = 65°, $\angle$PST = 65°, $\angle$TPQ = 25°,
$\angle$PQT = 25°, $\angle$PTQ = 130°, $\angle$TSR = 25°,
$\angle$SRT = 25°, $\angle$RTS = 130°, $\angle$TRQ = 65°,
$\angle$RQT = 65°, $\angle$QTR = 50°

4 a $\angle$BCD   **b i** $\angle$ADC and $\angle$ABC   **ii** 115°

c i   **ii**   **iii**

 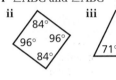

Page 163 Exercise 3.1

1 a $\angle$BAC and $\angle$DCE

b $\angle$PQT and $\angle$QRU, $\angle$TQR and $\angle$URS

c $\angle$FGJ and $\angle$GHK, $\angle$FGL and $\angle$GHM,
$\angle$JGH and $\angle$KHI, $\angle$LGH and $\angle$MHI

2 a 63°   **b** 135°   **c** $p = 128°, q = 128°$

3 $a = 27°, b = 55°, c = 55°, d = 125°$

4 The top two are parallel. 73° and 107° are supplementary

5 a/b

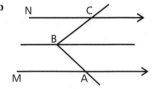

c 84°

Page 164 Exercise 3.2

1 a $\angle$CDA = $\angle$DAB

b $\angle$TQU = $\angle$QUP, $\angle$RSU = $\angle$SUP

c $\angle$LGH = $\angle$GHK, $\angle$JGH = $\angle$GHM, $\angle$KHI = $\angle$HIN

2 $a = 69°, b = 55°, c = 37°, d = 37°, e = 63°,$
$f = 63°, g = 131°, h = 131°, i = 86°, j = 86°$

3 a 43°   **b** 115°   **c** 39°

4 88°

5 $a = 151°$ supplementary;
$b = 29°$ vertically opposite;
$c = 29°$ alternate;
$d = 29°$ corresponding;
$e = 29°$ alternate

Page 165 Exercise 4.1

1 a i AO, BO   **ii** AOB   **iii** $\angle$OAB and $\angle$ABO
   b i CO, DO   **ii** COD   **iii** $\angle$DCO and $\angle$CDO

2 a $a = 32°$ **b** $b = 67°, c = 46°$
   c $d = 24°, e = 132°$ **d** $u = 30°, v = 30°$
   e $w = 47°$ **f** $x = 60°$
   g $s = 84°$ **h** $t = 78°$
   i $g = 70°$

3 a $u = 46°, v = 134°$
   b $w = 72°, x = 288°$
   c $a = 42°, b = 96°, c = 84°, d = 48°$
   d $d = 57°$

4 a i 134°
     ii 134°
     iii 23°
   b BAC and ACD are equal and must be alternate so AB and DC are parallel

5 a $x = 45°, y = 67.5°$
   b $v = 90°, u = 45°$
   c $m = 135°, n = 22.5°$

Page 167 Exercise 4.2

1 a i 30°   **ii** 120°   **iii** 60°   **iv** 60°   **v** 90°
   b i 36°   **ii** 108°   **iii** 72°   **iv** 54°   **v** 90°
   c i 45°   **ii** 90°   **iii** 90°   **iv** 45°   **v** 90°
   d i 65°   **ii** 50°   **iii** 130°   **iv** 25°   **v** 90°

2 a–c

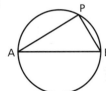

d 90°
g always 90°

3 a Isoceles triangle
   b angles in a triangle = 180°
   c $d = 180 - c = 180 - (180 - 2a) = 2a$
   d i angles in a triangle
     ii angles in a triangle
     iii $2b + 2a = 180 \Rightarrow b + a = 90$

Page 168 Exercise 5.1

1 a $a = 90°, b = 63°, c = 53°, d = 38°, e = 8°,$
$f = 71°, g = 53°, h = 74°, i = 45°$

2 a $v = 75°, w = 15°$
   b $p = 27°, q = 63°$
   c $r = 59°$
   d $s = 52°, t = 19°$

Page 169 Exercise 5.2

1 $j = 41°, k = 18°, l = 67°, m = n = 45°$

2 a $\angle$ACB, $\angle$CBD
   b $\angle$XYZ, $\angle$WZY
   c $\angle$QPR, $\angle$QTR
   d $\angle$ALB, $\angle$AJB, $\angle$LBJ, $\angle$LAJ, $\angle$LIJ, $\angle$LKJ

3 i ii

a

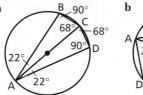

b

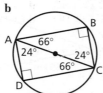

c

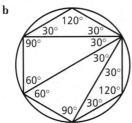

iii a kite   **b** rectangle   **c** square

4 a 120°

b

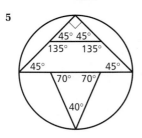

5

6 ∠BAE = 30°, ∠ABE = 90°, ∠ACD = 90°,
∠ADE = 35°, ∠EDC = 30°, ∠AED = 120°,
∠BEC = 120°, ∠CED = 60°

Page 171 Exercise 6.1

1 a OY, OX, OZ   **b** OV longer than OX
   c touches at 90°   **d** ∠OYW, ∠OYV

2 a i AC   **ii** B
   iii OB   **iv** ∠OBC, ∠OBA
   b i PR   **ii** Q
   iii OQ   **iv** ∠OQR, ∠OQP
   c i GF   **ii** G
   iii OG   **iv** ∠OGF, ∠EGT

3 a $x = 33$, $w = 90$ **b** $v = 90$, $y = 66$
   c $a = 28$, $b = 62$ **d** $c = 33$, $d = 57$, $e = 52$
   e $x = 130$, $y = 40$ **f** $p = 20$, $q = 20$
   g $m = 47$ **h** $i = 39$, $j = 51$

4 a $p = 62$, $q = 28$, $r = 23$, $s = 67$
   b $a = 66$, $b = 114$, $c = 33$, $d = 57$,
     $e = 123$, $f = 33$

5 a ∠OBC, ∠OBA, ∠BDE

b

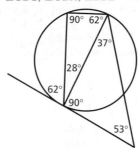

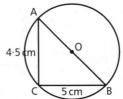

Page 173 Exercise 7.1

1 a 26 cm   **b** 20 cm   **c** 6·5 cm   **d** 7 cm
2 a 7·2 cm   **b** 12·2 cm   **c** 8 cm   **d** 48 cm
3 a

b 6·7 cm   **c** 3·4 cm
4 a 4·7 cm   **b** 2·2 cm
5 a 10·5 m   **b** 7·25 m

Page 174 Exercise 7.2

1 a 58·4 cm   **b** 14·0 cm   **c** 6·6 cm   **d** 2·0 cm
2 a 30·5 cm   **b** 132·3 cm   **c** 14·3 cm
3 a i 7·6 m   **ii** 6·3 m
   b i 12·8 m   **ii** 19·3 m
4 a 3·9 m   **b** 3·5 m   **c** 1·53 m

Page 176 Revise

1 $a = 43°$, $b = 48°$, $c = 41°$, $d = 122°$,
   $e = 117°$, $f = 51°$
2 $a = 69°$, $b = 146°$, $c = 44°$
3 a $a = 90°$, $b = 47°$ **b** $c = 90°$, $d = 66°$
   c $e = 90°$, $f = 57°$, $g = 57°$
4 2·6 m

11 Angles and triangles

Page 177 Exercise 1.1

1 a North-west (NW),
   North-east (NE),
   South-west (SW),
   South-east (SE)
   b i south-east
     ii north-east
   c i 90°   **ii** 45°
     iii 90°   **iv** 135°

2 240 m north, 250 m north-west, 400 m west,
   350 m south-west, 100 m south, 750 m east,
   100 m south-east
3 a 58°   **b** 29°   **c** 90°

4 a PR   **b** YZ   **c** DE
5 a $x = 0.5$ **b** $x = 0.5$ **c** $x = 1.3$ **d** $x = 7.2$
6 a $x = 35$
   b i $x = 24$ **ii** $x = 26$ **iii** $x = 4.5$
7 a pupil's own drawing   **b** PV = 70 km

Page 179 Exercise 2.1

1 a 090°   **b** 180°   **c** 270°
   d 225°   **e** 315°
2 a 010°   **b** 080°   **c** 310°
   d 250°   **e** 190°   **f** 110°
3 a pupil's own estimates
   b A 075°, B 110°, C 148°, D 233°, E 285°
4 a 080°   **b** 203°   **c** 300°   **d** 343°
5 pupil's own drawing

6 a   **b**   **c**

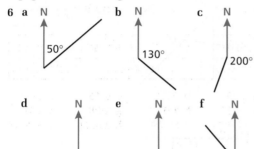

d   **e**   **f**

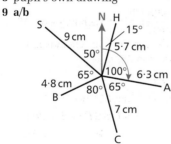

7 pupil's own drawing, with line AB = 6 cm
8 pupil's own drawing
9 a/b

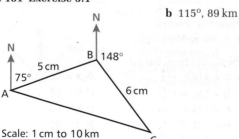

Page 181 Exercise 3.1

1 a   **b** 115°, 89 km

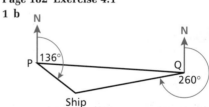

2 a i 50°   **ii** 140°
   b pupil's own drawing
   c i 10 km   **ii** 103°   **iii** 257°

3 a

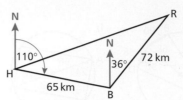

   b pupil's own drawing
   c i 109–110 km
     ii 071°

4 a

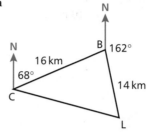

   b pupil's own drawing
   c 20.6 km, 291°

Page 182 Exercise 4.1

1 b

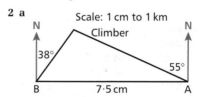

   c The ship is nearer P

2 a

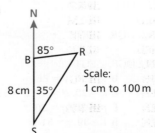

   b i 5.9 km
     ii 4.3 km

3 a

   b i 600 m
     ii 1040 m

4 a

b pupil's own drawing
c i 17·0 km   **ii** 18·8 km

5 a

b i 8·5 km   **ii** 6·8 km

6 a

b pupil's own drawing; a sensible scale would be 1 cm to 100 m
c 140 m

Page 184 Challenge
a i 215°   **ii** 243°
b i 305°   **ii** 328°   **iii** 030°
  iv 065°   **v** 100°   **vi** 120°
c i 232°   **ii** 280°   **iii** 010°   **iv** 140°

Page 185 Exercise 5.1
1 a i AC   **ii** BC   **iii** AB
  b i RT   **ii** ST   **iii** RS
  c i KM   **ii** KL   **iii** LM
  d i XY   **ii** XZ   **iii** YZ
2 a i UV   **ii** TU   **iii** TV
  iv TV   **v** TU
  b i GH   **ii** FH   **iii** FG
  iv FG   **v** FH
  c i LM   **ii** LN   **iii** MN
  iv MN   **v** LN
3 a 0·923   **b** 0·417
4 a i 0·800   **ii** 0·600   **iii** 1·333
  b i 0·600   **ii** 0·800   **iii** 0·750

Page 186 Exercise 6.1
1 a/b pupil's own drawings
  c columns 1 and 2: pupil's own answers; column 3 – the three answers should be approximately 0·81 when rounded to 2 decimal places

Page 187 Exercise 6.2
1 b $\tan A = \dfrac{CE}{AC}$ **c** $\tan A = \dfrac{DF}{AF}$
  d $\tan A = \dfrac{LT}{AL}$
2 a 1·33   **b** 0·23   **c** 3·43
3 $\tan B = \dfrac{24}{10} = 2\cdot40$ **a** $\tan B = \dfrac{9}{12} = 0\cdot75$
  b $\tan B = \dfrac{80}{18} = 4\cdot44$ **c** $\tan B = \dfrac{14}{48} = 0\cdot29$

4

Angle	10°	20°	30°	40°	50°	60°	70°	80°
Tangent	0·18	0·36	0·58	0·84	1·19	1·73	2·75	5·67

5 a 0·00   **b** 0·27   **c** 0·45   **d** 0·70
  e 0·90   **f** 1·00   **g** 1·88   **h** 4·70
  i 28·64   **j** 57·29   **k** 114·59   **l** 572·96
6 a/b

  c $\tan 45° = \dfrac{\text{opposite}}{\text{adjacent}}$ and for each angle of 45° the opposite side and the adjacent side are equal. Therefore, $\tan 45° = 1$.

Page 188 Exercise 7.1
1 a $\tan 36° = \frac{d}{5} \Rightarrow d = 5 \times \tan 36° \Rightarrow d = 3\cdot6$
  b $\tan 52° = \frac{d}{14} \Rightarrow d = 14 \times \tan 52° \Rightarrow d = 17\cdot9$
2 a 9·7   **b** 13·1   **c** 4·1   **d** 6·9
  e 16·6   **f** 5·1   **g** 10·6   **h** 27·6
3 a 4·6 m   **b** 3·5 m   **c** 5·5 m
4 a 12·6 m   **b** 41·5 m   **c** 14·4 m
5 a 2·4 m   **b** 3·7 m
6 9·0 cm
7 179·4 or 179·3 cm

Page 190 Exercise 8.1
1 a i $\tan x° = \frac{8}{9}$ **ii** $x = 42$
  b i $\tan x° = \frac{11}{7}$ **ii** $x = 58$
  c i $\tan x° = \frac{10}{14}$ **ii** $x = 36$
  d i $\tan x° = \frac{25}{18}$ **ii** $x = 54$
  e i $\tan x° = \frac{70}{24}$ **ii** $x = 71$
  f i $\tan x° = \frac{15}{36}$ **ii** $x = 23$
2 a 41°
  b i 48°   **ii** 42°
  c i 37°   **ii** 53°

3 9°

4 61°

5 9°

6 a ∠A = 67°, ∠C = 23°

7 ∠JLM = ∠KJL = 34°, ∠LJM = ∠JLK = 56°

8 ∠B = ∠C = 59°, ∠A = 62°

Page 192 Exercise 9.1

1 a $\dfrac{DG}{AD}$ **b** $\dfrac{EJ}{AJ}$ **c** $\dfrac{FK}{AK}$

2 b 0·80 **c** 0·96 **d** 0·53

3 a $\dfrac{12}{13} = 0.92$ **b** $\dfrac{45}{75} = 0.60$
  c $\dfrac{21}{75} = 0.28$ **d** $\dfrac{45}{53} = 0.85$

4

A	10°	20°	30°	40°	50°	60°	70°	80°	90°
sin A	0·17	0·34	0·50	0·64	0·77	0·87	0·94	0·98	1·00

5 a 0·00 **b** 0·26 **c** 0·71
  d 0·97 **e** 1·00

6 a–c

P, 30°, 60°, Q, S, R

d SR is half the length of QR, which is equal to PR so $\sin 30° = \dfrac{SR}{PR} = \dfrac{1}{2} = 0.5$

7 $\sin 34° = \dfrac{d}{5.8}$, so $d = 5.8 \times \sin 34° = 3.2$

8 a 5·4 **b** 5·4 **c** 4·4 **d** 3·2

9 a 2·7 m **b** 3·2 m **c** 3·7 m

10 a 16·4 m **b** 18·5 m
  c 19·1 m; kite **c** is highest

11 58·6 m

12 a 12·4 m **b** 5·1 m

Page 194 Exercise 10.1

1 a 30° **b** 20° **c** 54° **d** 90°
  e 53° **f** 17° **g** 38° **h** 51°

2 a i $\frac{5}{8}$ **ii** 39° **b i** $\frac{3}{10}$ **ii** 17°
  c i $\frac{7.5}{11.6}$ **ii** 40° **d i** $\frac{24}{26}$ **ii** 67°
  e i $\frac{18}{30}$ **ii** 37° **f i** $\frac{1.4}{5}$ **ii** 16°

3 a 30° **b** 43° **c** 41°

4 a 17° **b** 7°

5 053°

Page 195 Exercise 11.1

1 a $\frac{6}{11}$ **b** $\frac{7}{10}$ **c** $\frac{10}{26}$ **d** $\frac{4.8}{7.3}$

2 a i 0·80 **ii** 0·60 **b i** 0·66 **ii** 0·75
  c i 0·92 **ii** 0·38 **d i** 0·53 **ii** 0·85

3 a 4·5 cm **b** 9·8 cm **c** 5·9 cm
  d 8·9 cm **e** 18·4 cm

4 a 37° **b** 35° **c** 71° **d** 16°

5 a 0·7 m **b** 2·3 m **c** 2·3 m

6 12·8 m

7 18°

8 a 17·9 m **b** 25°

Page 197 Investigation

a

A	0°	10°	20°	30°	40°	50°	60°	70°	80°	90°
sin A	0·00	0·17	0·34	0·50	0·64	0·77	0·87	0·94	0·98	1·00
cos A	1·00	0·98	0·94	0·87	0·77	0·64	0·50	0·34	0·17	0·00

c 45°

d i cos 25° = sin 65° **ii** sin 41° = cos 49°
  iii cos 1° = sin 89° **iv** sin 27° = cos 63°

Page 198 Exercise 12.1

1 a i cosine **ii** 9·9
  b i tangent **ii** 3·7
  c i cosine **ii** 53°
  d i sine **ii** 16·2

2 29·4 m

3 a 5·7 m **b** 6·3 m

4 55·4 m

5 5·2 m

6 25°

7 a 12·2 m **b** 19·5 m

8 63°

9 a 34°
  b length is 11·5 cm, breadth is 9·6 cm

10 058°

Page 199 Exercise 12.2

1 a 25·4 m **b** 40·7 m

2 a $a° = 54°$, $b° = 69°$
  b RT = 63 cm, US = 94 cm

3 a 13·4 km **b** 12·0 km

4 a 8·2 m **b** 5·7 m

5 a 15·5 m **b** 26·3 m

6 a i 7·0 cm **ii** 12·2 cm
  b i ∠MNL = ∠NLK = ∠NMK = ∠MKL = 37°,
    ∠KNL = ∠KML = ∠NKM = ∠NLM = 53°,
    ∠NOM = ∠KOL = 106°,
    ∠NOK = ∠MOL = 74°
  ii 15 cm

Page 202 Revise

1 A 053°, B 108°, C 244°, D 298°

2

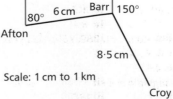

N, N, 80°, 6 cm, Barr, 150°, Afton, 8·5 cm, Croy

Scale: 1 cm to 1 km

3 a

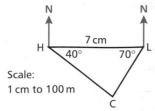

Scale:
1 cm to 100 m

b 480 m
4 19·6 m
5 53°
6 a 2·6 m   **b** 2·7 m
7 90·1 m

12 More statistics

Page 203 Exercise 1.1

1 a i 0·567   **ii** 0·583   **b** Burgh
2 a queue (frequency) 0(1), 1(5), 2(4), 3(6), 4(4)
   b i 4 cars   **ii** 4 times   **c** 3 cars
3 a 29 min   **b** 2·9 min   **c** 2 to 3 min
4 360
5 a i 47 mm   **ii** 2 mm
   b 2   **c** about 25 mm

Page 204 Exercise 2.1

1 a 6   **b** 25
   c 50·2   **d** 623·6
2 a £870·25   **b** 5
3 a £167·75   **b** 2
   c i £345   **ii** £142·43
4 a i £52   **ii** £65
   b £13
   c i £59   **ii** 5
5 a i 36 km   **ii** 36 km
   b i 4   **ii** 1
   c i means are the same
      ii but would appear to be more typical of
         Laura's performance than Sam's

Page 206 Exercise 2.2

1 a i 12, 35, 64, 9   **ii** 120
   iii 16   **iv** 7·5
   b i 20, 75, 150, 35   **ii** 280
   iii 10   **iv** 28
   c i 1, 10, 15, 7, 18   **ii** 51
   iii 12   **iv** 4·25
   d i 70, 80, 60, 120, 200   **ii** 530
   iii 20   **iv** 26·5
   e i 0, 30, 24, 60, 12   **ii** 126
   iii 15   **iv** 8·4
2 last column: 660, 480, 390, 280, 750; 12·8 years
3 a last column: 0, 6, 18, 15, 4
   b 25   **c** 43
   d i 1·72 passengers per visit   **ii** yes
4 a 20   **b** 37   **c** 1·85

5 a

Visitors	Freq.	Visitors × f
0	4	0
1	2	2
2	6	12
3	9	27
4	5	20
Totals	26	61

   b 2·35 visitors at noon per day
   c no
6 a 24 997 kg   **b** 499·9 kg   **c** yes

Page 209 Exercise 3.1

1 a 11   **b** 118   **c** 22 and 23
2 a red
   b cheese
   c Mon and Fri
3 a 31   **b** 4   **c** 15   **d** 4
4 a i 5   **ii** 8   **iii** 2
   b scientific   **c** arithmetic and scientific
5 a 7(1), 8(6), 9(4), 10(8), 11(7), 12(4)
   b 10
   c i 19   **ii** 11
   d no, about 37% scored below the target

Page 210 Exercise 3.2

1 a 6   **b** 0(2), 1(6), 2(8), 3(5), 4(4)
   c 2 videos   **d** tallest bar
2 a 14   **b** 28 sweets   **c** 30 sweets/packet
3 a 3 times   **b** 23   **c** Monday
4 a 0(1), 1(7), 2(0), 3(4), 4(6), 5(0), 6(6)
   b 4
   c i 1
      ii yes
      iii no, $\frac{2}{3}$ of time he was worse than this
   d i 3·3 late days/week   **ii** no   **iii** yes

Page 212 Exercise 4.1

1 a 8   **b** 37   **c** 98·5   **d** 49
   e 3·95   **f** 4   **g** 38·5   **h** 7·0
2 a i 5·5 min   **ii** 5·5 min
   b i 5·5 min   **ii** 16·75 min
   c median
   d i 4 min   **ii** 4·375 min; order of list was
         affected
3 a i 4 cm   **ii** 5 cm
   b i 4 cm unchanged   **ii** 1 cm large change
4 a i 7900 miles   **ii** 26 744 miles
   b i Earth   **ii** Neptune
   c 20 hours
   d i 4380 days   **ii** 21 971 days
5 a 6, 9, 9, 9, 12, 12, 12, 13, 13, 13, 14, 15, 18, 19,
      21, 23, 23, 24, 26, 26
   b i 9, 12 and 13   **ii** 15·85   **iii** 13·5
   c probably the median

Page 214 Exercise 4.2

1 a

```
Poppy size

3 | 0  1  4  6  7
4 | 0  1  1  4  5  6  8
5 | 0  0  1  1  2  3  4  6  7
6 | 0  4  5  7

n = 25     3 | 0 = 30 cm
```

b 50 cm

c 10

2 a i 11   **ii** 57

b 34   **c i** 32·9   **ii** 12

3 a i 18   **ii** 28

b the new model has a much higher median indicating possibly a better design

4 a i 10·8 cm   **ii** 10·3 cm

b i 8·0 cm   **ii** 8·0 cm

c i 13·2 cm   **ii** 13·4 cm

d with nutrient is marginally better

Page 216 Exercise 5.1

1 a 16 cm   **b** 97 s   **c** 37 days

d 187 kg   **e** 37 degrees C   **f** 22 degrees C

2 a 3634 million miles   **b** 3090 miles

3 a i 29 mm   **ii** 498 mm

b Canada

c i 30 degrees C   **ii** 2 degrees C

d i 25 degrees C

ii 74 mm

iii 33·5 mm/month

e Britain

4 a 1006·5 ml   **b** 54 ml   **c** 1004 ml

5 a Mel: range = 4, median = 12, Les: range = 19, median = 12, Don: range = 2, median = 8

b Don   **c** Mel and Les

d Mel   **e** Mel

Page 218 Exercise 6.1

1 a 11, 10   **b** 15, 20   **c** 11, 26   **d** 94, 15

e 3·7, 2·1   **f** 326, 4   **g** 1, 907

2 a 8, 4   **b** 15, 8   **c** 36·5, 72

Page 219 Exercise 6.2

1 a 5   **b** 54

c 2   **d** adequate

2 a 30   **b** 4

c 10   **d** at 10·3 mean is bigger

3 a i 8   **ii** 2

b 4   **c** Trumps 8·5, Reality 8·5

d although **i** the median number of points awarded each bike is the same **ii** enthusiasts were more consistent when awarding points to Trumps; overall, Trumps would seem to be the enthusiasts' choice.

4 a i 1   **ii** 3

b i 3   **ii** 3

c i without treatment 3 parasites; with treatment 1 parasite

ii without treatment 3·2 parasites; with treatment 0·9 parasites

d although the numbers are just as variable (having the same range) there has been a marked drop in both the mean and median number of parasites per bee.

5 a i 25 cm   **ii** 150 cm   **iii** 148·5 cm

b Peter is taller than average, both mean and median. He is 6·5 cm bigger than the mean and with a range of 25 cm you would expect the biggest height to be about 12 cm above the mean. Indeed there are only 2 in the class bigger than him.

6 a 35 years

b i 5 mm   **ii** 39 mm   **iii** 39·4 mm

c 41 mm is about 2 mm above average. With a range of only 5 mm you would expect the rainiest spell to be about 2 to 3 mm above the mean. So this year it has been a particularly rainy April.

Page 221 Exercise 7.1

1 a 1   **b** 0   **c i** $\frac{1}{2}$ **ii** $\frac{1}{2}$

2 a $\frac{1}{6}$ **b** $\frac{1}{2}$ **c** $\frac{2}{6} = \frac{1}{3}$

d $\frac{5}{6}$ **e** $\frac{1}{2}$ **f** $\frac{2}{3}$

3 a i $\frac{1}{8}$ **ii** $\frac{7}{8}$ **b i** $\frac{3}{8}$ **ii** $\frac{5}{8}$

c i $\frac{1}{4}$ **ii** $\frac{3}{4}$ **d i** 1   **ii** 0

4 a They add to 1   **b** $\frac{3}{5}$ **c** $\frac{31}{36}$

5 a $\frac{26}{52} = 0·5$ **b** $\frac{13}{52} = 0·25$ **c** $\frac{39}{52} = 0·75$

6 a 0·02   **b** 0·06

c 1 (to 1 s.f. it's certain)

7 a $\frac{5}{9}$ **b** $\frac{1}{9}$ **c** $\frac{1}{3}$ **d** $\frac{4}{9}$

Page 222 Exercise 7.2

1 a 20   **b** 2   **c** $\frac{1}{10}$

d i $\frac{3}{20}$ **ii** $\frac{7}{20}$ **iii** $\frac{12}{20} = \frac{3}{5}$

2 a i 30   **ii** 6   **iii** $\frac{1}{5}$

b i $\frac{1}{10}$ **ii** $\frac{11}{30}$ **iii** $\frac{19}{30}$

3 a 20   **b i** $\frac{3}{20}$ **ii** $\frac{9}{10}$ **iii** $\frac{1}{5}$

4 a i $\frac{9}{98}$ **ii** $\frac{42}{98} = \frac{3}{7}$ **iii** $\frac{12}{98} = \frac{6}{49}$

b i $\frac{2}{98} = \frac{1}{49}$ **ii** $\frac{68}{98} = \frac{34}{49}$ **iii** $\frac{2}{98} = \frac{1}{49}$

Page 225 Revise

1 a 3   **b** 3·2

2 a i 6 years   **ii** 15 years

b i 7 years   **ii** 14·5 years

3 a 4 wheels   **b** 8 wheels   **c** 3·7 wheels

4 a 6 degrees C   **b** 1°C

c 3, 5, 9, 14, 20, 22, 23   **d** 0°C

e 1 degree below median and 2 degrees below the mode is *about average* since the range is 6 degrees

5 a 1st fortnight
   i 7·14 hours   **ii** 7 hours   **iii** 4 hours;
   2nd fortnight
   i 7·14 hours   **ii** 7 hours   **iii** 3 hours
  b though both have the same mean and median numbers of hours of sunshine the first fortnight was slightly more variable (bigger range)
6 a $\frac{1}{4}$ **b** $\frac{28}{365} = 0·08$ to 1 s.f.
7 a 0·23   **b** 0·49

13 Chapter revision

Page 227 Revising Chapter 1

1 a 13   **b** 24   **c** 8   **d** 8
2 a 25   **b** 144   **c** 8   **d** 1
  e 81   **f** 4   **g** 7   **h** 1
  i 11   **j** 14
3 a 289   **b** 6·76   **c** 19
  d 2·7   **e** 4096   **f** 128
4 a 126   **b** $1\frac{1}{12}$ **c** $1\frac{7}{8}$ **d** $\frac{5}{28}$
5 a 8   **b** 7·0   **c** 1521
  d 2   **e** 1·6   **f** 3·8
6 $3·4 \times 10^3$ **b** $1·5 \times 10^7$ **c** 6×10^9
  d $2·3 \times 10^{-4}$ **e** 9×10^{-3} **f** $4·05 \times 10^{-7}$
7 a 4000   **b** 56 000 000
  c 0·0014   **d** 0·000 03
8 a Anna £12·50   **b** Ben £37·50
9 white 16 litres, green 4 litres
10 £16·53
11 a £1954   **b** £450·92
12 small 5·3p per ml, large 5·4p per ml, so small is better buy

Page 228 Revising Chapter 2

1 a false **b** false **c** true **d** false **e** true
2 a 4   **b** -2
3 $-7, -3, -1, 0, 3, 7$
4 a 6   **b** 1   **c** -7 **d** -4
  e -12 **f** 11   **g** -2 **h** -16
  i -8 **j** -54 **k** -40 **l** 0
  m -11 **n** -35 **o** -5
5 351 °C
6 a -140 **b** -5 **c** -2
7 a

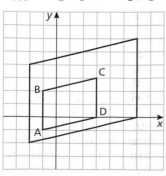

b A becomes $(-2, -2)$, B becomes $(-2, 4)$, C becomes $(6, 6)$ and D becomes $(6, 0)$
  c i see diagram for **a**
    ii a parallelogram
8 a 5 metres
  b i 1 metre
    ii -1 metre
    iii $-2·5$ metres
  c the 46th rung below sea level
9 a 13   **b** 18   **c** 36   **d** -11

Page 229 Revising Chapter 3

1 a $3x - 9$ **b** $7y + 35$ **c** $4b + 16$ **d** $3f - 15$
  e $7y + 21$ **f** $24 - 6y$ **g** $12 - 4x$ **h** $4e + 4f$
  i $9x - 9y$ **j** $10a - 10b$
2 a $18m + 15$ **b** $8k - 4$ **c** $21x + 6$
  d $10n + 30$ **e** $20y - 8$ **f** $45e + 27$
  g $27m - 36$ **h** $18h + 2$ **i** $25x - 10$
  j $56m - 21$
3 a $2n - 8$ **b** $13 + 3y$ **c** 15
  d $3q$ **e** $4y + 2$ **f** $8k + 1$
  g $8x + 8y$ **h** $11m + n$
4 a 2   **b** 3   **c** 7   **d** 4
  e 1   **f** 6   **g** 7   **h** 3
5 a $4(x - 3) = 20; 8$
  b $2(y + 3) = 14; 4$
  c $7(m + 8) = 56; 0$
6 a 7   **b** 7   **c** 5
  d 5   **e** 2   **f** 2
7 $3(x + 12) = 60; 8$
8 a i $3x + 10 = 6x - 2; 4$ **ii** 22 cm
  b i $6n - 4 = 20 - 2n; 3$ **ii** 14 cm
  c i $4(x + 2) + 3 = 23; 3$ **ii** 23 cm

Page 230 Revising Chapter 4

1 a £197·50   **b** £573·48   **c** £86·02
2 a i £1·74   **ii** £11·69
  b i £10·25   **ii** £68·84
  c i £25·77   **ii** £173·02
  d i £13·90   **ii** £93·35
3 A £98·13, B £17·17, C £115·30
4 a i £23·25   **ii** £52·64   **b** £75·89
5 a i 9·90 Swiss francs
    ii 396 Swiss francs
  b i £15·15   **ii** £328·28
6 £572·40
7 a i £673·40   **ii** £113·40
  b i £9799·54   **ii** £1800·54
8 £34·20

Page 231 Revising Chapter 5

1 a 1, 2, 3, 4, 6, 8, 12, 16, 24, 48
  b 1, 2, 3, 4, 6, 8, 9, 12, 18, 24, 36, 72
  c 1, 2, 3, 4, 5, 6, 8, 9, 10, 12, 15, 18, 20, 24, 30, 36, 40, 45, 60, 72, 90, 120, 180, 360
2 1, 2, 3, 6, 9, 18
3 23, 29, 31, 37, 41, 43, 47

4 2, 3, 5, 7, 11

5 a 9   **b** 8   **c** b **d** p
   e $2m$ **f** k **g** y **h** $3a$

6 a $1 \times 16, 2 \times 8, 4 \times 4$
   b $1 \times ef, e \times f$
   c $1 \times n^2, n \times n$
   d $1 \times 9ab, 3 \times 3ab, 9 \times ab,$
     $a \times 9b, 3a \times 3b, 9a \times b$

7 a $7(k - 2)$ **b** $8(n + 3)$ **c** $10(5 - n)$
   d $4(2 + 5xy)$ **e** $6(3 - 4b)$ **f** $6(2l - 3)$
   g $8(3e + 2)$ **h** $2(2ab + 3)$ **i** $2(2 + 5x^2)$
   j $2(y^2 - 11)$ **k** $8(2k - 3lm)$ **l** $2(16xy + 9z)$

8 a i $4pq$ **ii** $3p$ **iii** 1 **iv** $6p$
   b i $6x^2$ **ii** $2x^2$ **iii** $6x$ **iv** $3x$
   c i $6mn$ **ii** $4m$ **iii** mn **iv** 12

Page 231 Revising Chapter 6

1 a mint (15), coffee (3), toffee (1), orange (6)
   b i mint   **ii** toffee

2 a 90
   b i $\frac{15}{90} = \frac{1}{6}$ **ii** $\frac{36}{90} = \frac{2}{5}$
   c

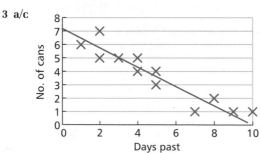

3 a/c

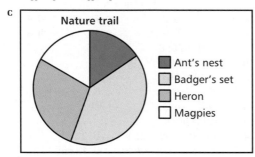

b negative correlation
d 3

4 a

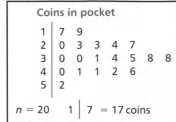

b 30s

Page 232 Revising Chapter 7

1 £14
2 15 pots
3 57·6 g
4 250 g flour, 125 g margarine, 50 ml water, 200 g jam
5 a 63 min   **b** 48 m²
6 a $H = 1·2t$ **b** 10·8
7 a $T = 0·2n$ **b** 56 min
8 a

(graph: Interest (£) against Money deposited (£), straight line through origin to point (500, 20))

b straight line passing through origin
c $I = 0·04D$
d £12·80

Page 233 Revising Chapter 8

1 only **b** could be true
2 a 42·7 cm   **b** 27·5 cm
   c 29·7 cm   **d** 83·9 cm
3 2·9 m
4 86·0 cm

Page 234 Revising Chapter 9

1 a 27 mph   **b** 6 hours
   c 3010 km   **d** 160 metres
2 a 48 km/h, 52 km/h, 38 km/h
   b i 6 hours   **ii** 271 km   **iii** 45 km/h
3 2 h 30 min
4 a 1·5 hours   **b** 60 km/h   **c** 18 05
5 a 150 km   **b** 30 km/h
   c i 12 00   **ii** 90 km
   d i 30 min   **ii** 90 km
   e 40 km/h   **f** tourer by half an hour
6 a 4·5 km
   b i 09 00   **ii** 09 50   **iii** 10 40
   c 20 min
   d i 09 20   **ii** 10 minutes
   e 9 km/h

Page 235 Revising Chapter 10

1 a $a = 58$ (complement of 32),
       $b = 109$ (supplement of 71)
   b $c = 43$ (vertically opposite and sum of angles in triangle)
   c $d = 49$ (supplement and alternate or corresponding angles)
   d $e = 26$ (sum of angles in triangle and alternate angles
   e $f = 23$ (alternate angles)
2 55° (isosceles triangle and alternate angles)
3 a 21°   **b** 46°
4 a 19·7 mm   **b** 6·6 mm   **c** 94·5 mm